THE
ASCENT
OF MIND

THE
ASCENT
OF MIND

ICE AGE CLIMATES
AND THE EVOLUTION OF INTELLIGENCE

WILLIAM H. CALVIN

BANTAM BOOKS
NEW YORK · TORONTO · LONDON · SYDNEY · AUCKLAND

THE ASCENT OF MIND:
ICE AGE CLIMATES
AND THE EVOLUTION OF INTELLIGENCE
A Bantam Book
Bantam hardcover published edition January 1991
Bantam trade paperback edition November 1991

ISBN 0-553-35230-X

Published simultaneously in the United States and Canada

Bantam Books are published by Bantam Books, a division of Bantam
Doubleday Dell Publishing Group, Inc. Its trademark, consisting of the
words "Bantam Books" and the portrayal of a rooster, is Registered in
U.S. Patent and Trademark Office and in other countries. Marca
Registrada. Bantam Books, 666 Fifth Avenue, New York, New York
10103.

PRINTED IN THE UNITED STATES OF AMERICA

BVG   0 9 8 7 6 5 4 3 2 1

For
Katherine Graubard

CONTENTS

FIGURE LIST

PREFACE

Back when I was trying on various book titles for size, I was temporarily attracted by several that, valued advisors assured me, were not properly serious for a book on human origins. *The Little Brain That Could* rightly emphasized the ape-to-human bootstrapping of brain size. It nicely contrasted with *The Cerebral Symphony*, wherein I emphasized how human consciousness now works (here I consider how it evolved in the context of ice-age climate changes—generation-to-generation evolution of mind, rather than its minute-to-minute operation). But *The Little Brain That Could* might have been shelved in the wrong section of the bookstore—and much as I would like to write for young readers, human evolution is a topic that requires the reader to have considerable experience with the world, a long attention span, and an ability to keep multiple possibilities in mind simultaneously—all while retaining the child's intense curiosity about origins.

Then there was *Our Gain in Brain Remains to Be Explained*. My advisors admitted that not many book titles can be sung in the shower, but wondered if that was really fitting and proper for the "greatest of mysteries." I was particularly attracted by *Our Gain in Brain* because, in *My Fair Lady*, Eliza Doolittle sings her famous line from the elocution textbook, the one about where it rains in Spain. And then the professor whispers in an excited aside, "I think she's got it!" Anthropologists and biologists know that, when attempting to explain what "caused" human evolution, such roles are invariably reversed. The professor tentatively starts with an excited whisper, "I think I've got it!" Whereupon a chorus complains, in a mighty refrain, that the matter *still* remains to be explained.

That's science for you, though our perfectly normal disagreements are often misunderstood by journalists and exploited by a certain type of religious fund-raiser. There is total agreement among the experts that evolution happened over millions of years, and that the apes are the group of animals out of which we evolved. But scientists haven't agreed on the exact course that prehuman evolution took—the *what*, *where*, and *when*—though hard-earned archaeological and fossil finds are sketching in the broad outlines. Nor can we yet agree on what drove it—those pesky *how* and *why* questions. Like Darwin, we keep getting into conflict with those who advocate a simplistic view of the world; not noted for their knowledge of elementary anthropology or evolutionary biology, they prefer miraculous "explanations." Of course, back when few antecedents were discernible, the scientists of three centuries ago also relied on the miraculous—but today, just saying "God did it" resembles peeking at the last page of a mystery novel, without savoring the buildup, climax, and explanation of all those incidents along the way. Even religious scientists tend to agree with the Greek philosopher Polybius, who, in the second century B.C., said: "Whenever it is possible to find out the cause of what is happening, one should not recourse to the gods."

WHATEVER THE ULTIMATE CAUSES of ape-to-human evolution, there are surely multiple proximate causes. The bootstrapping potential of technological problem-solving (toolmaking, hunting, etc.) is often mentioned as a way of working up from the apes. Other kinds of cleverness might also work, such as the social problem-solving that affects reproductive success (the most formidable problem typically faced by a chimpanzee is to figure out what fellow chimps are going to do next). And climate change, besides biasing evolution in certain directions, also affects the rate at which other "causes" make progress.

Each proposed cause—even if true—seldom convinces other scientists that it is more important than their own favorite candi-

date from the multiplicity. Even if you only try to explain the
changes in brain, body, and behavior since we last shared a
common ancestor with the chimpanzees, many things appear potentially important. And because human evolution only happened
once, all of the happenstance of that seven million years can, by
some stretch of the imagination, be held to be essential for the
making of modern humans ("We wouldn't be human without it"
goes that refrain).

Worse yet, there are some seductively attractive processes
that might have sufficed, given enough time, to do the job of
enlarging the brain fourfold. Our gain in brain is certainly the
most central, compelling "fact" of post-ape evolution (though that's
largely because, until recently, it was about all that could be
measured from fossil skulls). Size—even relative size—may not be
the most important aspect (more on that later). But surely the
most commonly noted brain-enlarging process since Darwin's day
is "Bigger-than-average brains are smarter, smarter individuals
survive better, therefore a bigger brain will evolve gradually."

Good old compound-interest reasoning, sheer intelligence bootstrapping itself, little by little. Physicists who make grandiloquent
statements regarding life in the universe are particularly prone to
such one-sentence summaries. But such "universal truths," rising
above the messy details, are what science is supposed to be all
about, right?

Yet even if true (and I would caution that bigger-than-average
brains aren't necessarily smarter-than-average), such reliable-
sounding causes could well have been superseded, rendered totally
irrelevant. Why? *A fast-but-chancy track often preempts the slow-
but-sure tracks in the evolutionary race for a new ecological niche.*
Like patent protection, the evolutionary inventor may be rewarded
with a winner-take-all protected niche, so that even-better (but late-
arriving) candidates are locked out for quite a while. There are also
"windows of opportunity," such as the boom times when competitive
rules are suspended. They are brief intermissions in the grind of ordinary times when interesting things happen. (I am reminded of them
each time that I get bored with a play or concert and discover that
the production has no intermissions, that I cannot escape gracefully.)

Evolutionary explanations involve a lot of such messy details,
threatening the grand generalities. Since the unique history is

important, piecemeal answers are inevitable. Unfortunately, a patchwork quilt of little correct explanations does not readily constitute one grand answer (and so the complaining chorus chants its refrain once more). We keep wishing for a sturdy framework on which to hang the pieces.

THERE ARE SEVERAL THINGS that I hope to contribute to the debate about human evolution through this book. Individually, each may seem a little mundane, hardly an obvious "antecedent to consciousness." But they do hang together in a way that helps explain how the more elegant human abilities might have emerged.

The *first* is that where the rain falls is surprisingly important (and in Spain, it falls mainly in the mountains, not the plains). As droughts demonstrate, climate is fickle; "sudden-death play-offs" can happen within a matter of a decade or so. Abrupt climate change makes versatility, often a virtue, a necessity. There were many abrupt shifts during the last 2.5 million years of fluctuating climate known as the Ice Ages, quite in addition to the slow advance and retreat of the continental ice sheets. That 2.5 million-year period is exactly when our brains enlarged and reorganized beyond the ape standard, exactly when tool-making became prolific. Given the greenhouse problems coming up, one might almost call those several dozen ice ages "the qualifying rounds."

A *second* involves how hominids might have discovered hunting. I have touched on this in earlier books (and, in *The Cerebral Symphony: Seashore Reflections on the Structure of Consciousness*, elaborated on the spare-time uses of throwing's mental machinery, which is quite handy for augmenting insight, foresight, and language abilities). But here I emphasize how the projectile predator niche might have been invented and bootstrapped with the aid of toolmaking (I will even touch on something which an early reader nicknamed "the killer Frisbee").

Third, I suggest that there is a three-part cycle of evolutionary alterations in body proportions. This cycle can be rerun, something like a college course that can be repeated for additional credit; it involves several different sets of genes that regulate fetal and childhood growth. One likely result of the selection cycle I propose is a bigger and bigger adult brain; another predicted result is a considerable fluctuation in adult height during ape-to-human evolution.

That cyclical subscenario also illustrates that any explanation, to use a baseball metaphor, has to touch a lot of bases along the way. Any adequate explanation must propose a framework whereby we could have evolved from an upright-walking hominid with an ape-sized brain to the fully human cave painters of the last Ice Age. My modest attempt at this is in the form of a multimillion-year scenario, paced by the cyclical subscenario and (during the last 2.5 million years) by the ice-age rhythms. The bases one should touch are, of course, part of the explanatory problem. My selections overlap with those of modern anthropology while adding some nudges and constraints from climate and brain.

While I naturally hope that my scenario will turn out to be correct in both outline and details, the more realistic aspiration is that it might demonstrate the *breadth* of explanatory power that theories need. The anthropologists' favorites of the last few decades are rather narrow. They are known via static images, like tableaux in a museum: seed-eating, "Man the Hunter," homebase, "Woman the Gatherer," and scavenging. Not unreasonably, they tend to emphasize either animal behavior or "stones and bones."

But R. G. Collingwood noted in 1939 that history "is concerned not with events but with processes. Processes are things which do not begin and end but which turn into one another." Each is a continuing development involving many changes; the drying climate that changed forests into savannah in East Africa is probably the anthropologist's favorite process. I hope to demonstrate that the harder-to-depict *re-entrant process* is particularly important (what goes out the front door is eligible to reenter the back door and take another pass through the transformation). Indeed, an adequate explanation of human evolution will need a wide range of processes (both re-entrant and one-shot) from ecology, climatology, developmental biology, evolutionary biology, immunology, and from my own fields, physiology and neurobiology. The people piecing the story together will probably come from ethology, primatology, developmental psychology, the cognitive sciences, philosophy, linguistics, systems modelers—as well as anthropology. The correct portrayal of the prehuman path (if we ever agree on one) will probably be too multifaceted to state in one sentence, and so we will yearn for the good old days of "Bigger-is-smarter-is-better gradual Darwinian improvements." The story surely won't sound as elegant as "The Rain in Spain."

IT IS WINTERTIME IN SEATTLE as I finish this book. The relentless sound of rain on the roof reminds me of the incorrigible leak that again imperils my collection of *Current Anthropology*; the downhill path to disorder is threatening my view of the uphill record. But then the typically snowy nature of wintertime elsewhere in these middle latitudes is the *fourth* important "cause" of our brain boom that I have found so fascinating. "Think Snow" is a bumper sticker (much favored by waterlogged would-be skiers) which I would commend to those paleoanthropologists fixated on the tropics, as a slogan emphasizing a golden opportunity.

I suppose that we could have quadrupled our brains without the virtues of winter, but I'll bet that it would have taken forever. So much brain enlargement in a mere 2.5 million years is awfully quick by the standards of evolutionary biology. Yet winter once a year, an abrupt climate change every few millennia, and an ice age every hundred thousand years will speed up things ever so nicely—at least if you've got our kind of brain, rather than a bear's. Or so my story goes.

W.H.C.

Seattle, Washington

— 1 —

FOLLOWING THE GULF STREAM TO EUROPE: TRACKING CLIMATE CHANGE AND HUMAN EVOLUTION

Carried away, perhaps,
by His matchless creation,
the Garden of Eden,
He forgot to mention that
all He was giving us
was an interglacial.
ROBERT ARDREY, 1976

Matching wits with the fickle climate is how we became human. Or so I reflect, while waiting for the London-bound flight to depart from New York. "Delayed by unseasonably severe weather," a disembodied voice proclaimed an hour ago. My fellow passengers speculate about whether the greenhouse climate has already arrived.

Well, there really isn't a threshold of some sort—whenever the ice ages temporarily recede, the carbon dioxide starts climbing. It's more a question of how badly we are augmenting the overheating tendencies. And what sort of trouble we'll make for ourselves with major climatic change.

It usually works in the other direction: climate change affecting humans in a big way, rather than vice versa. Major climatic changes—particularly the ice ages—have meant quite a lot, when it comes to human evolution from the apes.

Back before the ice ages started 2.5 million years ago, we were upright and even looked pretty human, if seen from a distance. Yet up close, it would have been apparent that behind that large face was an ape-sized brain. Then the ice ages started. Great continental ice sheets built up and then they melted off, dozens of times. During all that, we evolved much faster than in the preceding few million years. We now have smaller faces, though with a notable forehead. Seen in side view, however, there is a big difference. That's because our brains have quadrupled in size over the early model hominid.

Why? Nothing similar happened to any other animal during the ice ages. With the brain's enlargement and reorganization, we acquired some beyond-the-apes abilities that we value most highly: a versatile language and a plan-ahead consciousness that enables us to feel dismay when seeing a tragedy unfold, enables us to develop ethics.

What was it about climate change that pumped up brain size, that somehow augmented intelligence? Surprisingly, severity of

weather, as such, probably wasn't the key. Rather, it's those repeated boom times that early hominids had the opportunity to
exploit. Some of the stories now emerging about the ice ages
demonstrate the challenges and opportunities faced by our ancestors. For example, two particularly dramatic events occurred
about 11,000–12,000 years ago, just as the last Ice Age (the one
that began 118,000 years ago) was ending and half the accumulated ice was already gone. Until very recently, no one had been
aware of either the American or the European story. And while
these two climatic episodes probably didn't affect brain size very
much, some of their predecessors likely did.

IN CANADA, TWO GIANT ICE SHEETS had been pushing
against one another, head to head: the one pushing west from
Hudson's Bay, the other grinding eastward, coming down from
the Rocky Mountains. They met in the eastern foothills of the
Rockies. With the melting, they each pulled back a little, allowing
some grass to grow. And this opened up a north-south route from
northern Alaska down to Montana.

It's called a corridor because corridors have walls: I tend
to think of this as something like the biblical parting of the
Red Sea. The grazing animals discovered the new grass growing in the corridor, and their predators followed them. Brown
bears migrated south, as did the humans who had reached
Alaska sometime earlier by crossing the Bering Strait from
Asia.

This corridor had only one exit. When the hunters reached
the southern end of the corridor about 12,000 years ago, at about
where the U.S. border is now, they discovered the Americas
largely uninhabited by humans. It was ripe for big-game hunting
and, thanks to living in Arctic latitudes where gathering was
scarce, they were experienced big game hunters, even felling
mammoth and mastodon in addition to lighter fare.

So they had themselves an enormous baby boom, thanks to
this previously untapped resource. A few dozen generations later,
about 11,000 years ago, these hunting families were all over the
continent, judging by their propensity for losing their favorite
spearheads, the so-called Clovis points (one has even been found
in the rib cage of an extinct mastodon). Their descendants are,

with the exception of a few latecomers such as the Inuit (Eskimo), the present-day Indians of both North and South America.

IN EUROPE at about the same time, there was a more established prosperity, as hominid hunters had been living off the grazing animals there for many ice ages, more than a half-million years. By the beginning of the most recent Ice Age, about 118,000 years ago, *Homo sapiens* had probably evolved from the earlier model, *Homo erectus*. Brain size may have already reached the modern size by then; the main change during the last glaciation can be seen in the teeth, but only if you look very carefully.

Teeth became about 10 percent smaller, seemingly a consequence of the food technologies invented during this last Ice Age; they dropped another 5 percent when agriculture came along. Cooking came first, judging from the charcoal that appears on cave floors starting about 80,000 years ago. Food preparation involving pottery improved things even more. We start to see skulls that indicate even the toothless could survive, suggesting both food preparation and a level of care of the disabled that was not seen in earlier times. Late in this glaciation, between 37,000 and 20,000 years ago, the life of the mind grew: Carved ivory and cave paintings became popular. By 11,500 years ago, these European hunters might have been starting to practice herding and agriculture (which was certainly imminent in the Middle East).

But, as the new Americans were thriving, the more established Europeans got a big surprise, and I doubt that they liked it very much. I wouldn't be surprised if linguists someday show that the phrase "the good old days" dates back to 11,500 years ago.

THERE WAS A EUROPEAN GENERATION who in their youth enjoyed the warming climate. New grass was growing everywhere along the glacial margins, and the herds were gradually getting larger. It wasn't a boom time for humans, as in the Americas, but both animals and humans were probably doing well because of the North Atlantic's warming trend that had suddenly started 1,500 years earlier (this "Allerød event" was about 13,000 years ago).

This same generation saw things change. One year, the winter rains were scant, and it seemed colder. It wasn't as cloudy as usual in the spring, and the summer was bone dry. The good grazing was exhausted early, and animals started exploring un- likely places in search of food. By the time the winter snows started, both humans and animals were in poor condition; more than the usual numbers died that winter. Was it just a drought?

The next year was even colder and drier. And the next. The next 20 years saw dramatic changes, far greater than in the "Little Ice Age" of a few centuries ago. Forests died and weeds took over. It became more dusty as severe storms stirred up the dry topsoil. The herds surely dropped to a fraction of their former sizes.

And the human tribes likely did poorly in consequence. Half of all children tended to die in childhood, even in the best of times before modern sanitation and medical care, but poorly fed children succumbed even more readily to childhood diseases. If anyone had had time to notice while scratching around for food, they would have seen glaciers advancing once again. In Scotland, where gla- ciers had already completely melted off, they started to re-form as the summers became too cold to melt much of the winter accumulation.

People didn't live half as long as we do, back then. A 40- year-old person often looked old and worn out. Children, who had never known those warm days of plentiful food on the hoof, surely wondered what the old folks kept talking about. When the genera- tion that had seen the transition died out, the stories may have persisted for a while, and the good old days were perhaps incorpo- rated into the creation myths as a form of heaven on earth.

(A few decades ago, modern scientists looked at the accumu- lated layers of a lake bottom in Denmark. In a deep layer, they saw the sudden introduction of the pollen of an arctic plant called *Dryas* that had no business being in Denmark, and named this cold snap after it: the Younger Dryas climate.)

And then—it ended even more suddenly than it had begun. There was a generation about 10,720 years ago, the great-great- (repeat that 29 more times)-grandchildren of those people who were absolutely sure about the good old days, that experienced the change. They grew up in a cold and dry Europe, and then saw the warm rains suddenly come back over the course of just a few years and melt the ice. The grass prospered, and the remaining

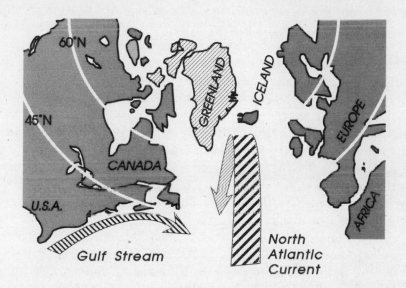

Gulf Stream

North
Atlantic
Current

grazing animals began a population explosion. It became a boom time for those Europeans who had survived up in the land of hard winters, just as it had become a boom time for the Arctic-adapted hunters who reached the end of the North American ice-free corridor a thousand years earlier.

It was as if a switch had been turned off. And then back on again. Or perhaps faucet is the apt metaphor, since the key to what happened is the Gulf Stream's European relative, the North Atlantic Current.

AFTER LEAVING NEW YORK at sunset, our London-bound airplane followed the Gulf Stream to the northeast, up over familiar Cape Cod haunts in the dusk, then just offshore of the Nova Scotia peninsula. We saw the entrance to the Gulf of St. Lawrence, where the overflow from the Great Lakes makes its way out to sea, and saw many fishing boats as we passed over the Grand Banks fishing grounds off the large island of Newfoundland. Finally, during the night, we followed the eastbound Gulf Stream out over the North Atlantic proper.

Before dawn, we flew over the North Atlantic Current, which sweeps northward up toward Iceland. But even after we passed over the current, I continued to see its effects, in the form of rain clouds drifting eastward toward Europe. I saw southern Ireland in the dawn light, great green patches between the storm clouds. Home of the Irish elk, the deer with the giant wingspan—at least for about 1,500 years (the Younger Dryas wiped it out, a good 1,600 years before humans arrived in Ireland).

Seen through the scattered clouds, London at six in the morning is glowing in the early-morning sunlight, and the streets shine from the spotty showers; a few delivery trucks cast long shadows while driving on the wrong side of the street. The green parks and the tennis courts are empty. But it's the London of William Shakespeare, Isaac Newton, Dr. Johnson, Charles Darwin, Bertrand Russell, and George Bernard Shaw.

And London is a puzzle, since it is 51.5° north of the equator. It is hard to imagine any city in Asia or the Americas, that far from the equator, becoming such a center of culture and commerce. None has, so far: not Calgary, Alberta (where parking meters have electric outlets, so you can keep the car warm enough to restart). Nor Moosonee, the town at the bottom of Hudson's Bay. Or chilly Puerto Arenas at Tierra del Fuego, equally distant from the equator to the south.

Indeed, most of Europe is at Canadian latitudes. Compared to the populous parts of the United States and Canada, mostly between the 30° and 45° lines on a globe, the populous parts of Europe are shifted 10–15° to the north, mostly between 40° and 60° latitudes. "Southerly" Rome lies at the same 42°N as does "northerly" Chicago. Paris lies at the latitude of Vancouver, British Columbia, about 49°N. Berlin is up at 52.5°N, Moscow at nearly 56°. Oslo, Stockholm, and Leningrad nestle up just under 60°N, where the sun makes only a brief midday appearance during December—about the same as in Alaska's coastal cities.

The reason that Europe is warm and wet, where Canada is cold and dry, is largely due to the North Atlantic Current and how it differs from similar major currents in the Pacific Ocean. All those rain clouds I saw this morning were caused by the copious evaporation from the warm ocean surface of the North Atlantic Current.

But what if something were to happen to the North Atlantic Current again?

THE BEST-KNOWN CLIMATE CHANGE in the offing is the global warming that is occurring from the greenhouse effect. It isn't minor, as this 1989 summary notes:

> Computer-modeled predictions of greenhouse warming suggest that global mean air temperatures may rise by 5°C [9°F] over the next 30 years, with amplified rises of up to 12°C [22°F] in polar regions. This is comparable with the temperature increase from the last glacial period to the present interglacial, and the projected rate of increase is probably greater than at any time since then.

The best-known consequence is the rise in sea level that threatens coastal populations. But *climate need not change gradually*. We now know that, in the past, other climatic changes have flipped on and off, without much of a middle ground. The North Atlantic Current's on-and-off tendencies are only one example of the more general problem of "modes" of behavior.

It has long been known that the climate could, in theory, become trapped in extreme states. The "White Earth Catastrophe" scenario could happen if ice extended over enough of the Earth's surface to reflect a lot of arriving sunlight back out into space. the Earth could freeze and never recover, short of volcanos covering the white surface with some dark lava. And the "Greenhouse Catastrophe" scenario would occur if the carbon locked up in the sediments (not just coal and oil but also that frozen tundra of Arctic regions) were released to the atmosphere in quantities sufficient to form a greenhouse layer of insulation, allowing the atmosphere beneath it (and oceans, and land, and us) to heat up catastrophically.

In the 1980s, the Swiss climatologist Hans Oeschger suggested that, in addition, the Earth's climate had several modes of interaction between the oceans, the atmosphere, the biosphere, and the ice sheets. These aren't extreme (indeed, we're in one mode now) but the transitions between them could be uncomfortably sudden. There had been hints of fairly sudden minor transitions. After all, people periodically rediscover that monsoons can simply be omitted some years.

There are drought cycles that repeat every few decades, but some are much shorter: South American fisheries and the bird

populations of many Pacific islands are dramatically depressed
every half-dozen years by the warming changes in the ocean
currents, known as El Niño. Evidence has been accumulating that
North American droughts are secondary consequences of equatorial ocean currents turning colder, the so-called La Niña condition. But what Oeschger was talking about was more than minor:
he suggested that the climate had major modes, some lasting
many centuries. These bistable styles of operation may pose far
more of a threat than the slow loss of coastal real estate to rising
sea levels.

Modifying the Earth's climate with greenhouse warming may
well exaggerate such mode-switching—*or leave us stuck in the
"wrong" mode for centuries*, as has happened before. Paradoxically, you can get cold from heat, as the Younger Dryas demonstrates: a warming trend can apparently cause a prolonged cold
snap. Most people have a tendency to dichotomize climate change
into warming or cooling, and forget that both can happen
simultaneously—but in different places.

Ice layers preserved under Greenland's glaciers show that
more than 20 regional chills, each lasting centuries, have occurred
in the last 120,000 years. The Younger Dryas was simply the most
recent and the longest-lasting (almost a thousand years). Though
detectable along the east coast of the United States and Canada,
it was most pronounced in Europe and southern Greenland; you
won't see it in the deep ice cores from Antarctica. It was probably
triggered, in part, by the dilution of the salt water by all that
freshwater glacial runoff. But how were the other 19 cold snaps
triggered? Might something like a greenhouse warming provoke
another one? Those are the kinds of questions to which we ur-
gently need answers.

SUDDEN REGIONAL COOLING during a global warming trend
probably happens because the circulating ocean currents switch
into a new mode, as when the North Atlantic Current no longer
warms and waters Europe in its customary way. And Europe
without the North Atlantic Current would be about like Canada:
they both have a comparable amount of fertile agricultural land at
similar northerly latitudes. Indeed, Europe gets Canada's air second-
hand, a week or so later, as Europe periodically rediscovers

whenever a forest fire in Canada makes European skies hazy and sunsets dark red.

You might surmise that Europe's population ought to be something like Canada's 27 million people. But France alone has twice as many people as Canada. Europe, to the west of the Soviet Union, totals more than 500 million people (twice the U.S. population), and there are another 200 million people in the western parts of the Soviet Union that share Europe's climate (the Younger Dryas climate reached as far as the Ukraine). That Europe presently supports about 26 times as many people as Canada is largely attributable to the beneficent influence of the North Atlantic Current, warming all that cold Canadian air crossing the North Atlantic, before it reaches Europe. And thus loading it with a lot more moisture, to be dropped on Europe as rainfall.

What will the "extra" half-billion people of Europe do, should the North Atlantic suffer another hiccup, returning Europe to a Canadian climate? If one could reliably forecast this situation, with a lead time of a hundred years or so, perhaps those Europeans would move elsewhere peacefully or develop a reciprocal symbiotic economy with some Third World countries that could feed them. Yet mode-switching cooling can happen as quickly as the onset of a minor drought, and no one knows how to predict it, much less control it. The first few years, there would be an "economic response": Europeans would buy grain elsewhere and ship it in, cut back on meat. But what would happen in the long run?

Remember how poorly the economic response worked for Ireland in the mid-nineteenth century when the potato crops failed? And what happened during Europe's last Great Depression a half-century ago: Germany's *lebensraum* excuse for territorial expansion, a professed need for "more living space?" Europe is technologically competent, compared to today's Third World or nineteenth-century Ireland, and a starving population isn't going to die quietly. They will move instead. A little glitch in the North Atlantic, similar to those of the past, is the most serious, least avoidable scenario for global warfare that I can imagine.

Whether it is a greenhouse-induced rise in sea level threatening the half-billion people relying on low-lying areas of the Indian subcontinent, or a cooling-and-drying Europe in need of *lebens-raum* for a half-billion people, or the projected return to dust-bowl conditions in the American Midwest and the loss of irrigation water in California (whose agriculture already helps feed Eastern Europe and the USSR in their bad years), climatic change is not likely to be peaceful. "Disruptions" is hardly the word for it.

We are very overextended, with far more population than we can support (even in the off-years of our current climate, as those Third World famines have repeatedly demonstrated). Major climate change, whether ice age or greenhouse warming, means a considerable "contraction" in the human population that the planet can support, unless new technologies fix up things very well indeed. An *abrupt* Dryas-like climate change, however, could easily destroy the stable civilizations that such large-scale innovative technologies require.

BUT WE HUMANS THRIVE on challenges, and a prolonged series of climatic changes probably played a leading role in how we evolved the neural mechanisms for those aspects of our *consciousness* that exceed those of the apes.

The most unique aspect of our consciousness is "thinking ahead," our ability to spin scenarios that try to explain the past and forecast the future. Often these strings of concepts make little sense (such as our nighttime dreams); other times, we shape them up into a thing of quality (such as a poem or a logical argument) and then act on it. Planning ahead in other animals is mostly a hormonal thing, hoarding behaviors being triggered by the shortening daylight hours of autumn which prolong the nighttime release of melatonin from the pineal gland. But we humans are capable of planning decades ahead, able to take account of extraordinary contingencies far more irregular than the seasons.

Since the prehuman brain enlarged only when the ice ages came along, the betting is that climatic challenge had something to do with the Great Encephalization—probably not so much because of a more severe climate but because the constant disruptions created opportunities and slowed "optimizing." Shaping up a body plan to the environment, efficiently dealing with its opportunities and hazards, is the usual anthropological concept of Darwinism, but fickle climates can add another dimension to the story.

Give evolution enough time to shape up things for efficiency, and jack-of-all-trades abilities will be eliminated—we'll get a stripped-down, lean-mean-machine version optimized to the existing climate. Fortunately, evolution is slow. Climate often changes faster than biological evolution-for-efficiency can keep up—*and so a brain that can function in various different climates has an advantage over one that is merely efficient in a single climate.* Retaining those jack-of-all-trades abilities is a lot easier if the climate keeps switching around unpredictably.

Ever since the major buildup of ice caps started 2.5 million years ago, the world climate has been oscillating markedly every 10,000 years or so (and more often in some regions), with major meltbacks of the northern ice sheets every 100,000 years (like the one 13,000 years ago that heralded the development of agriculture and then civilizations). This book makes the argument that we owe our versatile brains to these first-one-thing-and-then-another challenges of the ice ages—and the boom times that often followed.

That doesn't mean, however, that another major climatic challenge will pump up the brain some more. There has been a little change in scale. The human population has increased a thousandfold since the end of the last ice age: that's what agriculture, animal breeding, and technologies have made possible, compared to the days of hunter-gatherer bands wandering around. Having large numbers of individuals tends to buffer biological change, to slow it down.

EXPLAINING THE CLIMATIC PAST, forecasting our climate's future—those are some urgent tasks for our newfound mental abilities. But since human behavior plays the major role in generating the problems we now face—all those boom-time birth rates that lead to more population than can be fed in the drought years, our live-for-today and let-tomorrow-take-care-of-itself mentalities that lead to more pollution—understanding our evolutionary past may be just as important as building those big computers that will make working models of the global interactions between ocean, atmosphere, and ice. The way to make plausible plans for the future is to know what's worked in the past, and what hasn't. Navigating in tight spots means knowing the currents.

The inhabitants of planet Earth are quietly conducting a gigantic environmental experiment. So vast and so sweeping will be the consequences that, were it brought before any responsible council for approval, it would be firmly rejected. Yet it goes on with little interference from any jurisdiction or nation. The experiment in question is the release of CO_2 and other so-called "greenhouse gases" to the atmosphere. . . . Because of our lack of basic knowledge, the range of possibility for the greenhouse effects remains large. It is for this reason that the experiment is a dangerous one. We play Russian roulette with climate, hoping that the future will hold no unpleasant surprises. . . .

My impressions are more than educated hunches. They come from viewing the results of experiments nature has conducted on her own. . . . Earth's climate does not respond to forcing in a smooth and gradual way. Rather, it responds in sharp jumps which involve large-scale reorganization of Earth's system. . . . Coping with this type of change is clearly a far more serious matter than coping with a gradual warming.

the climate researcher WALLACE S. BROECKER, 1987

---2---

INCREMENTING INTELLIGENCE: A PRINCIPLE OF NATURE?

Who taught the raven
in a drought
to throw pebbles
into a hollow tree,
where she espied water,
that the water might rise
so as she could come to it?
FRANCIS BACON (1561–1626)

Brain size. Cleverness. Intelligence. Versatility. Being "smart," thoughtful, able to plan ahead. What do they all have to do with one another? There is clearly much overlap in the connotations of such words. Since they are also self-congratulatory, we have to watch out for anthropocentric tunnel vision as we try to get a grip on the problem by comparing various animals, seeing what's so good about innate intelligence.

Brain size seems especially crude as an index, as if the brain were only a container for what was really important, rather than the working machinery of consciousness. We know that our way of thinking isn't simply a matter of absolute brain size: individuals with a two-liter brain aren't twice as smart as those with a one-liter brain. If you correct for body size (the ratio of brain weight to body weight is the usual measure, though obviously inadequate), you get a somewhat improved correlation of size with some aspect of cleverness. But there are still all sorts of exceptions: the squirrel monkeys, fairly average among the New World monkeys, have a much higher brain/body ratio than all other monkeys—but the capuchin monkeys seem by far the cleverest of the New World monkeys, almost apelike in some respects.

And cleverness? Intelligence? What do they mean? Except for the great boost that language gives us, are we humans all that much more clever than the apes? An airplane flight from London to Budapest gave me plenty of time to think about this (despite the nice view of London after takeoff, Europe was entirely covered by clouds, undoubtedly contributed by the North Atlantic Current). I already had plenty of incentive to reflect on it, given that I was shortly scheduled to explain the evolution of intelligence to a group of astronomers who were gathering to discuss the prospects of detecting extraterrestrial life forms.

GENES NEED ONLY be approximately correct, as a little behavioral versatility can do the rest. While this versatility during life may not alter the genes passed on to offspring, it does serve to shape up those genes: behavior can drag along anatomy. This was recognized by three scientists in 1894; though often called the Baldwin Effect, it probably ought to be called the Morgan-Baldwin-Osborn Effect. Perhaps we would understand it more intuitively were it called the Old-Family-Recipe Effect.

Anyone who has ever asked for a copy of "that wonderful recipe" knows that the recipe card is always faded, flour-encrusted, written in a style of handwriting favored by some first-grade teacher of long ago, and smeared by several ancient droplets of an unknown fluid. And so when you transcribe it onto a new card to carry home with you, some copying errors are likely.

What's worse, the donor of this recipe has long since stopped consulting the recipe card: she just bakes from memory and, over the years, has improved the cake (or whatever) considerably beyond what would result from faithfully following her written recipe. Indeed, she has no idea how much her "handful of flour" departs from the half-cup that the recipe calls for, or how inaccurate the temperature setting on her oven has become. Still, she has found the winning combination (you did, after all, ask for the recipe) and so her point-of-departure version of the recipe comes to be copied with an unintentional mutation or two.

This commonplace situation suggests a simplified scheme for how cake-baking contests at county fairs could "cause" better cakes to evolve. Pretend for a moment that success in baking cakes obeys the following rules:

1. Each participant inherits a randomly altered copy of her parent's recipe for a cake. Perhaps a teaspoon of baking soda is changed into a tablespoon's worth. Or the 385°F baking temperature into 335°F. Or some other such alteration in the mix of ingredients, amounts, times, and temperatures.
2. The cook can modify the recipe during her lifetime, but only by memory, not by amending the recipe card. Indeed, since the recipe card is merely the point of departure for experimentation, it need never be consulted again (until finally copied).

3. There are contests to select the better cakes, and the winners and runners-up are the ones most likely to have offspring attracted by the cake-baking contests in some future decade. Note that winners don't train offspring at cooking (in this simplified scheme): they only pass on their point-of-departure version of the recipe. The only thing that experience, i.e., the recognition of good variations, does in the long run is to make the winners' offspring more likely to become contest-minded cake bakers.

4. The judging doesn't change criteria over the years ("good taste is eternal").

The recipe's mutations are usually worse than the original. In any generation, of course, an off-on-the-wrong-foot cook who is, none-theless, skillful at fiddling the recipe may hit upon the combination that constitutes the optimal recipe; inheritance is not fate (but she cannot pass on this winning combination as such, just the degraded recipe card). Yet on the average, the copying errors that move away from the optimal make it less likely that unwritten variations in the recipe ("a lifetime of experience") will hit on the optimum.

Because losers tend not to have offspring that participate in such contests (the losers don't get asked for a copy of their recipe), diverging recipes are more likely to die out. And so there will be a slow convergence in copying errors toward the optimal combination, just by carving away the other combinations. The optimal recipe may never be written down, but the population of written recipes in use gets closer and closer to the combination of ingredients, amounts, times, temperatures, and assembly procedures that will satisfy the expert tasters of cakes.

Allowing a son or daughter to learn the parent's hard-earned variations on the recipe would, of course, represent Lamarckism: inheritance of acquired-during-life characteristics. This "Training Effect," of course, happens with real cooks and their offspring; we encourage this mode of transmission with schools and books. But we theorists may temporarily leave such influences out of expla-nations, just to demonstrate that the whole population of written recipes (or whatever) can nonetheless shift closer and closer to the unwritten optimal even without the additional Lamarckism (in the case of biological inheritance, we also leave instruction out because there is little evidence for it).

Adding some version of Lamarckian shaping has two interesting effects: cakes converge on the optimal even more quickly, but the written recipes converge more slowly than they would otherwise. (In the terminology of evolutionary biology: With Lamarckism; the phenotypes evolve faster but, paradoxically, the genotypes evolve slower!) Should there be a "lost generation" that never learns to cook from their expert parents, the grandchildren will have to start over from instruction cards that haven't been shaped up anywhere as far as they might otherwise have been.

While shaping up the "written version" may be safer in the long run, one has to first survive the short run—and climates often shift so rapidly that survival depends on changing food-finding strategies just as quickly (in the cake analogy, suppose that next year's judges went sour on sugar, all trying to lose weight because of a new preventive medicine campaign against obesity). And so both the Old-Family-Recipe Effect and the Training Effect may prove essential in the short run because the judging criteria are so inconsistent.

In the analogy, the individual ingredients-and-procedures are the genes, the recipe is the sperm-or-ovum, and the whole population of cake recipes is the genome. And, of course, the cake is only the recipe's way of getting a copy made of itself. The Selfish Recipe has struck again.

THE ABILITY TO DO SOMETHING COMPLEX isn't, by itself, a sign of intelligence. The Earth's ocean-atmosphere-ice cap system is quite complex, without even being alive. Spiders weave complex webs but are hardly versatile designers. Ants build high-density dwellings that are air-conditioned with a sophistication that, until this century, was beyond the engineering abilities of mere humans. Learning and memory are not necessarily signs of sophisticated abilities either. All sorts of animals, such as earthworms, can learn and exhibit long-lasting memories. Pigeons have even learned quite fancy category discriminations, learning to pick out pictures of sad humans from happy humans. But when an animal does something both novel and complicated—after only several unsuccessful attempts—that's at least clever.

Observation learning is the most obvious case of such speed-ups in acquiring abilities, where one animal imitates the novel actions of another. Insight is another, where an animal seems to contemplate the situation and then does the effective thing without any trial-and-error. A dog on a leash, who is prevented from getting to food because its leash has become snagged around an intervening tree, may never solve the problem except by rambunctious trial-and-error. A chimp, on the other hand, can take one look at the situation, immediately retrace its steps, and disentangle its leash from the obstruction.

> *Man is an imitative animal.*
> *This quality is the germ*
> *of all education in him.*
> *From his cradle to his grave*
> *he is learning to do*
> *what he sees others do.*
> THOMAS JEFFERSON, *Writings*

LEARNING BY OBSERVATION AND IMITATION is not uniquely human. As the cats demonstrate. Psychologists had a hard time training cats to press bars or run mazes; rats do such things easily. Since the number of trials that it takes to produce flawless performance is the basic measure of learning among comparative psychologists, the recalcitrant cats were coming in last, behind the slowest rats in the ratings.

This contradicted common sense, so psychologists persevered and finally found a cooperative cat that would consent to learn their task. And the way they trained the *next* cat was simply to allow it to be a sideline spectator, while they put the trainable cat through its paces. When the spectator was then placed in the apparatus, it naturally tried out the tricks for itself. And so got the idea very quickly, faster than a rat would have done. The bar-pressing problem posed by the psychologists just wasn't sufficiently interesting by itself; the way to engage a cat's attention is to let it observe another animal.

Observation learning is probably how the neighborhood cats have discovered our pet cat's entrance to the basement. I had constructed this hole in the wall such that our cat had to jump the height of a countertop in order to reach the opening, thus breaking the scent trail that other animals could easily follow. And this indeed cuts down on the number of midnight marauders who require evicting. The raccoons still come to visit (we see their muddy paw prints on the glass of the front door, from where they peered inside during the night) but it has been a decade since one ransacked our kitchen, back in the days of a ground-level cat door. Yet once a year, a neighbor's cat will appear in our kitchen, with that tentative "just looking around" poise, shortly after our cat has arrived indoors. It probably saw the leap to the opening, and mimicked the behavior.

FORESIGHT LIES BEYOND INSIGHT (if one were to attempt to construct a rating scale for animal cleverness) but only if there is something unique about the plan. A squirrel hoarding nuts for wintertime at the behest of its hormones doesn't count. But as I discussed in my previous book, *The Cerebral Symphony*:

Chimpanzees come the closest to human-level novel planning when they engage in little deceptions (a behavior rarely observed in monkeys). A chimpanzee who comes upon a bountiful food resource—say, a tree full of ripe fruit—usually utters a joyful "food cry" that quickly attracts the other chimpanzees of the band, who similarly exclaim in delight upon seeing the bounty. But if the first chimp sees that there are only a few fruit to be had, it may keep quiet, attempting to silently eat all the fruit before any other chimp wanders along.

Foresight-prompted deception occurs when the lone chimp, hearing the approach of other chimps and worried that it will be deprived of the rest of its feast, leaves the limited bounty, casually strolls over in a different direction, and issues a food cry in the midst of dense foliage—where there is no food! This decoys the other chimps away from the limited supply of fruit. While the others are excitedly looking around the false site, the first chimp circuitously returns to the true site and finishes off the feast.

So it seems as if the chimpanzee can foresee the scenario of losing its remaining feast to competitors, and that it can spin a decoy scenario that involves "telling a lie." One might argue that these deceptions are only occasionally novel: losing food to a higher-ranking animal is an everyday occurrence, and most decoy deceptions are probably just repeats of an earlier success. But still, there is some element of novelty in the animal's "first lie" that begins to look like the scenario-spinning deceptions common in humans.

Now if all chimpanzees did such things, we might simply consider it an innate behavior, wired into their brains before birth. And if we knew that the chimp had learned to do this by mimicking the success of a frequent companion, we also might be less impressed. Only if we were convinced that a chimpanzee spun alternative scenarios, picked and chose between them, spun more scenarios when dissatisfied with the early choices, etc., would we worry that apes were closing in on the uniquely human scenario spinning abilities that we associate with contemplative consciousness.

And when we say *intelligent* rather than merely *smart* or *clever*, we are often implying a substantial amount of looking-ahead, judging the probable consequences of a novel course of action. Doing something nonstandard, rather than what your genes tell you is the appropriate thing to do, is usually risky. Just as most gene mutations are not an improvement (many lead to spontaneous abortions), most behavioral innovations are disastrous, absent foresight. The only way that humans get by with so many inventive behaviors, performed for the first time ever, is that we can do a lot of trial-and-error in our heads as we contemplate acting, as we "get set." We simulate a course of action before acting, provided that we have the time to spare. And we discard most of the plans before acting on them, rating them unsafe, inappropriate, or uninteresting.

Another key aspect of intelligence is the ability to perceive order in a situation that appears disorderly, all those collections of objects where you're supposed to deduce the feature that characterizes all but one, so as to spot the odd man out. What's been surprising is how often a chimpanzee can solve the ones that two-year-old babies can solve. Pigeons do surprisingly well, too.

THE ANIMAL INTELLIGENCE PROBLEM has caused some investigators to emphasize that animals can do almost anything that humans can, *except* use language to express the results or pose the questions. They suggest that the appropriate "null hypothesis" is that language is the main difference between apes and humans, that most of the "intelligence" differences are merely secondary to the mental structures that come with language.

The great neurologist of a century ago, John Hughlings-Jackson, said: "We speak not only to tell other people what we think, but to tell ourselves what we think." But don't animals think, and without our kind of language? Yes, all animals "think" to some extent—all can decide what to do next, evaluating their environment and choosing between standard alternatives—but without language we lose the richness of the choices available to the thoughtful person, and we miss out on much of our ability to invent novel alternatives.

The tragic problems of "feral children" are sometimes used to illustrate this point, but they always have a multitude of social and medical problems caused by the neglect. Children born deaf, and never exposed to sign language, illustrate how an otherwise-normal human upbringing that omits language leaves the unfortunate child lacking in basic abilities. The neurologist Oliver Sacks described such an 11-year-old deaf boy who was never exposed to sign language:

> Joseph saw, distinguished, categorized, used; he had no problems with *perceptual* categorization or generalization, but he could not, it seemed, go much beyond this, hold abstract ideas in mind, reflect, play, plan. He seemed completely literal—unable to juggle images or hypotheses or possibilities, unable to enter an imaginative or figurative realm. And yet, one still felt, he was of normal intelligence, despite these manifest limitations of intellectual functioning.

Joseph's deafness escaped diagnosis and compensatory early education in sign language; he was considered "retarded" or "autistic" for most of the critical years of his childhood. Language allows far greater levels of abstraction, permits us to build up mental models for how the world works, allows us to pose questions, craft answers.

How does the brain organize itself to do that? How do we weave together that linear tapestry that we call a text or a speech?

BRAINSTORMING techniques illustrate one explicit way of syn-
thesizing a sentence or proposition. This way of thinking is one
that we probably don't share at all with the apes (even if they
should have the neural machinery, they're usually too impatient!).
We attempt to generate dozens of ideas, the wilder the better—
but hold off evaluating them until quite a few have been gener-
ated. That way, we get a lot of variations on a theme out on the
table. Then we shape up the best ones a little further, using our
factual and aesthetic judgments.

This creativity-promoting technique is a lot like the processes
of Darwinian evolution, where a boom time serves to suspend
judgment until a lot of variations are out there, broadening the
characteristics of a species (like those dozens of unevaluated ideas).
And then judgment time arrives, usually in the form of a worsen-
ing climate, and only the versions survive that perform well in
that particular climate. Might the brain be using Darwinian techniques most of the time, not merely when formally brainstorming?
Might the subconscious be the dozens of mostly nonsense candidates, vying to be what we are conscious of?

Deciding what to say next is a simple example of the brainstorming technique, though we usually do it so unconsciously as to
be unaware of most intermediate steps. Imagine four planning
tracks, each able to hold on to a string of words, keep them in
order. Start with a series of words that are in the forefront of
your short-term memory, probably because you've recently used
or heard or read them; they'll each have some connections to other
words in your vocabulary (*cat* might evoke *dog*, *bite* might evoke
eat, etc.). Stringing some of them together in a random order will
usually yield nonsense (pretend that the four tracks are merely
the best out of a hundred such tracks). But some will approximate
reasonable sentences, when you judge the string of words against
your long-term memories of reasonable English-language sentences. Most of those will be inappropriate to the situation you're
currently in, so that current-situation judgment will deflate your
"good" ratings of otherwise reasonable sentences.

Now try another round of brainstorming: erase those low-
rated strings, take the top-rated string of Round One ("The dog
bit the mailman"), and try variations on it—which you store in the
erased tracks. This "noisy copy" makes mistakes just like the ones

Vocabulary in Short-term Memory

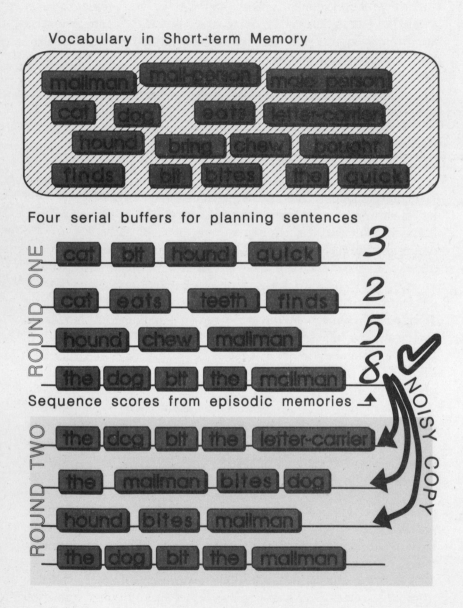

Four serial buffers for planning sentences

Sequence scores from episodic memories

in genetics, sometimes using a related word instead of the original (as in a thesaurus). And so you'll get *mailperson* as an occasional substitute for *mailman*, or perhaps *letter-carrier* or just *person*. There will be a hundred such strings in the hundred planning tracks: the original plus 99 variations on its themes, of which the top four might be worth talking about. These 99 new tracks are again judged against your memories of what might be grammatical and what might be suitable. If you prefer letter-carrier to other related words, you might wind up with "The dog bit the letter-carrier" as your most common string of words. If it seems good enough to cross your personal threshold for converting thought into action (perhaps because it has finally cloned itself into a majority of the planning tracks), you might even speak the sentence.

Many rounds of this shaping-up process would likely yield more literate sentences, and occasionally novelty: concepts that had never been linked together before. It's very much the way in which natural selection shapes up a population of biological individuals, which is why I call it a Darwin Machine.

The various Darwin Machines are each characterized by a somewhat different sequence of information units. A sequence of DNA nucleotides, in the case of genes. Amino acid sequences, in the case of an individual antibody of the immune system. And, in the case of mental plans for what to do next, we are creating new sequences of sensory schemas (e.g., nouns) and movement subprograms (e.g., verbs).

Besides the obvious usefulness for our kind of beyond-the-apes language, this Darwin Machine shaping-up method is also handy for scenarios, devising plans of action that involve many linked steps. Most random scenarios won't work, and it is nice to be able to figure that out before acting. If you've done exactly the same series of actions before (as that deceptive chimp might have done), fine—but what if the scenario is unique? Novelty in biological evolution usually results in spontaneous abortions; in behavior, most novel actions will get you into trouble. Making a working model of what is likely to happen next, inside your head before acting, is the way to have your cake and eat it too.

While remembered environments are less detailed than real ones, this off-line simulation and testing operates in milliseconds-to-seconds rather than the centuries-to-millennia of biological spe-

Vocabulary in Short-term Memory

ciation. If you've time to contemplate the problem, you can do thousands of generations, shaping up alternatives. Unless you are as unfortunate as the deaf Joseph, you can create a metaphorical world in your head, within a matter of minutes—and using the same techniques as Darwinian evolution took to evolve the biological world in eons.

But where might humans get those hundred planning tracks, that ability to shape up better and better plans? Why don't apes do the same thing? Our best clue is whatever evolved our left-brain's special ability to order things serially.

IS THE ELABORATION OF FORESIGHT, good old think-before-you-act, the particularly human aspect of intelligence that evolution somehow augmented, not language per se?

There are three main theories for where this foresight has come from, in evolutionary terms. The English psychologist Nicholas Keynes Humphrey, for example, would emphasize that social intelligence is all-important: that an up-and-coming chimp is always trying to predict what a dominant animal will do in response to an initiative, is often recruiting help by building coalitions, and otherwise solving social problems (that influence access to mates) rather than environmental ones (that affect survival). On this theory, social foresight bootstraps cleverness. This would make it analogous to the way the gorilla's harem mating system tends to exaggerate male body size.

A second theory is that augmented foresight (and, indeed, language) resulted from a conversion of function, that the natural selection was *not for foresight itself* but rather for the forerunner function, before conversion. However, let me start with a few words about the third, which is the conventional "natural selection" reasoning for becoming smarter and smarter—and a few more words about why one cannot be satisfied with it, which I like to call the Fermi Principle.

THE LAKESHORE TOWN of Balatonfüred in Hungary, an hour or two southwest of Budapest, was the scene of the International Astronomical Union's bioastronomy symposium. "Bioastronomy" is sometimes considered the IAU's euphemism for what is commonly known as the search for extraterrestrial intelligence, or

SETI (actually, it is quite appropriate: they are searching for biology in general, not intelligence in particular). About 150 scientists met for a week. We were mostly radio and optical astronomers, plus some chemists, and a few odd brain-behavioral people like me.

I suspect that many of us were curious to see the Hungarian culture that had produced so many mathematicians, scientists, artists, and composers. However, the visitor to Hungary is immediately disoriented by discovering that the language is completely impenetrable, totally unlike any familiar European language (though there is a distant relationship to Finnish and Estonian). Fortunately, many of the highway and railroad station signs are bilingual—Hungarian and German.

Hungary was a particularly appropriate place for a SETI discussion, given that famous quip by the Hungarian physicist Leo Szilard a half-century ago. Once at lunch, the Italian physicist Enrico Fermi tried to point out the absurdity of the favorable estimates of intelligent life elsewhere by asking, "If they are so probable, then where are they? They should be here already, we should have seen them by now." After all, there are stars far older than ours: life elsewhere could have had a ten-billion-year head start.

After a pregnant pause, Szilard answered, "Perhaps they are already here. But we call them *Hungarians*."

EXACTLY THE SAME OBJECTION as Fermi's can be raised to our common assumption that becoming intelligent, or at least smart, is what evolution is all about. It seems so self-evident that being smart is better than not. But, if so, we should now be surrounded by smart animals, exploiting sheer intelligence rather than brute strength and low cunning. Where are they?

Well, the primates, and indeed many of the mammals, are often clever. But really useful features tend to be reinvented by evolution. Photoreceptors have been independently invented over 40 times in various invertebrate lineages: partway out a branch on the tree of species, photoreception will appear and persist. Powered flight was invented at least three times after the insects did it: by the flying dinosaurs, by the bats, and by the birds (not to mention all the jumping spiders, gliding mammals, "flying" fish, even a snake that glides between tropical treetops). Is being smart a similar sterling feature of evolution, rediscovered many times?

If ape levels of cleverness are your criterion, then the answer is no. Even lowering your standards to the abilities exhibited by monkeys and bears still yields only one major lineage: mammals. But if we take a somewhat lower standard of intelligence, say the cleverness of a rat or raccoon, we can find several more lineages besides the mammals. The birds have gone on to develop clever crows, ravens, gulls, and vultures; the Egyptian Vultures bomb ostrich eggs with stones when the eggs themselves are too large to haul aloft and crack by dropping them. The big-brained crows and ravens are mischievous in ways that tend to suggest they get bored. And one invertebrate phylum, the mollusks, has also gone on to develop cleverness of a rat-raccoon level: the octopus has impressed researchers with its versatility, especially when it comes to catching crabs.

So count three examples of the independent evolution of rat-raccoon levels of cleverness, all probably associated with omnivorous diets and the necessity for a dozen different techniques for detecting and outsmarting prey. Why might there be a "varied diet" requirement for evolving cleverness? There are, of course, some clever animals that presently have monotonous diets, such as the marine mammals that presently make their living in the same manner as the fish-eating fish. The big brains of the dolphins and whales don't seem to be currently needed for many of their characteristic food-finding behaviors, given that fish-sized brains suffice. The land-dwelling ancestors of the marine mammals probably specialized in eating shellfish in the intertidal. They gradually learned to swim well enough to exploit schools of fish offshore, and finally miniaturized their limbs and converted to streamlined body forms via a thick layer of fat, rounding out their shapes (sea otters, who rely on fur rather than fat for insulation, have probably returned to the sea rather recently, compared to the 100-million-year time scale of the seals, dolphins, and whales).

But having a mammalian brain means that they can sometimes invent clever techniques, the way that orca ("killer whales") may herd small fish into a corral of bubbles. They swim around blowing bubbles, to create a circular curtain that causes the fish to turn around and head back toward the middle. Then the orca

soar up through the corral toward the surface, mouths wide
open, scooping up fish. Laying down a bubble curtain is exactly
what hatchery workers do when wanting to net a lot of fish—but
I think that orca invented the technique, long before humans.

The big brain of the gorilla isn't really needed for its
60-pounds-a-day diet of leaves and bamboo. And while they can be
playful, wild gorillas exhibit little of the behavioral versatility of
the chimps and haven't been observed to do anything as fancy as
the orca's funneling of fish. Gorillas (and, for that matter, orang-
utans and the lesser apes) seem to have retreated into a vegetar-
ian niche that severely limits where they can live. Given the low
quality of the food, they need dense forest to provide the needed
quantities (and an enormous gorilla-length gut to digest them).
Humans who retreat from our ancestral diet that valued meat to
being vegetarians can at least cook their food (which expands the
choice enormously, via inactivating toxins and softening bonds).

Obviously, cleverness isn't just useful in finding food and
avoiding predators. It can also facilitate acquiring mates, surely
one of the major advantages of social intelligence. In societies
with a dominance hierarchy, the position in the hierarchy tends to
influence reproductive success—and so the ability to build alli-
ances, pacify the angry, get around a watchful alpha male and
consort with a female unobserved, will all aid reproductive fitness.

The most obvious aspect of male competition for females is
body size—the bigger gorilla tends to win the fights with smaller
males, and so a harem-type mating system leads to an arms race
in body size. But since a gene augmenting testosterone production
is located on the male-only Y chromosome, it's mostly bigger
bodies for the males (they're now about twice the size of females).
In contrast, male cleverness in winning females in other spheres
of action should tend to improvements in both male and female
cleverness in following generations (there is only room for several
genes on the Y chromosome, so most are located on the 22 pairs
and X chromosome common to both males and females), just as
female cleverness in keeping sick infants alive has undoubtedly
benefitted both sexes, not just females.

Thus both environmental selection and sexual selection could
operate on cleverness and so shape up the population to evolve
into increasingly more clever animals. Even a minor improvement

can eventually confer a major advantage. Consider the fourfold brain size increase of humans over the apes, most of which happened in the last 2.5 million years: it only required an average increase of one-millionth of a percent per generation. Compound interest has done the rest. Or so the story goes.

Why should not Nature have taken a leap from structure to structure? On the theory of natural selection, we can clearly understand why she should not; for natural selection can only act by taking advantage of slight successive variations; she can never take a leap, but must advance by the shortest and slowest steps.

CHARLES DARWIN, *On the Origin of Species*, 1859

SUCH IS THE STANDARD REASONING for intelligence by adaptations, the argument why, given enough time, biology *ought* to evolve our kind of intelligence: We just used increments in cleverness for more efficient food-finding, predator evasion, or creating mating opportunities.

The efficiency type of argument always seems to point to inevitable progress. "Since evolving intelligence is a general principle of nature, we don't need to bother with the details—it'll happen, one way or another." Perhaps that is a little exaggerated, but it is what the physicists and astronomers rely upon, when they argue the probabilities of finding intelligence "out there."

Why, then, are the evolutionary biologists so uniformly skeptical about the SETI story? It's not that they believe intelligence is surely rare elsewhere—they just point out that progression in intelligence is a suspect proposition, that efficiency leads even more often to dead ends. They are better acquainted with all those branches of the tree of animals that don't seem to be going anywhere, those stabilities into which evolution settles.

A familiar stability is embodied in the Peter Principle, the late Lawrence J. Peter's humorous suggestion that all experienced bureaucrats are incompetent. This is because, as a reward for past service, they've finally been promoted to a level for which their abilities prove insufficient. And so they receive no further promotions, limited by reaching their "level of incompetence." This stability means, in Peter's formulation, that the higher echelons of the bureaucracy are filled by people who are well-suited to one level *below* their final rank. Biological evolution isn't quite like that (nor are real organizations!), but there are many stabilities that similarly limit progress. Indeed, species often "paint themselves into a corner" by overspecialization.

Evolution is also full of *good-enough solutions* that remove a feature from exposure to natural selection—and so a Rube Goldberg scheme may persist without improvement. "Satisficing" is Herbert Simon's term (from satisfy, as opposed to optimize) that he uses to describe the analogous situation—the failure to optimize seen in psychology and economics. Satisficing is probably why only three lineages have developed rat-raven-octopus levels of cleverness: most were clever enough for their way of making a living and the brain changes that did chance to come along had as many liabilities as they did advantages.

But, assuming that dead-end stabilities aren't reached, how fast will evolution progress toward cleverness? It depends on exposure to natural and sexual selection. As the Younger Dryas story suggests, there are sometimes severe waves of natural selection (in the following chapter, I will elaborate on the various selection cycles that may have played a role in our evolution). But what else influences the speed with which new functionality develops?

Evolution isn't just "shaping up" via adaptations, though that is the first explanation we always try out for size, when contemplating a feature that evolution has produced. There are at least two other major routes to new functionality: 2) sometimes a feature is shaped by natural selection for another feature, one that is linked to the first feature because they share a common developmental mechanism (as when selection for precocious puberty also serves to produce shorter stature and smaller adult teeth). And 3) sometimes a new function is simply invented, a new use emerging for old anatomy. One hesitates to invoke these less common explanations until the simple adaptationist reasoning is tried out.

Yet sometimes the simple route just doesn't work very well. I like to imagine what Nicholas Copernicus would have been subjected to, had there been scientific meetings of our modern kind in sixteenth-century Europe: "But my dear Copernicus, surely it is simpler to assume just *one* rotation, that of the sun around the earth? Occam's Razor says we should pick the simplest explanation, does it not? Why this messy, unaesthetic business of assuming *two* rotations, the absurd postulate of the earth rotating in orbit around the sun, plus the earth rotating around some axis through the frozen northlands? Gentlemen, if the earth were spinning like some child's top, I'd fly off my feet and out that window! And I assure you that my feet remain planted firmly on the ground." No wonder Copernicus was reluctant to publish until he was dying—he could imagine the pointed questions.

Simplicity is relative: it depends on how many things you're trying to explain at once. Just imagine what you'd have asked Copernicus or Galileo at a scientific meeting if you didn't much care about those occasional retrograde motions of the planets across the night sky, didn't think them very important compared to the sun and moon. We see a closely analogous situation when attempting to figure out what happened in human evolution: with adaptations one can usually, given a sufficiently good imagination, figure out a plausible reason why a feature might have been useful. We explain things one feature at a time— just like that fellow Ptolemy, the Roman astronomer of the second century A.D. who simply added on another "epicycle" for each problem that needed a solution, building up a descriptive model of the motions of the heavens with dozens of rotations around different centers (rather than Copernicus' two).

One can, presumably, "explain" everything in human evolution in that mosaic manner—but how enlightening will that be? Explicating many disparate features with one stroke of the theorist's pen, proposing an explanatory structure that not only explains with economy but is framed to be fallible (potentially falsifiable)—that's considered the sign of a more promising theory. In contemplating our present task, we see that there are easily a hundred features by which we humans differ from the apes—not just language, but also plan-ahead intelligence, accurate throwing, concealed ovulation, relative brain size, hand anatomy, body hair. Not to mention pseudo-monogamy and our predilections for wagering and playing all sorts of serial-sequential games. Were there a hundred different lines of improvement, as the prevalent Ptolemaic adaptationist reasoning seems to envision—

or just a few basic inventions, each of which had multiple effects via developmental linkages or conversions of function?

WORSE YET, efficient adaptations can actually slow down the evolution of complex behaviors. That is because a major stimulus toward more elaborate organisms has been the fluctuating climate: if evolution were fast enough to track it, we'd likely see body styles fluctuating back and forth along the same path that the weather takes—getting bigger or smaller, more or less hairy, earlier or later maturing. But with little sustained, long-term trends.

Yet evolution is often too slow to track the Earth's climate, especially given those episodes of abrupt climatic change like the Younger Dryas where the climate shifts dramatically within one generation. That generation either has what it takes, or it dies.

And so those variants that happen along, capable of surviving various extremes of climate, will have an advantage over those aforementioned one-climate-at-a-time efficient trackers. The very slowness of evolution relative to climate change serves as a drive toward more complex organisms, those with the machinery for handling both kinds of environment. And complexity is the overall trait that underlies intelligence, primarily because new capabilities emerge from combinations of mechanisms: rather than compound interest, we have compounded mechanisms, such as those dozen behavioral strategies that omnivores need for finding their various kinds of food. The SETI meeting in Hungary offered a perfect example of what compounded mechanisms might provide, which I incorporated into my talk.

We humans track the seasons by varying the clothing we wear. When we travel to Hungary in the summer, I noted, we have the problem of guessing whether or not we will need warm clothing. (This brought an appreciative chuckle from the audience at Balatonfüred, as the first few days of the conference had been too chilly for swimming or windsurfing offshore at lunchtime.) Those who always carry both winter and summer outfits will be safest. Those who carry only enough for one climate at a time will be less burdened. Because carry-on luggage may suffice, they may get the only available taxicabs while the cautious await their checked baggage. If the weather was completely unpredictable, then everyone would have to carry along both winter and summer clothing. As long as climate fluctuations occur slowly, the more efficient packers may outreproduce those clothing-for-all-seasons types burdened by the need to be so versatile.

But sometimes new properties arise from having both sets of clothing available at the same time (perhaps a winter coat or umbrella could be pressed into service as a sail for summer windsurfing on Lake Balaton?). And sometimes compounded mechanisms confer new "emergent" properties, quite unlike anything existing. They are true innovations, not just predictable improvements.

This means that capabilities occasionally arrive unheralded by gradual predecessors. In the familiar case of bird flight origins, natural selection for thermal insulation shaped forelimb feathers up to the threshold for flight. Natural selection for a better airfoil shaped feathers thereafter. But the switchover from one track to another was presumably a surprise, leaving the protobirds to explore their newfound abilities rather as we might try to figure out a holiday gift that arrived without an instruction manual. The protobird's experiments were very different from adaptations, where the animal already knows how to perform and the improvement is merely a matter of efficiency.

Inventions are the novelties in evolution, though you'd think that shaping-up streamlining was what it was all about, when reading most of the literature (most of the people doing the arguing are primarily concerned with bone-based comparative anatomy, not the broader viewpoint of comparative physiology). But adaptations are only improvements on a basic design; what we're talking about is the invention itself before streamlining, which is often a matter of a conversion of function. Nature does take leaps, and the physiological conversions of function are even faster than those anatomical leaps envisaged by proponents of punctuated equilibria and hopeful monsters.

> *In considering transitions of organs,*
> *it is so important to bear in mind*
> *the probability of conversion*
> *from one function to another. . . .*
> CHARLES DARWIN, 1859

THIS SECOND MAJOR ASPECT of evolutionary change is something that people often forget, fixated on what Darwin said about "a leap from structure to structure" being unlikely. But that's *structure*: Darwin also emphasized the role of conversions of *function* without anatomical change. Adaptationists often conflate the two, probably because their focus is on bones where structure is indeed closely related to function. There's more to bodies than bones.

Darwin's teaching example of a functional conversion was the fish's swim bladder: a fish extracts gases from the blood and inflates the swim bladder just enough so the fish neither sinks nor floats to the surface (pilots will recognize this as a biological version of the "trim tab" on a rudder). Darwin suggested that when fish crawled ashore, they started exchanging blood gases with the outside air by converting the swim bladder's then-obsolete function to the new one, breathing air. For efficiency, many lobes of the swim bladder were developed and, somewhere along this path, we rename it "the lung." But a conversion of function, as in the case of those reptilian feathers on forelimbs, need not initially require an anatomical change (though, of course, they tend to follow as the new function comes under natural selection for efficiency).

Life coming ashore surely involved quite a lot of compounding of mechanisms, as intertidal animals have to survive both in the water and in drying conditions; they acquire compounded mechanisms in consequence, organs for both environments not unlike the way that some animals (such as humans and horses) have both hair for insulation and sweat glands for getting rid of excess heat. When finally ashore, early land animals had some obsolete organs available for conversion, such as the swim bladder and the salt glands.

Might intelligence have been aided by some conversions of function, perhaps in brain machinery?

THE BRAIN IS PROBABLY BETTER at new uses for old things than any other organ of the body. Sometimes two digestive enzymes, which each evolved separately for a different food, can act in combination to digest a third foodstuff; occasionally, *nature really does provide something for nothing*. (Yes, I know that this is profoundly anti-Calvinist; there is a Puritanical streak in modern evolutionary thinking that seems to require us to look for a function's antecedents in their usefulness to that very function, not some other one.) But a brain can easily combine sensory schema and movement programs in new ways, since it tends to use a common currency.

From whatever source, an excitatory or inhibitory input is first converted into positive or negative millivolts; nerve cells then add and subtract in this substitute value system. For one input to substitute for another, it only needs to produce similar voltage changes in the relevant nerve cells. One can add apples and oranges to get so many pieces of fruit.

This means that omnivores, with their compounding of behavioral programs for detecting and outmaneuvering many kinds of prey, can make innovations more easily than an animal evolved for eating a monotonous diet. Indeed herbivores have smaller brains than omnivores of the same body weight. Horses and bears have similar body size, but the bear's brain is somewhat larger and it is forever outsmarting the human designers of garbage cans for national parks.

It is hard to talk about "basic units" of brain function but, for the present purpose, sensory schemas and movement programs will suffice; even if you haven't heard of them separately, you've heard of their combination, the reflex. Schema is the general term for the template inside the mind that detects a sensory pattern in time and space; movement programs such as breathing can often be decomposed into subprograms, such as for inspiration and expiration. When a schema and movement program are firmly linked, we tend to call the combination a reflex, as when the silhouette of a hawk overhead causes a baby bird to crouch down in concealment. We once thought that all movements were guided by reflexes; now we know that some are innate, capable of being executed spontaneously and without any sensory guidance. Feedback tends to be important when first learning a new task, or when the task is quite varied (each time I pick up my teacup, its weight is somewhat different and my posture has probably altered too)—feedback helps shape up the movement program.

What is surprising about schemas is what seems to suffice—some are quite crude, not even the equivalent of a cartoon sketch. Some shore birds, for example, may recognize their own young by

proximity to the nest: let a chick stray outside the parents' territory, and it will be attacked when it returns, as if a total stranger.
Male flickers (a colorful woodpecker) have a black "moustache"
stripe on the side of their heads; paint such a stripe on a female,
and her mate will attack her as if she were a total stranger. The
cuckoo practices parenthood piracy successfully because the "foster parents" fail to recognize their young except via a brightly
colored throat, which cuckoo chicks mimic and so are fed, even
when absurdly larger in size than the foster parents. Some birds
will preferentially incubate the larger eggs in a nest—and so one
can see a small bird sitting atop a large chicken egg placed in its
nest by experimenters, ignoring its own small eggs.

Absurd? Evolution often is—that's because good-enough solutions may suffice (Simon's "satisfice"), and evolution never gets
around to finding solutions for the occasional problems. Our first-
generation household robots are going to be characterized by
similar stupidities, and we will tell each other stories of how our
robot threw out the umbrellas with the trash, mistaking the
umbrella stand for a wastebasket.

INBORN SCHEMAS certainly exist, but the hawk-overhead pro-
tective crouch shows how indirectly the detection may be accom-
plished. We eventually realized that chicks initially crouch down
when *any* bird flies over, but soon habituate to the more familiar
species that they see every day. Then only rarely seen birds
trigger the reflex. Some birds are rare because they are exotics,
just passing through. But other species are few in numbers because they are at the top of the food web; birds that eat other
birds cannot be as numerous as their prey species. So the simple
habituation serves, at the cost of some false alarms, to tune up the
chick to the local predator species, whatever it is. Thanks to the
population statistics of various species in the food web, all it needs
as "inborn" is the generalized bird-overhead template, an ability
to learn new schemas (special cases of the more general inborn
type), and the ability to use learned schemas to cancel the primi-
tive reflex.

Movement programs can be tuned up too, enhancing and
suppressing features with both genetic variations and learning
within individual lifetimes. The horse's "pacing" gait, where both

left legs move forward together, then both right, is infrequently seen in nature, but selective breeding can bring it out. A few humans have the ability to wiggle their ears, and it seems likely that many others could learn to do so with sufficient shaping by a skillful coach. Some movement variations turn out to be useful in certain situations; a dog that tends to circle a few times before lying down would, in the context of grasslands, create a better nest for itself. Charles Darwin saw this potential for variation and selection of such behaviors in his 1872 book on the expression of emotions.

Nature is always throwing up new variations, thanks to the shuffling of genes when making new sperm and ova. We tend to think of the unusual phenotypes as "defective" (the 15 percent of children who have difficulty learning to read) or as "gifted" (unusual musical and artistic abilities)—but we are all just variations on a series of themes, thrown up for the present environment to evaluate. We are all nonstandard *because there is no standard* (that "escape from the Platonic essence" was the initial ingredient of Darwin's great insight that allowed him to conceive how evolution works). When the variations are easy to see (thin and fat, short and tall, light skins and dark), we give them names—but when they just involve brain wiring, as many of them do, then they are less readily recognized.

When a new way of making a living comes along, perhaps extracting insects from holes with a probe, these brain variations make it easier for some individuals to learn the new task. Perhaps they have a predisposition to chew on the ends of sticks (like some children I know) and so are likely to manufacture better "fishing" sticks. More of their offspring survive than others, and so variations on the new theme get tried out, some of which are even better at fishing for insects. Eventually some body features change, in addition to the more subtle brain features, as when the precision grip modifications are made to the fingers.

Because learning within an individual lifetime is easier than brain-wiring variations in successive generations, which are in turn easier than gross body changes, behavior tends to lead the way in exploring new evolutionary pathways. Squirrels that seek food in the tops of trees may have to climb all the way up a tree, then all the way back down, and across the ground to another tree. But if its ability to leap across rocks on the ground can be extended to leaping between branches in the treetops (perhaps because a variation arose that had less fear of heights), then it might become a more efficient food-finder, despite the fraction of the population fatally injured by falls. If the climate then cooled, so that the forest thinned out, squirrels that could glide between trees would become the most efficient at feeding their offspring. And so we might see the squirrel's skin become flabby, as those with that variation would now have a more suitable airfoil for gliding from the top of one tree to halfway down a neighboring tree. They'd get to the food faster, and outfox the foxes watching from the ground for a squirrel to descend. It's The Old Family Recipe Effect at work.

SO OUR KIND OF INTELLIGENCE may not be the inevitable outcome of some general principle of nature. And, while it might happen via gradual adaptations, surely there were a number of speeding-things-up surprises along the way as animals discovered previously untried combinations of sensory schemas and movement programs that proved handy for new ways of finding food, avoiding predators, or acquiring mates.

The natural history of intelligence may turn out to be a prolonged version of the progress we've recently seen from special-purpose computers to the modern general-purpose computer. The basic techniques evolved in the nineteenth century with the programmable Jaccard loom, the punched card sorting machines, and the mechanical hand-operated calculators. By the time of World War II, special-purpose computers were constructed for pointing antiaircraft guns and breaking ciphers—and these machines were internally so similar that we began to see general-purpose computers, able to switch from one task to another. In less than a half-century, schoolchildren possess computers far more versatile than those once nurtured in air-conditioned warehouses by legions of experts.

Did we get our general-purpose brains, capable of tasks like reading that were never involved in their evolution, via a similar series of special-purpose adaptations for finding fruit and catching meat? Did our fruit-finding ancestors owe their versatility to something similar? Certainly developmental coupling, mechanism compounding, and functional conversions are—each of them—a theme as important as the usual adaptationist efficiency. But we must look at the interaction between a flexible diet and a changeable climate to see how hominid brains might have been "pumped up." It doesn't take climate change as abrupt or dramatic as the Younger Dryas to pump up behavioral versatility; the ice ages have had plenty of merely rapid changes as well.

And even if we explain the origins of *Homo sapiens*, there is still the problem of accounting for how Hungarians happened.

[As] my conclusions have lately been much misrepresented, and it has been stated that I attribute the modification of species exclusively to natural selection, I may be permitted to remark that in the first edition of this work, and subsequently, I placed in a conspicuous position—namely at the close of the Introduction—the following words: "I am convinced that natural selection has been the main but not the exclusive means of modification." This has been of no avail. Great is the power of steady misrepresentation. . . .

CHARLES DARWIN, in a late edition
of *On the Origin of Species*

The great synthesizer who alters the outlook of a generation, who suddenly produces a kaleidoscopic change in our vision of the world, is apt to be the most envied, feared, and hated man among his contemporaries. Almost by instinct they feel in him the seed of a new order; they sense, even as they anathematize him, the passing away of the sane, substantial world they have long inhabited. Such a man is a kind of lens or gathering point through which thought gathers, is reorganized, and radiates outward again in new forms.

LOREN EISELEY, 1973

3

FINDING A FAST TRACK TO THE BIG BRAIN: HOW CLIMATE PUMPS UP COMPLEXITY

D'où venons nous?
Que sommes nous?
Où allons nous?
Where have we come from?
What are we?
Where are we going?
PAUL GAUGUIN, 1897

T he old joke goes, "But you can't get there from here!" (This was the response given by the laconic farmer to the city motorist who was lost in the backcountry and asking for directions.) I'm reminded of it because of our attempts to find a certain restaurant in the hills near Lake Balaton. We asked questions—in German, translated from American English—of Hungarian pedestrians and eventually discovered that we had to drive back downhill to the lakeshore and then take a different road back up into the hills.

But, of course, you can get there from *almost* anywhere (when in the company of astronomers, one has to make allowances for the improbability of ever escaping from a black hole). It's just that the path may be a little roundabout, requiring a lot of detailed description about backtracking to some other junction, rather than a simple "That-a-way." Progress sometimes requires a temporary dose of *regress*. The evolutionary path from an apelike ancestor to *Homo sapiens* also requires a lot of detailed description, including backing up a few times. Indeed, if intelligence is not one of those much-sought "general principles" of the universe, the details of the path are all-important.

Yet self-congratulatory generalizations are about all we've got in the way of explanations for hominid evolution—such as "Man the Toolmaker" or the "bigger is smarter is better" pseudoexplanation of why brains enlarged fourfold. What we need is a good idea about each leg of the journey to humanity, the opportunities and provisions along the way, the hazards and how our ancestors coped with them, plus some notion of how we avoided drifting back to where we started. And we've got a lot more to explain than mere cleverness or brain size—for instance, ethics, art, music, compassion.

We've come a long way from the apes. There is no animal currently around that can serve as a suitable stand-in for our common ancestor with the apes. But, if you imagine the common ancestor as a composite of the chimpanzee and gorilla, you're not likely to be far off. While all ape species have surely changed as well during the last 5–10 million years, they haven't made the major transitions that separate us from our common ancestor: walking upright, concealed ovulation, elaborate language, extensive tool use, accurate throwing for hunting, and the big brain.

Attention has naturally focussed on how we evolved from an ape level of language and intelligence to that exhibited by the remaining hunter-gatherer bands of today—and on the acquisition of a fourfold larger brain along the way. Did toolmaking drive the brain boom, as anthropologists once proposed? The usefulness of language, as the linguists propose? The psychologists are naturally in favor of intelligence as the *raison d'être*. And at least one neurophysiologist thinks that it is mostly due to the brain-muscle coordination needed for hunting with projectiles (although I'm not a sports fan, we neurophysiologists are fascinated with rapid movements of all kinds). If you asked a reproductive biologist, there would surely be a key role for concealed ovulation (no more estrus behaviors advertising the time of maximum fertility, promoting pair-bonding but also social cleverness). All of us could be right. Unlike the tale of the blind men and the elephant, there is more than one right answer—because everything in biology has multiple "causes."

There may be multiple ways to be "right" but there are even more ways to be wrong. And eliminating incorrect explanations is a key way in which science progresses in many fields. As the economist Kenneth Boulding once said,

I have revised some folk wisdom lately; one of my edited proverbs is "Nothing fails like success," because you do not learn anything from it. The only thing we ever learn from is failure. Success only confirms our superstitions.

For some strange reason which I do not understand at all a small subculture arose in Western Europe which legitimated failure. Science is the only subculture in which failure is legitimate.

For example, it was once thought—quite reasonably, I might add—that upright posture was caused by the need to "free up" the hands for toolmaking and, in addition, that a bigger brain was required for manual dexterity. Thus toolmaking should precede upright posture and the brain boom, and parallel their changes. The sequence was even embedded into popular thought by the opening scene of the movie *2001*. Now, thanks to a lot of hard work in the hot sun by the paleoanthropologists and archaeologists and geologists, we know that, instead, upright posture *preceded* prolific toolmaking by several million years. Some fossil footprints of a bipedal hominid dated to 3.5 million years ago are virtually identical to those of present-day South American Indians who habitually go barefoot. Though the facts eliminated that hypothesis for upright posture, they unfortunately didn't explain what "caused" the posture to shift to upright.

EVENTS DURING HUMAN EVOLUTION

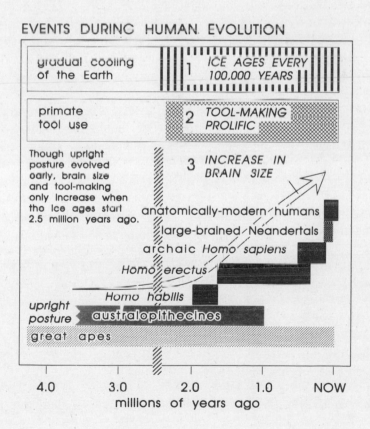

And we now know that about 2.5 million years ago, three major trends started up, all at about the same time: prolific toolmaking, brain enlargement, and the ice ages. Was one the "cause" of the other two? I can't imagine how anything done by a hominid could have affected the ice ages (at least back then—we surely can cause an ice age now, should by-products of our technology increase the marine cloud cover enough). So that reduces the possibilities to:

1) toolmaking-to-encephalization,
2) encephalization-to-toolmaking,
3) ice age-to-toolmaking, and
4) ice age-to-encephalization

if one ignores such other issues as language (and the null hypothesis: that they all happened independently of one another!).

Some crucial archaeological evidence is now available concerning the first possibility. While brain enlargement accelerated to achieve the fourfold mark by about 0.1 million years ago in *Homo sapiens*, toolmaking had a more fitful course. From about 1.5 until about 0.3 million years ago, the brain size of our ancestors doubled—but toolmaking suffered from a lack of major developments; the Acheulean toolkit stayed about the same. So it becomes hard to argue that innovative toolmaking was what rewarded any bigger-brain variants in the genome. So eliminate #1.

That encephalization might have eventually facilitated toolmaking (#2) will surprise no one, but it seems a very slow path to me. That the ice ages might provide a stimulus to toolmaking (#3) is similarly possible but slow, and the argument is not as sound as one initially supposes. So did the ice ages drive the brain boom (#4), which secondarily facilitated toolmaking? That's still a very interesting proposition—indeed, what the rest of this book will examine. This isn't some general evolutionary principle at work: that's because the ice ages do not seem to have affected other mammalian brains in a similar way. One has to examine this possibly unique journey in great detail, looking for connections between Pleistocene ecological opportunities and the hominid skills not shared with the apes. And while concentrating on "progress," one must remember to look around for opportunities conferred by regression as well.

THE CLOSER WE LOOK at apes in the wild, the more we notice that we share many features of their social lives. The African apes are clever, both in manipulating tools and in social manipulations of each other—including both cooperation and deception, both aggression and peacemaking. Patiently trained to use sign language in the laboratory, apes exhibit the ability to use language with about the complexity shown by a two-year-old child—a vocabulary of a few hundred words and simple sentences that make no demands on syntax—though in the wild, the apes use only a few dozen exclamations and a variety of body postures and facial expressions. That shared body language and gesture is still used by humans—when language fails (as by Americans in Hungary) or just redundantly (as by Italians in Italy). We have greatly elaborated communications with our serial-sequential languages—but just how important might that have been for finding food, defending against raiders?

What about some of the ecological-niche candidates for shaping up modern man? More than a million years ago, hominids learned to live outside the tropics and subtropics, which means that they could cope with winter. This required some new skills. Clothing for insulation, fire-making, and shelter would take on considerable importance. Yet none would seem to require much more intelligence than our ape cousins demonstrate—more patience, perhaps, but not much more cleverness.

The big problem with living through the winter is food: the choice becomes very restricted for a few months each year because the gathering is so thin, plants having shed their edible leaves, and the snow masks what's left for the taking. To get yourself, much less dependent offspring, through the winter usually means one of two strategies (though there are some exceptions): hoarding a surplus from the summer, or being able to eat grass, which remains nutritious through the winter, whether bundled as "hay" or dormant on the ground. The grazing animals manage to find enough grass beneath the snow, and they have evolved the teeth and digestive enzymes they need to utilize it. Humans haven't, but they have managed to eat animals that eat grass by becoming skillful enough at hunting.

Hoarding sometimes works, but usually only with hunting as a backup: sometimes the harvest is insufficient, sometimes the rats break into your grain hoard, or the wolves discover the frozen carcass and gobble up the meat on which you were relying to get through the last half of winter. Living in the temperate zones tends to suggest that hominid hunting techniques had become more reliable than those opportunistic snatch-and-grab tactics used by chimpanzees.

But what do hunting skills have to do with our more valued aspects of humanity: language, consciousness, ethics, music? Actually, thanks to the neural machinery needed for accurate throwing, quite a lot—because all of the aforementioned happen to be aspects of the serial-order behaviors in which the brain's left hemisphere specializes. Perhaps, when not throwing projectiles or swinging a club, the neural sequencing machinery can be used for speaking a sentence, or planning for tomorrow, or feeling dismay when seeing a tragedy unfold (or laughing at the surprise ending, counter to your expectations). Some such neural machinery is secondarily useful for composing a melody, or playing chess, or dancing, or kicking. Spare-time use of machinery in the off-hours for secondary uses didn't start with playing games on the office computer: conversion of function is a major mechanism of evolution, described by Charles Darwin in the middle of the nineteenth century. Natural selection acting on any *one* serial-order skill might tend to improve *all* of them, just because they all utilize the same neural machinery for creating novel sequences of muscle commands.

WHICH WAY TO OUR BIG BRAIN? Given all the advantages of being smart, there is surely more than one way to become intelligent. Indeed, those who have thought about the SETI problem often observe that "Surely X would be useful." And the theorist of evolutionary intelligence can seldom rule out that route, in the manner that a physicist manages to rule out 99 percent of the theories offered to explain a phenomenon, just showing that X would also cause Y to happen—and it hasn't, therefore rule that one out too. In biology, there are always multiple causes of everything we study, so we can't have the physicist's kind of confidence in our attempts to eliminate causative factors.

But one way to make progress in clearing away the minor causes and concentrating on the major movers is to ask, "Yes, but how fast would such a change happen?" In biology, fast tracks tend to preempt slow tracks. And sometimes, evolution happens so rapidly that only a fast track could have done it.

Our big brains are a prime example of rapid evolution: they have increased fourfold in size in a mere 2.5 million years. That's almost unbelievably fast by the standards of evolutionary biology. *The rapidity itself is a clue as to the evolutionary causes of brain size increase.* It tends to rule out slow tracks such as smarter-is-better, where the incremental payoff for each 10 percent increase is small indeed.

So what controls evolutionary rates? Some factors are: producing individual variations (via mutations and permutations). The severity of selection (droughts every decade). The rate of evolutionary inventions (those conversions of function, the compounding of mechanisms). The invention of a new niche, or finding an empty one, makes for boom times (of which, more later). The prevention of backsliding (via reproductive ratchets and similar stabilities). And more.

The hominid's Great Encephalization is so rapid that one tends to look for scenarios that incorporate a number of these factors. We may not have used every possible way of speeding up our brain changes, but we likely used quite a few of them.

TO SHOW HOW SELECTION shapes up populations, short of writing a textbook on all these factors, one can try telling a bedtime story about a bear. Bears are popular here in central Europe; they're "emblematic," as the anthropologists might say. My exemplar bear will henceforth be known as Mama Bear.

At the opening of Act I, we see Mama Bear and her two baby bears, gambolling about in the summer sunshine. So ends Act I (and the traditional version of the bedtime story; the following might be considered a revisionist adult version).

Act II is a year later. Mama Bear weaned the two baby bears after a half-year of suckling them. Then after putting up with them for a winter of hibernation, she kicked them out into the real world to fend for themselves. This is Mama Bear's summer for getting pregnant again; next winter she will again give birth to another pair.

Act III is another two years later, with another two half-grown bears let loose on the world. Mama Bear may do this five or ten times during her lifetime, if she stays healthy.

Unfortunately, a little arithmetic shows that this story doesn't have a happy ending. How many bears can the environment feed? Obviously, that's the average bear population. And that means, on average, only two babies per mother get to grow up and become a parent, out of the dozen or two that she produces. The maximum population level is not set by the birth rate but by the number of job slots afforded by the environmental niche occupied by bears. And that is a complicated function of food availability, suitable nesting sites, predator populations, pathogens, parasites, and such. Only in boom times does birth rate have much to do with it.

That means the average Mama Bear is raising five to ten times more baby bears than can possibly survive, absent, of course, miracles—approximately what one might call it when a new niche happens to open up, either by new territory becoming available (as when the Alaskan brown bear discovered the ice-free corridor, at the same time as the Paleo-Indians) or when a new way of making a living is discovered (as when bears learned to go fishing in streams for salmon migrating upstream). For cats and dogs, the waste is even worse: say, six per litter, and five or ten litters per mother, but only enough adult food for two of them to survive. I know one cat, living in optimal circumstances, who has given birth to more than 200 offspring, a hundred times her quota. So again (at least in nature) there are a lot of animals that are going to die of starvation, becoming food for a predator.

Why does Mama Bear spend all that effort raising many times more offspring than the market will bear (no pun intended)? It's called "keeping up with the Joneses." For Mama Bear to have a *gene Q* for doing less would result in fewer such *gene Q*'s in the next generation; this gene would "work itself out of business." Indeed, this situation is like an arms race; if a variant arises that can successfully raise triplets, her genes will soon take over the population, replacing the two-at-a-time genes, making triplets the new standard, and so on to even bigger litters.

If triplets don't happen now, it's probably only because each would be so stunted in size from crowding *in utero* as to be less competitive; three scrawny ones being worse than two of the standard twin-size. The bigger the litter, the higher the percentage of manufacturing defects—and the less postnatal parental

attention per offspring. In boom times, all offspring might survive—
and indeed both bears and humans shift to larger litters when
resources are bountiful.

This is an Alice-in-Wonderland sort of principle: the Red
Queen told Alice that you have to keep running just to stay in the
same place. The Red Queen is one of the reasons we talk of a
naturalist fallacy. "What's natural is good" is, alas, another example of substituting upbeat wishful thinking for familiarizing
oneself with the available evidence. Across many species of mammals, the amount of effort devoted to reproduction bears little
relationship to niche size. Nature just hasn't developed a way of
limiting overproduction of baby bears (or any other species, although humans may yet become an exception), and most animals
spend nearly all their life just raising youngsters with which to
feed the predators and pathogens.

THIS UNHAPPY STATE OF AFFAIRS (by humane standards)
provides, however, the raw material on which natural selection
operates. Though we usually focus our attention on the adult population, it's really the young (after their parents cease to care for them)
that are the prime objects of natural selection. The young are where
the action is. The young are comparatively inexperienced in critical
areas—and there are many more of them, compared to adults.

While predators also cull the old, that's not an example of
natural selection at work: whatever genes the older animals are
going to get into the next generation is determined earlier in their
life, so whether they die now or later isn't going to shape up the
ongoing population of genes. This is why there hasn't been much
natural selection against late-developing aspects of gene repertoires, such as Huntington's chorea, or cerebrovascular disease,
or Alzheimer's senility, or the inability to digest milk that sometimes develops in the mid-thirties.

Predators also cull the sick. That, however, promotes natural
selection for the immune system's capabilities. Natural selection
doesn't just work through predators and food availability but also
via childhood diseases: it takes years to build up immunity to the
common diseases, which is why older workers have fewer respira-
tory infections than younger workers. In one sense, you actually
become healthier as you grow older!

But in the real world of Darwinism, if an animal becomes weak from a virus, a predator eats it. If the animal becomes weak from inability to find food, a predator dispatches it. The young are comparatively inexperienced in both areas. Lacking a change in the average environment (of which, more later), the top 10 to 20 percent of the young bears survive—which is quite a shaping-up. Some of the others make it too by accident, and some of the top ones die by being in the wrong place at the wrong time, as when struck by lightning.

Droughts make selection even more severe, but the overproduction among mammals causes a lot of severe natural selection, just as a baseline. Somehow, I doubt that more severe selection (e.g., harder winters during the ice ages) was the cause of the Great Encephalization, especially given that other animals' brains didn't similarly enlarge during the ice ages.

EVEN THE BABY BEARS that escape natural selection for a normal adult lifespan may still have a big problem. Another form of selection operates because not all get to breed.

In most animals, nearly all surviving females get to bear offspring (there are some exceptions among social insects and dog packs, where a dominant female may inhibit the reproduction of subordinate females). In many types of mating systems, however, quite a few males are locked out of propagating their genes. Harems are the most obvious example.

What determines which males get their genes into the next generation? Sometimes, brute force decides: head-to-head competitions between males for control of a harem, where male body size and armaments count heavily. In some other mating systems, there is female choice, typically for healthy-looking males. This potentially augments the tendency of natural selection to promote improvements in body styles. But health isn't always judged by something truly relevant, such as having the prospective suitors run a marathon or collect a week's food for a family. There is usually some substitute indicator of health used, some stand-in— perhaps agility in a mating dance, or the condition of a male bird's plumage.

And this can lead to appearance mattering more than reality, with some cosmetic trimmings all-important. If shiny plumage is the criterion by which a female bird selects one male over another, you can see an arms race in plumage, such as the iridescent peacock tails. Sometimes it is feather length—and so you see some absurdly long tails in species such as the bower birds and magpies.

So *sexual* selection is based, not on the elements of the natural environment such as food availability, predators, pathogens, nesting sites (those are the elements of *natural* selection, though it might be better called *environmental* selection), but on reproductive peculiarities, many of which no longer function in any reasonable way. Those absurdly long tails may impede flying abilities and those bright feathers tend to give away one's location to predators (and so sexual selection may conflict with natural selection, balancing each other out). Male gorillas are so heavy as adults that they cannot take to the trees when a predator approaches, in the manner of the adult females and adolescent males— they have to stay and fight! One presumes that some such counterbalancing with natural selection is why sexual selection doesn't often keep proceeding to absurd lengths.

WHAT CONTROLS EVOLUTIONARY RATES, and so the length of time it takes to shape up a new feature? Most people would immediately suggest mutation rate, how fast the cosmic rays or mutagenic chemicals can introduce errors into the DNA strings. While an extra dose of radiation can indeed augment variability in offspring, gene *permutation* is probably the most important aspect, that shuffling of the chromosomes that takes place during crossing-over as new sperm and ova are made. From generation to generation, far more variability in offspring is created by permutations than by new mutations.

Furthermore, evolution above the one-cell level didn't really get going until crossing-over was invented by eukaryotes about one billion years ago; promptly thereafter, multicellular life developed in a big way, inventing about 50 major ways of structuring a body plan during the next half-billion years. Mutation didn't accomplish that: it was permutation. What affects the rates at which genes come to stick together, or develop new points at which to break apart during crossing-over? That's one of the unsolved problems of basic biology.

Among other factors, the reproductive arms race and its wastage must partially control the opportunity for natural selection to act on the variants thrown up by gene shuffling and mutation: everything else being equal, cats ought to evolve faster than bears because they overproduce more (their top 5 percent might survive, rather than the bear's top 10–20 percent). But fortunately we can avoid discussing the "cannon fodder" principle ("the more waste, the faster we evolve!"), because climate is the most obvious variable when it comes to fast vs. slow evolution.

The most rapid of environmental cycles are the daily ones associated with day-night and with the tides. Any planet is going to have solar tides, so long as it has oceans and doesn't keep one face always toward its gravitational attractor. If a planet has two attractors (as does ours), that's even better for speeding evolution. Thanks to the moon's tidal forces adding to (and then, for half a month, opposing) the sun's gravity, there are also monthly and yearly cycles of extreme low tides. The tides serve to select for intertidal plants and animals that can survive in a second kind of environment for longer and longer intervals—perhaps until becoming land-dwellers.

WHILE LAKE BALATON is Hungary's largest body of water, the tides here are about as conspicuous as the Hungarian Navy. One sees only wind-driven waves of greater and lesser proportions, keeping the shoreline wet. But it reminds me of the shorelines back home in Puget Sound, where the sea level varies each day over an average range of more than one story high, and so a lot of beach alternates between being underwater and being temporarily above water, drying out in the sunshine.

At some such intertidal zone of 450 million years ago, life came ashore. A species exposed to the monthly low tide series was undergoing natural selection for mechanisms that would keep it going in two different environments, both free-flowing water and up in the air. For the intertidal species, the tides provided daily waves of selection for the abilities needed to survive extreme variations in moisture, pH, salinity, oxygenation, and temperature. Had such tidal selection instead happened once per century, the fanciest land animal these days might be a floundering lungfish.

*It takes a swamp-and-tide-flat zoologist to tell you about life;
it is in this domain that the living suffer great extremes, it is
here that the water-failures, driven to desperation, make
starts in a new element. It is here that strange compromises
are made and new senses are born. . . . [In] the mangrove
swamps by the Niger, fish climb trees and ogle uneasy natu-
ralists who try unsuccessfully to chase them back into the
water. There are things still coming ashore.*
LOREN EISELEY, *The Immense Journey*, 1957

ONCE ASHORE, there are some yearly variations in environment outside the tropics—better known as the seasons. Thanks to
axial tilt and land surface in the temperate zone (mostly Northern
Hemisphere these days, the tip of South America excepted), we
have had yearly cycles of selection for species able to survive both
summer and winter weather (most species simply stick to the
tropics).

But for those who do evolve the mechanisms to endure both
winter and summer extremes, there will be yearly waves of selection, operating upon that huge overproduction of the Mama Bears
of the temperate zone. While not as frequent as the daily and
monthly cycles of the tides, wintertime selection cycles might
cause more rapid evolution in the temperate zones than in the
tropics—at least for winter-related body features. And for the
behavioral traits needed in the wintertime (predation skills are
particularly important in many animal species, as plant life becomes dormant).

THANKS TO CYCLES in the atmosphere-ocean system, we have
multiyear cycles of drought. Somewhat understood are the mon-
soon variations in the Indian Ocean, and El Niño's twice-per-
decade cycle in the weather systems of the Pacific Ocean. Among
human populations, the families of South American fishermen are
most affected—but the bird populations of many Pacific islands
crash to ten percent of their usual numbers. Recently, some of the
U.S. midwestern droughts have been linked to El Niño as well.

Pathogens also have multiyear cycles, as in the shellfish population crashes. Forest fires occur every few decades and, near a
shoreline or watercourse, floods occur several times each century

(if not more often). Less systematic are the meteor strikes and
volcanos that darken the atmosphere (though some of the more
famous examples of post-volcanic cooling, such as the year-without-
a-summer in 1816, may yet turn out to be unrecognized visitations
of El Niño).

Those trying to live on the margins of a habitat are the
hardest hit. In Europe, most traces of people who lived at low
population densities have been lost by the reuse of sites by the
peoples that followed. But in the New World, one can do better:
many "stone-age" sites have been discovered relatively intact. For
example, in the U.S. Southwest, rainfall improved about A.D.
1050 and many new Anasazi villages sprung up all over the area;
by 1130, they were all abandoned and even the major population
centers were dwindling. So the archaeologist gets to see a window
in time, largely uncontaminated by what followed. Boom and bust
is common in nature, not just in economies.

THE LAST FIVE MAJOR ICE AGES

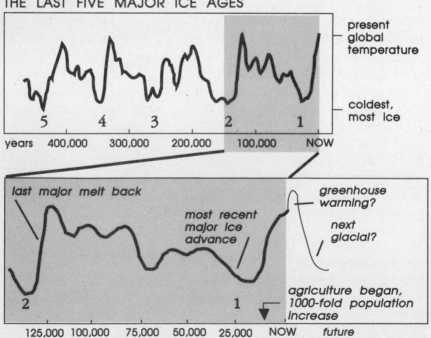

THANKS TO VARIATIONS in the Earth's axial tilt and the drift in the season when perihelion is reached, we've had 100,000-year-long major climatic cycles to shrink and expand the temperate zone populations. Of which, more later.

There is also lots of back and forth within each ice age, with perhaps five minor retreats in the ice sheets between each major meltback. Back and forth. So that means a major climate change about every 10,000 years (and within just the last 120,000 years, "cold spikes" have also occurred about every 6,000 years in the North Atlantic region alone).

And we know that there are centuries-long fluctuations within this as well. The Little Ice Age was a period of cooler climate between about 1200 and 1800, made even worse on occasion by some volcanic eruptions that clouded the atmosphere and cooled the weather for several years at a time.

[There] are two ways in which a creature can seek to survive in a jungle environment. One way [known as wedging] is to compete fiercely and successfully for an existing niche with other creatures that are trying to occupy it. The other way is to find a wholly unoccupied niche. . . .

HERBERT A. SIMON, 1983

MASS EXTINCTIONS also affect evolutionary rates, thanks to whatever happens every 28 million years (volcanos, asteroids, and meteors are possible, but some favor comets since a scheme has been suggested whereby the recurrences would cycle every 28 million years). After each mass extinction, whatever its cause turns out to be, there are opportunities for new species to fill vacated niches. This is an extreme case of boom and bust, and so it is worth examining it in more detail.

Darwin realized that evolution could be slow if efficiency was the only factor. An improving species (say, one better able to utilize a particular food) would have to wedge its way into the niche of another species already utilizing the resource. This metaphor of the wedge is very useful, but some of the major advances in evolution occur when no wedging is needed—because of the empty niches. Some empty niches are just there, waiting to be found: there are no woodpeckers on New Guinea despite dozens of species of woodpeckers on Borneo and Sumatra in similar forests. And filled niches can be emptied, as occurs in an extinction.

In periods of rapid diversification, a whole series of empty niches are discovered—as when some uninhabited islands are discovered, as has happened on both land and sea after the mass extinctions of 250 million years ago and 65 million years ago (those were merely the biggest extinctions; minor ones seem to happen about every 28 million years, the last one about 10–11 million years ago). After the dust clears, competition within a species is not important for a while; nearly all the offspring get to live and reproduce, allowing for variations that would ordinarily be culled by natural selection to survive and, indeed, be elaborated in successive generations. And so body styles vary widely; when the niches start to fill up, many will be eliminated and a more standardized model will take over.

But some variants may become associated with a stable niche. If they no longer interbreed with the parent species, as often happens in such situations, then they will constitute a new species. This serves as a ratchet, preventing backsliding to some average body style. Much evolution, in the sense of change in body form, has been temporary because it did not find a new stable point from which backsliding was prevented. Speciation, i.e., inability to interbreed effectively or *reproductive isolation*, is the prime (though not the only) means by which stratified stability occurs.

BUT BEFORE SPECIATION OCCURS, isolation has usually happened by more temporary means. Because the environment is often patchy, there are subpopulations of a species that mostly interbreed within their group. They could interbreed between groups, given the opportunity, but they don't—usually because of some geographical barrier such as a mountain range, or a wide expanse of territory lacking their kind of food resources. And so the members of a species are often found in dozens of relatively independent colonies: call the effectively interbreeding group a *deme* if you like, though *population* or *subpopulation* or *colony* will also suffice.

When natural selection has been episodically severe, a population may be completely eliminated and the territory's resources may go untapped until straying members of another population discover it—and have themselves a population explosion, founding a new deme.

Consider, however, what happens in less severe population crashes. Anyone who regularly visits a natural setting from year to year, as I do at the Friday Harbor Labs's nature preserve in the San Juan Islands, must be impressed with the yearly fluctuations in the number of common species such as deer and rabbit. Some years, there will be a dozen rabbits outside the front door of the main labs, mowing the lawn; other years, you're lucky to see two rabbits when walking around the entire several acres of lab buildings and housing units (and the maintenance personnel have to crank up the lawnmowers that year). Some years, there will be a dozen deer grazing amidst the buildings; other years, none are seen for days at a time. Some years, the raccoons are particularly prominent.

These fluctuations are not due to variations in food resources or nesting sites. Some are due to hard winters. But most, I suspect, are due to diseases that nearly decimate the island's population within several years. The survivors are the few whose genes allowed their immune systems to cope with the infection. Some of their offspring will inherit those genes, and so the population may start rebuilding even in the continued presence of the virus.

Over a century, a population will be exposed to quite a few similar episodes. If the population is modest in size, its genes may be severely edited by such episodes, and not just those for the immune system. Those whose constitutions are particularly robust will survive illness better, and so the plague years (as we would call them, were this a human population) also shape the genome in the direction of a specialty in this island's environment: its climate, its food resources, etc. Illness, by weakening the individual, sharpens the importance of that island's natural environment. Populations on other islands may be shaped somewhat differently, both by chance and by the differing environment there.

Boom-and-bust cycles edit small island populations far faster than they would a mainland population. You can see why a Mama Bear that produced triplets rather than twins would spread her

triplet genes around rapidly, given the occasions where an island's
bear population had been depleted by a virus. On the mainland,
the adjacent populations unaffected by an epidemic could later
move into a depleted area, the merely lucky competing with the
offspring of the survivors who had "earned" the chance. Large
mainland populations buffer rapid change—and incidentally help
insure against the loss of valuable genes, as can easily happen in a
small island population.

Back in the millennia long past, when humans were sparsely
located over the surface of the Earth, each tribe was effectively on
an island. Now evolution is slowed down to a crawl, simply because there is little isolation anymore. A large population evolves
slowly in comparison to a small deme.

AGRICULTURE GREATLY REDUCED the influence of natu-
ral selection on most humans (while we still die, the evolutionary
issue is *who* dies when). "Being better" now shapes up the human
gene pool rather slowly. And that's probably been true on most
continents for the last few millennia, perhaps most of the period
since the continental ice sheets melted about 12,000 years ago.
Which is not to say that evolution ("change") won't occur in the
future, only that traditional Darwinian processes will perhaps play
a minor role in guiding it, compared to biotechnology and such
environmental novelties as air pollution.

So the combination of transportation (allowing different demes
to intermarry more easily, which can have the advantage of hybrid vigor) and agriculture (serving, along with sanitation and
medicine, to allow most variants born to survive and reproduce,
for yet another round of variation) give rise to a conclusion about
future human evolution that is very different from the Social
Darwinism views of the late nineteenth century and the eugenics
views early in this century. The eugenicists (not, interestingly,
most geneticists) thought that artificial selection was important to
improve human bloodlines, preventing the mentally ill and the
epileptic from reproducing, and encouraging marriages between
those possessing favored traits.

Given the successes of animal breeding, eugenics was in many
ways a perfectly reasonable hypothesis, considering how little was
known at the time. I think few people realized how slowly things

worked—absent that Mama Bear scale of wastage, absent new niches to explore. Incorporating this early scientific speculation into German nationalistic slogans says more about the need for morale-building than it does about science.

By the time the Nazi government got hold of the eugenics idea (or at least its vocabulary), many geneticists and evolutionary biologists had backed off from any support of the eugenics movement. Scientifically, concepts were changing. Geographic isolation leading to reproductive isolation and speciation, etc., are insights from the thirties and forties, particularly from mathematical types such as Sewell Wright, and the early forties saw the emergence of the Modern Synthesis of Darwinism with genetics. It took a while for this news to spread. The major German societies of physical anthropologists indeed collaborated with the Nazi program of racial hygiene. And in the United States, awareness was not markedly better: Even in 1939, the American Association of Physical Anthropologists tabled a proposed resolution condemning Nazi racial myths (as the 1989 president of that association, Matt Cartmill, has recently noted in a sobering book review).

Part of the problem was that news travels surprisingly slowly between different disciplines—in this case, evolutionary biology and anthropology. Even today, I am surprised at how little some anthropologists concerned with hominid evolution seem to know about evolutionary biology of the kinds summarized thus far; their major concepts such as the savannah and scavenging are seldom evaluated in terms of anything other than slow adaptations, Darwin's original valuable insight. Fortunately, ignoring fast tracks and isolation opportunities (or developmental linkage, or compounding, or conversions of function) has none of the potential for societal misuse, at least when compared to transplanting animal breeding considerations into the human sphere.

Ignorance doesn't merely slow science down: ignorance also leads to mistakes. One of the seldom-realized benefits of science has been what knowledge has allowed us to avoid: the quack remedies and their tendency to delay effective action until too late, the buildings that collapse from trial-and-error construction methods, the invasion of pests because of having ignorantly killed off a natural predator. If history is any guide, our changing concept of human origins will enable us to avoid some of the problems in education and health care occasioned by our ignorance of how we humans function.

EVOLUTIONARY CHANGE is not only more rapid in small groups, but it is more likely to become "permanent" in a temporarily isolated setting. That is to say, something may happen that makes interbreeding less likely, even when the geographic barrier is removed (as when an ice age's lower sea level reconnects all of the islands in the San Juan Archipelago with one another).

Sometimes this is a chromosomal rearrangement in an island's population; mating between individuals with the rearranged and regular chromosomal patterns may have a high rate of spontaneous abortion or, if there are offspring, they may be sterile and so fail to propagate the lineage. Other times, there is simply less of a tendency to mate with a member of an out-group: behavior can effectively keep descendants of an island's population, now expanded over a broader landscape, from mating except with one another. The classic example is when mating seasons have shifted: on a mountainous island with late-melting snow, the mating season may have become a month later than usual, as those variants had offspring which survived better. And so that island's population, when mixed up with the general population by lowered sea level, still tend to mate with their original group for millennia thereafter, simply because the two groups are never sexually receptive at the same time.

Such prevention of backsliding might be called a reproductive ratchet. While mere "attractiveness" of physical appearance contributes to this tendency, culture tends to augment it: Erik Erikson noted the "excessive" amount of human energy that preliterate peoples spent in simply being different from one another. He calls it "pseudospeciation."

Reproductive isolation that is truly persistent is another way of saying that a new species has been formed: the traits shaped up by that island *have* to stick together, because they are simply unable to mix with those of the parent population. Various traits may have altered in an island's population that have nothing to do with reproduction—but they too will be protected against the dilution caused by mixing with the main population. A reproductive ratchet speeds evolution.

SPECIES TEND TO DIVERGE a bit after reproductive isolation occurs because of the Exclusion Principle: one species per niche. If two species tend to make their living in exactly the same way, are subject to about the same viruses and parasites, and so forth, then after enough time has passed, one of those species will probably decline in numbers and eventually go extinct in the area where the two species' ranges overlap. They won't be equally adept at utilizing the resources: one species will be more efficient.

There may, of course, also be some antagonism between such closely related species: if you see two species peacefully coexisting, they are probably not competing with one another for resources or nesting spots, etc. The antagonism speeds up the decline of one species, but efficiency is the most fundamental cause of such an extinction. This competition *between* species, certainly the usual nonbiologist's image of natural selection at work, is, however, fairly infrequent; most competition is *within* a species, involving things such as superior child-rearing.

Animals with a broad ecological niche, such as monkeys that can efficiently eat many different kinds of fruit but at different seasons, may so exclude more species than a narrow specialist like the bamboo-eating panda does. And humans have one of the broadest ecological niches of all, so it is not surprising that we have few close relatives left (and all five of the ape species are now endangered by human activities). We have created a wide swath of exclusion, and can only lessen the damage by substantial conservation efforts.

When bigger-brained species of prehumans formed on some island (real or virtual), they were probably capable of making their living in new ways or of exploiting former resources more efficiently, e.g., through food preparation technologies. If they were reproductively isolated from their parent species, they would tend to take over in local regions after a few millennia, even without antagonism between the two groups.

WHEN THE ICE AGES came along, the lowering sea levels caused a lot of islands to be reconnected with each other. And melting later caused new islands to form—not only literal islands, but some virtual islands as well: those mountaintop "islands" in the tropics to which the mountain gorilla is limited (by its need for 60 pounds of food a day!) tend to shrink and expand with the climatic changes seen even in the tropics when the ocean currents rearranged themselves.

And then, of course, there are the geographic barriers created by the ice sheets themselves. As Ernst Mayr notes, they are likely to induce speciation:

During the height of the glaciation, the ranges of many temperate-zone species contracted into small pockets, so-called glacial refuges, which persisted south of the area of glaciation. In Europe, for instance, the Alpine and northern ice caps approached each other to within 300 miles, separated by icy windswept steppes. The forest animals retreated into southwestern or southeastern Europe. When conditions improved at the end of glaciation and the populations in the refuges expanded northward, the isolates in southwestern and southeastern Europe had, in many cases, become sufficiently distinct from each other to form hybrid zones in central Europe.

Animals that could survive in the steppes were on small "islands" indeed. But the animals that needed forest were pushed toward the Iberian Peninsula and Greece, effectively divided by the Alps from opportunities to interbreed. These "islands" were much larger than the ones between the ice sheets, but apparently still small enough for speciation to occur. "Pleistocene forest" refugia also occurred in the Americas to the south of the ice sheets: mountains in Arizona, for example, were a refuge for temperate-zone species forced south from Canada.

In fact, Hungary is right near the boundary between the group of birds associated with the Iberian refuge and the group associated with the Balkan refuge. The experienced bird-watchers among us could probably find some hybrids right around Lake Balaton, crosses between Iberian and Balkan peninsular species, living evidence of the icy wedge that disappeared 12,000 years ago.

SO A SPEEDY SCENARIO for hominid encephalization would likely be set in the temperate zone, where every year the winter speeds up natural selection. The temperate zone would provide exposure to the ice age's tendencies to create islands on which evolutionary change is faster—and incidentally enhance speciation opportunities and reduce backsliding.

The ice ages also provide a lot of empty niches to fill, simply because they are forever changing the landscape. Near a glacier, only grasses grow. Farther back, forests get started. Birds find them quickly, but mammals take a little longer. Each species that comes upon a big uninhabited area enjoys a population boom. Sometimes an "adaptive radiation" occurs, diverse forms arising while the competitive rules are inoperative. The big brain is expensive (not just in terms of blood supply, but apparently in terms of a long vulnerable childhood), and it might have taken a profound dose of "good times" to allow it to develop, some major new resource becoming attainable (such as being able to eat meat every day, rather than once a month).

We tend to emphasize the conditions in Africa when talking of hominid evolution. The older fossils are found there and adaptationist theory tends to emphasize local adaptations to local environments (rather than carryovers from more distant former environments). One of the minor points that this book has to make is that ice ages cause temperate-zone traits to become far more important than one might initially think. Except near a few mountains, cold weather plays little role in Africa; during an ice age, while equatorial regions may house glaciers high on volcanos, most species can easily escape natural selection for cold climate by retreating to a lower elevation, an option not always available in the temperate zone (especially Europe, where southern retreat is often limited by the Mediterranean).

Hominids spread out of Africa, on the present evidence, about 1.4 million years ago and, as more digs are conducted in the temperate zone, the dates will likely become even earlier. Indeed, we are faced with the probability that after such a date, the African models of hominid may have been developed elsewhere: that some of their features were shaped up in the temperate zone, and later spread back into Africa. That would mean that such "African" hominids had some temperate-zone specializations that weren't really essential in the tropics. And the big brain may be one of them.

I JUST LAUGHED, remembering the time when I was teased about "walking on water." It was in the bottom of the Grand Canyon, rafting on the Colorado River. Trying to pull the boats into the beach near Phantom Ranch, we encountered a large sandbar offshore—basically a standing wave of sand, providing a narrow ridgeline just under the water's surface but rapidly falling off into over-your-head depths. And so I finally got out of the boat, stood ankle-deep atop the sandbar, and pulled the boat down to where there was a break in the sandbar. Then I sloshed back up the sandbar to help a second boat that was stuck. One of its occupants couldn't resist: "Say, Doc, while you're at it, suppose you could change this canteen of water into some wine?"

This is surely standard repartee among even devoutly religious fishermen, repeated many times over the centuries. And so I couldn't help wondering, when I visited the Sea of Galilee, if there were sandbars. One winter day, I sat there on the southern shore near its outlet into the River Jordan, eating a picnic lunch while facing into a cool onshore breeze, looking out over the large lake with the snow-covered uplands of the Golan Heights as its backdrop, remembering the 1.4 million-year-old traces of *Homo erectus* found a few kilometers to the south in the Jordan Valley, between the Galilee and the Dead Sea—right on the path out of the bottleneck from Africa into Asia.

And I remember contemplating the shallow bottom and the wind-driven waves that often produce sandbars. Walking across sandbars is, when you know your way around, a shortcut that saves much time over the long circuitous route along the shoreline. A hidden standing wave, no less. If visitors don't know about the submerged sandbar, it must look pretty strange.

In paleoanthropology, one concentrates on the stones and bones, hoping that they will yield some clues to function, what was serving to shape up the new species. But functions have shortcuts too, hidden structure that supports a new way of making a living.

We have learned all the answers, all the answers:
It is the question that we do not know.

ARCHIBALD MacLEISH

At the moment we are an ignorant species, flummoxed by
the puzzles of who we are, where we came from, and what we
are for. It is a gamble to bet on science for moving ahead,
but it is, in my view, the only game in town.

LEWIS THOMAS

4

NEANDERTAL COUNTRY: SOME CONSEQUENCES OF A FICKLE CLIMATE

Scientific inquiry is successful because it is, like the evolutionary process, a powerfully selective system. Scientific theories, by design, are always vulnerable to destruction just like a species, subjected to environmental pressure, is subject to extinction. Because of that vulnerability, scientific truth has the strength that comes of survival in a challenging environment. . . . Even when scientific theories fail to survive . . . their evolutionary progeny carry the best "genes"— the ideas that still work—of the previous theory intact. Ironically, it is the willingness to risk everything, even existence itself, that is the guarantor of survival.

the physicist HEINZ PAGELS, 1988

The Hungarian Academy of Sciences's library in Budapest was the scene of one of the most important, albeit unlikely, episodes in our understanding of the ice ages. It was where Milutin Milankovitch was a prisoner of war during the First World War. A Serbian mathematician who briefly saw service as an officer of Serbian troops invading the Turkish Empire, he was subsequently captured by Austro-Hungarian troops in 1914 while visiting his hometown of Dalj. Taken to the Esseg fortress as a prisoner of war,

> The heavy iron door closed behind me. . . . After a while I happened to glance at my suitcase. . . . My brain began to function again. I jumped up and opened the suitcase. . . . In it I had stored the papers on my cosmic problem. . . . I leafed through the writings . . . pulled my faithful fountain pen out of my pocket, and began to write and count. . . . As I looked around my room after midnight, I needed some time before I realized where I was.

His jailers later received a telegram ordering them to remove Milankovitch to Budapest. There he was paroled on the condition that he report once a week to the police station. A Professor Czuber, having learned that the mathematician had been imprisoned, had petitioned for his release.

When settled in Budapest, Milankovitch walked over to the Hungarian Academy of Sciences where he was welcomed with open arms by the library's director, the mathematician Koloman von Szilly. Milankovitch spent the next four years in the library's reading room, making a mathematical model for the climate of a planet whose axial tilt varies and whose elliptical orbit changes, stopping by the police station periodically to demonstrate that he hadn't escaped.

Milankovitch didn't know what we know now: that the first major ice buildup started about 2.5 million years ago. That means, on his 100,000-year cycle, that there were several dozen—but each of the several dozen ice ages also contains a lot of back-and-forth in addition to a major meltoff. The last major meltoff was about 13,000 years ago, though the previous one was at 128,000 years ago—just to show you that 100,000 years is only approximate.

The evolutionary changes that produced our big brain had mostly happened in earlier ice ages; this Ice Age's theme is primarily concerned with takeover rather than innovation. One can, however, see processes at work that would have been important in evolving the basic *Homo sapiens* body and brain during the back-and-forth of any ice age of the several dozen that Milankovitch's theory addressed.

BETWEEN BUDAPEST AND SEATTLE, there are no nonstop flights—but Copenhagen isn't far off the great-circle route. I've managed to get a geologist's seat (defined as a window seat in front of the wing) for both legs of the trip, Budapest–Copenhagen and Copenhagen–Seattle.

After lifting off from Budapest, the plane follows the Danube upriver. The river country soon gives way to the low mountains of Czechoslovakia—classic Neandertal country, as I explained to the Danish couple seated alongside me (they had inquired about what was so interesting outside the window). Beyond these mountains are the plains of Poland, flattened by the glaciers that periodically sat atop them—but hardly any Neandertals have been found north of the line from the Netherlands to Czechoslovakia (nor south of the Mediterranean) and no earlier than about 100,000 years ago (nor since about 33,000 years ago).

Though we are accustomed to thinking of hominids (all of the species since our common ancestor with the chimpanzees, about six million years ago) as originating in Africa, the Neandertals seem to be primarily European—though not like the modern Europeans. If you've ever seen a professional football team walk through an airport or hotel lobby, and compared them with some other collection of young men such as a group of soldiers out of uniform, you'll have the general idea about the size differences between Neandertals and ordinary *Homo sapiens*—but you'll have

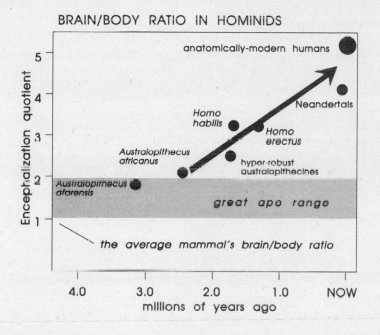

BRAIN/BODY RATIO IN HOMINIDS

to imagine the football players' faces as massively rugged around the eyes and cheeks to understand that Neandertals weren't just big.

While their brains were somewhat larger than ours (perhaps 15–20 percent), so were their bodies. As were the brains and bodies of their European competitors, early modern *Homo sapiens*. Most of us today are smaller than both types of Europeans that battled the ice, just as most aboriginal groups are smaller than the Eskimos. As a consequence, we have smaller brains (if size counts, it's probably *relative* to body size).

Though Europe was their home (and there is no sign of them having originated in, or spread to, Africa), Neandertals are occasionally found elsewhere. Like the birds pushed into ice-age refuges in the Balkans and the Iberian Peninsula, ice-age Europeans might have also been forced to the southeast and southwest. Certainly they occasionally spread to the southeast as far as the Caspian Sea. One of the most rugged-looking Neandertal skulls I've ever seen is from Mount Carmel, near Haifa, and is one of the first exhibits to greet you as you enter the Israel Museum in

Jerusalem. The Crusaders weren't the first Europeans to invade the Middle East.

To the southwest of central Europe, there are many Neandertal remains, and one can imagine them isolated on the Iberian Peninsula, trapped between the ice and the sea. An "island" is a classic setup for developing specializations such as robustness, such as behavioral predispositions that tend to minimize interbreeding with a parent population once the geographic isolation ends. Europe was being covered and uncovered by glaciers all the time; it was all frontier country, grassy steppes near the glaciers giving way to forests a bit further away. Megafauna such as mammoth grazed and browsed on those glacial frontiers. *Homo sapiens*, both modern-type and Neandertal, probably made a good living by hunting the big animals.

But the Neandertals lived with much more stress, probably due to episodes of starvation diets; you can see evidence of disrupted growth in their teeth. Certainly, they died far earlier; only 8 percent of adults made it past 35 years of age, compared to about 50 percent in aboriginal populations. A possible reason: three out of four adults that lived past 25 years of age had some evidence of healed bone fractures, compared to perhaps one in four in modern aboriginal populations. Trauma that quickly killed the individual isn't counted, as it is difficult to tell fresh breaks from postmortem breakage; only partially healed fractures are distinctive enough to count with confidence, so the percentage is undoubtedly even higher. And, of course, infant and child mortality meant that many didn't even make it into adulthood at all, to be counted by such statistics.

That so few Neandertal adults survived to 35 years, and that so many of them were maimed by injuries, suggests a life full of hazards not faced by the groups to which we compare them. Perhaps their methods of hunting involved getting too close to the angry animal. Perhaps they hunted only deer and the like rather than a wide range of species (and so were hurt by their bad years). Perhaps there was bloody rivalry between different bands of Neandertals for hunting territories. Conflict with early modern *Homo sapiens*, the invariable focus of popular discussion, is unlikely to explain very much of the Neandertal's short, brutal lives, as most would live their lives without ever seeing the other version of *Homo sapiens*.

The early modern *Homo sapiens* were doing something better than the Neandertals: they certainly lived longer as individuals and ultimately survived as a subspecies, whereas the Neandertals disappeared as an identifiable group. Starting about 50,000 years ago, early modern *Homo sapiens* began moving west from the plains of Poland into Neandertal's home grounds. The Neandertals were last seen about 33,000 years ago in western Europe. After surviving two major glaciations, Neandertals died out before the last one (which peaked 20,000 years ago); they lasted at least 70,000 years.

MODERN-TYPE *HOMO SAPIENS* was around during most (if not all) of this last Ice Age, which started 118,000 years ago; we might well date from the 10,000-year-long population boom that probably occurred during the major respite between glaciations, when all this land of northern Europe and Asia opened up to hominid habitation. We have more information on this Ice Age than the several dozen earlier ones, but it is well to remember that the last 100,000 years is merely the last 2 percent of the evolutionary period for getting from the apes to humanity—and that Neandertal-like variants lasting only about 70,000 years might have often happened in earlier times, confusing our view of the "progression."

While Neandertals may have evolved out of early modern *Homo sapiens* in some isolated refuge such as the Iberian Peninsula, both forms could have evolved out of archaic *Homo sapiens*, which date back to the penultimate Ice Age and somewhat earlier (400,000 to 100,000 years ago, very roughly). Archaics are a large-brained transitional form, not very well defined, which evolved out of the somewhat smaller-brained *Homo erectus*. Those latter ancestors got started about 1.7 million years ago in Africa, appeared in the role of "Java Man" about a million years ago, and were last on stage as "Peking Man" 225,000 years ago.

Between the DNA-dated common ancestor with the chimpanzees at 6–7 million years and the earliest of *Homo erectus* at 1.75 million years are several major types of upright but small-brained australopithecines. Between 2.0 and 1.8 million years ago, there was *Homo habilis* with its enlarging brain. But who is ancestor to whom? That's always controversial, and *Homo habilis* is not the best-defined of species either. The australopithecines were seen almost 4 million years ago, overlapped with *Homo erectus* for a while, and died out by about 1 million years ago. They are frequently subdivided into a gracile and a robust form (slender and thickset, e.g., the difference in appearance between basketball and football players); indeed, a hyper-robust form of australopithecine developed and died out.

The two types of the australopithecines are somewhat reminiscent of the difference between the slender "pygmy chimpanzee" (often called the bonobo) and the more robustly built common chimpanzee. And between the early modern *Homo sapiens* and the Neandertal. Such contrasting body types are actually a fairly common theme in zoology: while bigger is often better, boom times may allow lightweight variants to arise and come to dominate.

A not uncommon mechanism for this switchover involves early sexual maturity. Because there is less time between generations *and* it's a boom time, this allows the fast maturing to outreproduce the standard-maturity main population in the race for the extra allowable population slots; that's how their percentage in the population increases over the centuries. The other major consequence is that the adult body size and shape of the fast maturing becomes "gracile," reminiscent of how the robust adults looked when adolescent. That is because sexual maturity tends to slow down body development to a crawl (just compare ages 10–19 with 20–29!), and so one gets a "juvenilized adult."

In average times, the gracile variants may not be able to feed their dependent offspring as well as the average type. Among mammals such as the hominids, you can see some reasons why. While bigger males might be more successful in something such as hunting, I suspect that the females are the key because, back in the good old days, fasting was more than just a voluntary religious exercise. A woman's body fat can be converted into mother's milk, and so protect an infant from the bad weeks when the adults involuntarily go hungry. A bigger mother has more resources and can keep an infant healthy for longer, despite going hungry herself; a steady diet is particularly important for infants because they are so often sick, not having built up their immunity yet. Fat was surely beautiful.

In hard times, the robust forms may come to dominate again despite their slow maturity. Shorter generation time may count for little when the overall population isn't booming but rather contracting. And so, even if the juvenilized graciles have become a majority, their dominance slips a little in average times, even more in hard times. The Neandertals seem to have typically lived in hard times, given those appalling trauma and longevity percentages, given that tooth pathology caused by going hungry so often—not at all the sort of situation depicted in novels about the Ice Age.

NEW SPECIES presumably arise from just such boom-time broadening of species characteristics. The old climate might only support a robust type of body and a conservative sort of brain. The boom time might broaden out the species, so as to support both robust and gracile bodies, both shy and bold personalities, as extremes of a bell-shaped distribution. After the boom time is

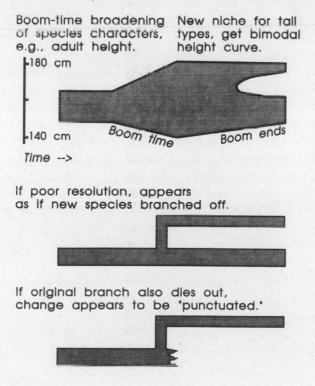

Boom-time broadening of species characters, e.g., adult height.

New niche for tall types, get bimodal height curve.

180 cm

140 cm

Boom time   Boom ends

Time -->

If poor resolution, appears as if new species branched off.

If original branch also dies out, change appears to be "punctuated."

over, so the usual reasoning goes, the graciles ought to shift back toward the robust standard.

Should the extreme graciles discover a new way of making a living, thanks to their juvenile playing-around tendencies or some other aspect of gracile bodies or juvenilized development, then they might persist even when the climate worsens once again. The two extremes of the bell-shaped distribution might continue, but the middle disappears, not optimized for either niche.

This sort of scenario (and it is hardly restricted to the robust-to-gracile spread of characters) illustrates how a species might split into a *Y.* If the original species dies out simultaneously, the new would seem to replace the old. "Windows of climatic opportunity" can be quite rapid on the geologist's time scale, and so such boom-time splits might seem sudden. The "tempo and mode" of evolutionary change is especially important, as Darwin recognized:

> [The] periods during which species have been undergoing modification . . . have probably been short in comparison with the periods during which these same species remained without undergoing any change.
>
> CHARLES DARWIN, from later editions of
> *On the Origin of Species*

There was a "boom" in punctuated equilibrium research until it was realized that a geological time resolution of only several centuries was probably going to be needed to test alternative hypotheses; stratigraphic layering just isn't that precise. Surely, however, species characteristics need not take a jump: in most cases, there was likely a hard-to-resolve broadening of characters that preceded the "new species."

THE OBVIOUS WAY TO GET A BIGGER BRAIN has always been juvenilization. Juveniles have a larger brain/body ratio than adults, which suggests this simple recipe: Declare the juveniles adult (good old early maturity), slow down their somatic development to a crawl as usually happens after puberty, and presto! You'll have an adult with a relatively bigger head. An example:

[T]he talapoin, a dwarfed relative of the rhesus monkey, has the largest relative brain weight among monkeys. Since within-species brain curves have substantially lower slopes than the two-thirds value for the marmoset-to-baboon curve, evolution for a smaller size by backing down the within-species curve would yield a dwarf with a far larger brain than an ordinary monkey of the same body size.

STEPHEN JAY GOULD, 1986

Backing up isn't just biological; these days, it is also a major cultural phenomenon. One often remarks on adults who are attempting to look younger than they really are, using a variety of cultural strategies such as eye-size-enhancing makeup, dieting to an adolescent profile, and hair dyes. Evolutionary processes can also make an adult look juvenile, by the standards of earlier generations.

This idea is usually subsumed under the term *neoteny*, though, in many people's minds, that term means more than juvenilization of features: it also indicates a concomitant slowing of somatic development (so that it takes a child weeks longer than average to gain the next centimeter of height). But I think that, in the hominid case, precocious puberty eventually leads to such slowing of development, which is why we often see them as linked.

THERE ARE EASILY a hundred features by which humans differ from the apes. Thanks to various linkages, some of the features group into families, such as neoteny's group of linked traits. Then there are the fat-salt-water features of the aquatic theory, though the savannah theory (a proposal that hominids went through a period of making their living in open country away from the forest, and that this shaped up a group of features such as eating seeds and perhaps partially upright posture) is probably the best-known example of a common cause for many features.

Although they accept the linkages implied by the savannah theory, most anthropologists seem to be generally dismissive of the aquatic ape theory and its analogous group of linked traits. The physiologist Alister Hardy proposed in 1960 that early hominids must have gone through a period of making their living by shoreline foraging, given all those unapelike features that we share with the more thoroughly aquatic mammals such as seals and whales. We have lots of subcutaneous fat (and those rounded body contours of the aquatic mammals), we have the salt-and-water-wasting kidneys (which force us to stick close to fresh water and seek out salt if not eating enough meat), plus a variety of other oddities such as tearing (likely related in part to the salt glands used by aquatics to get rid of excess salt).

Dismissing this makes about as much sense as totally dismissing the savannah theory, merely because a few facts can be found that cannot be explained by the savannah's selection pressures (such as those subcutaneous fat layers). I think it a mistake to consider aquatic and savannah as competing theories, which is reminiscent of the blunder seen in post-1900 genetics. Those pioneering geneticists made the false dichotomy of mutations *or* Darwinian selection; we now know that both are correct—but still not a complete view.

I suspect that we will come to see that both aquatic and savannah are correct but not complete. I'll bet that aquatic came first, then a savannah phase (and that a more recent temperate-zone, winter-driven phase will eventually be recognized once the fossil record improves). Certainly from the viewpoint of evolutionary theory, it is a serious mistake to treat either aquatic or savannah as anything other than a *partial* theory.

Both aquatic and savannah theories are an effort to reduce the hundred features to a few processes, each of which affects a multitude of features via linkages. And so is the neoteny theory, though in a different way: the neotenic features may be tied together by *developmental* linkage, not by a common *environment* such as aquatic or savannah. A selection pressure involving one feature (such as shortened generation time, when the niche is expanding in a boom time) may haul along a number of other features, such as smaller teeth and flatter faces, even though there is no positive selection pressure on those ancillary features.

The aquatic theory, the savannah theory, and the neoteny theory together serve to "explain" many of the hundred features, and so focus attention on the remaining features for which some additional selection pressure was probably required. To say that neoteny cannot explain the descent of the larynx (ours is located several vertebrae lower down than in apes, making the throat a

more versatile vocal filter), or all that unapelike fat that is added
to a fetus in the last months of gestation, is not to say that
"neoteny is wrong" but only to raise the possibility that yet
another selection pressure may be needed besides the ones leading to the major groupings.

Reducing the laundry list to manageable proportions, and so
singling out the oddities, is an important function of such partial
theories. Some scientists make the mistake of assuming that the
function of neoteny or aquatic ape theories is like that of a
theory in physics: to be an all-purpose explanation ("One thing
explains all!"), so that finding something "wrong with it" can
be used as a pretext for dismissing it completely. They do not,
fortunately, make the same mistake with the savannah theory;
they have not discarded it when finding some comparable feature
that they cannot explain. That the aquatic ape theory derives from
comparative physiology, and the neoteny theory from developmental biology, probably has something to do with this unequal
treatment, as most anthropologists are far more comfortable talking
about comparative anatomy and primate behavior (such as changing a monkey's anatomy and social behavior into those of a baboon
by moving from the trees to a savannah, as a model for what
hominids might have once gone through).

Simple adaptationist reasoning is usually the first thing
we try, but we must examine the possibility that ape-to-human
mosaic evolution involves only a half-dozen important selection
pressures, rather than a different one for each of the hundred
distinguishing features. And we must examine the processes that
spread a new feature around to other parts of the world.

GLACIERS ADVANCE AND RECEDE like a disease with occasional remissions. That has some important consequences for
demography, thanks to another aspect of episodic boom times.
The fluctuations in the climate serve to magnify the effect of
natural selection in certain locales, so as to make a small minority
into a widespread majority. One implication: natural selection in
one locale affects population characteristics elsewhere, indeed in
places where such natural selection is quite weak. The ice ages
provide an easy example.

When Europe and northern Asia were uncovered, a lot of

new land was opened up for human habitation—about 20 percent of the hominid-habitable land area of the Old World lay under the ice sheets at their maximal extent, so the meltback expanded the remainder by 25 percent. That is a lot; one would expect quite a population boom (say, for the sake of illustration, a 25 percent population increase).

Still, by today's standards (Kenya's population is expanding at the rate of 4.2 percent per *year*), it was a very slow population boom, so sluggish that no one could have known it was happening. Even in the fastest part of the meltback, the land area was only increasing at the rate of 0.4 percent per *century*. It wasn't like the Oklahoma Land Rush of 1889, when the existing population suddenly spaced itself out to occupy the "vacant" land. The new land surely went to the offspring of the people who lived near the ice-age frontier: they would have been able to successfully raise somewhat larger families than the world average because of the increasing productivity of the nearby land (more grass, therefore more grazing herds, consequently more meat for hunters).

And those inhabitants of the ice age frontier likely had a gene pool somewhat different from the world average: because the frontier was in the temperate zone, they may have required some adaptations to get through the winters, such as somewhat larger bodies. The large bodies of the Neandertals and early modern *Homo sapiens* are suggestive of such an adaptation to life on the ice-age frontiers of Europe during the most recent glaciation, for about the same reason that polar bears have especially large bodies: when you're caught out in a blizzard, core temperature loss is slower if you're big. Stature tends to increase with latitude among present native populations. Note, however, that height isn't always the best indicator of "body size"; the tall and slender Masai on the equator demonstrate how body shape can be important for heat loss by sweating (the more skin area, the better), and the more compact bodies of the Inuit suggest heat conservation. What, besides thermal adaptability, does one need in order for an ape to live in the temperate zone year-round?

All temperate-zone aboriginal peoples utilize hunting in the wintertime (even if hunting is currently out of fashion among anthropological theorists). Obviously, somewhere along the way, we've improved the typical ape's flinging skills into the baseball pitcher's throwing skills. Projectile predation is very rewarding, compared to snatch-and-grab hunting of the kind that baboons and chimpanzees practice—action at a distance is safer for the hunter, and accuracy improves the yield.

While a nice invention, hunting isn't usually essential; most preagricultural aboriginal populations get the majority of their calories from gathering plant products such as leaves, fruit, and nuts. Hunting is of restricted importance in the tropics because hunting failures can usually be offset by more gathering. While this is also true in the temperate zones for most of the year, wintertime means sharply restricted gathering opportunities: plants become dormant, snow hides much of what is left. This creates an annual do-or-die wave of selection for hunting skills.

While hunting involves all sorts of skills, most of them are shared with the carnivores and baboons and chimpanzees: teamwork (and the body-language communication that goes with it) and outsmarting the prey have often been mentioned as aids to selecting for prehuman communicative skills and plan-ahead intelligence—but they were well-developed in other social animals (dogs, baboons, etc.), presumably before hominids came along. The only area in which humans seem to have enormously augmented primate hunting skills is in projectile predation: we seem to have invented "action at a distance" killing (well, reinvented: archer fish spit at insects flying just above the water surface). So the temperate zone population might also have had some of the brain reorganization and enlargement that facilitates precision pitching.

Still, the temperate zone must have supported only a small fraction of the total hominid population—say, 15 percent. The annual wave of selection for wintertime skills would keep the subpopulation shaped up, and people moving around would spread some of those genes south to the tropics.

Diffusion back from the frontiers is, however, a very slow way to change the world-average hominid—absent, that is, a little pumping of the periphery. Therein, I suspect, lies the true importance of the ice ages per se for human evolution.

ONE STROKE ON A PUMP HANDLE usually doesn't yield any water. You just hear the water trickling back down. Only by repeated strokes on the pump does any water flow. The second stroke catches the water from the first before it can escape, and boosts it a little higher.

While evolution doesn't work exactly like that, it has some properties that you'd never guess just from studying static populations, just as you might never guess how to pump water uphill by contemplating a still pond. As Darwin noted, relatively static situations mean that new species have to "drive a wedge" between old species in order to eventually take over. It is very slow going. But climatic *fluctuations* provide pumps. They not only promote complexity but they speed up change via boom times. They occasionally even have ratchets to prevent backsliding.

"In the variations lay the insights" is a scientific principle that stands in contrast to all post-Platonic efforts to define the "essence" of what makes a monkey a monkey, and so forth. Many of the most important insights into nature have been made by scientists who looked instead at deviations from the "average type." Newton and followers discovered that the really workable way to define a *force* was as the rate of change of momentum (itself the product of mass and velocity), that anything which caused momentum to change would henceforth be defined as a force. Darwin and followers looked at the variations around the "typical" and saw in them the needed raw material for evolution. Einstein and followers looked at Brownian motion—that random walk of bits of dust illuminated by a sunbeam—and saw in it a way to derive the gas laws that predict your tire pressure increase on a hot day. And in the 1980s, climatologists took a second look at those cold spikes in the ice-core records of the last glaciation that they had previously discarded as just "noise" and discovered in them a mode-flipping tendency of the Earth's climate.

Over and over again, in matters large and small, the variations turn out to be more important than we thought. Now we look at the back-and-forth ice ages and see in them not just overblown winter but a way of *amplifying* the effect of the wintertime natural selection that takes place up on the sparsely populated frontiers.

THE ICE AGES PROVIDE THE PUMP—though not, as most people initially assume, because of more severe selection during

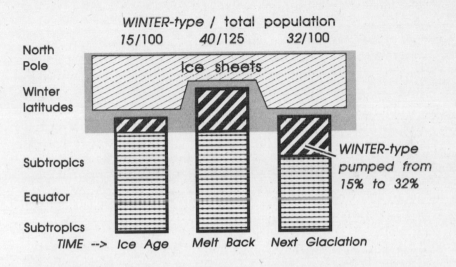

WINTER-type / total population
15/100   40/125   32/100

North Pole

Winter latitudes

ice sheets

WINTER-type pumped from 15% to 32%

Subtropics

Equator

Subtropics

TIME --> Ice Age   Melt Back   Next Glaciation

the ice age itself. Rather, it is because of those population booms that occur with a meltback.

When the population increases by 25 percent, it all comes from the temperate-zone version of hominids: they are the ones living up near the new land as it becomes available. And so the winter-specialized hominid subtype goes from being 15 percent of the population at the peak of the glaciation to being 32 percent of the expanded total (15/100 expands to 40/125) when the meltback is complete.

With the next advance of the ice, the habitable land shrinks. Plants cannot pick up and move; they are plowed under. But animals can move south as the glaciers cover up land. There will be more hominids than the reduced land area can support, so the population will drift back down to the original total over the generations. Will the percentage of temperate-zone body styles also change?

If there were farmers defending their fenced-off fields, the frontier people might have been caught between a glacier and a hard place. But both temperate and tropical types were mobile populations of hunter-gatherers, always milling around, and their territories were likely flexible in the manner of the American Indians. The crowding would force some temperate-zone hunters into lower latitudes, where they didn't absolutely require their temperate-zone adaptations. Yet the hunting skills they had would be handy for exploiting semitropical resources that the less winter-adapted hominids weren't utilizing, such as meat that can run away from you, such as the gathering high in the subtropical hills where the chilly weather discouraged the tropical types. The larger body size of the temperate veterans would make them more likely to win arguments when defending desired hunting territories, but one need not make an analogy to the "Out of the North" hordes such as the Viking and Mongol invasions of Europe (facilitated by boats and horseback riding, respectively): simply running off competitors for hunting grounds with thrown rocks and the like would have sufficed. The temperate-zone types would be better at that, whether the competition was a wolf or another hominid.

So in the population contraction that accompanied the advancing glaciers, the winter-specialized subtype might well stay at 32 percent—and perhaps they even did better. And now a majority of the winter-specialized subtype is no longer living in the temperate zone but at lower latitudes without winters, mixing with the general population.

LET THE CYCLE REPEAT: a meltback slowly expands the population by 25 percent once again, and the 32 percent winter-specialized subtype increases to 46 percent via all those "extra" frontier babies. When the population contracts during the next ice advance, they remain 46 percent of the reduced total if they hold their own. Expand again, and they go to 56 percent—and 65, 72, 78 percent and so forth. Thanks to the slow meltback giving them the extra babies, the temperate-zone subtype soon becomes the dominant type in the world population.

Actually, it probably went faster than that. You have to remember all of those "minor" back-and-forth movements of the glacial frontier *during* each major ice age. Four expand-and-consolidate cycles of only 10 percent each takes the original 15 percent winter-specialized subtype up to 42 percent of the world population, then the big 25 percent meltback jacks it up to 54 percent. So *the winter-specialized subtype goes from being a 15 percent minority to being a 54 percent majority* in only one 100,000-year ice-age cycle.

And all this while, the annual round of natural selection for getting-through-the-winter abilities is further changing that 15 to 32 percent of the population that still lives in the temperate zone. So as fast as hunting abilities can be shaped up into biological adaptations via form-follows-function on the frontier, they can be spread to the lower-latitude main population with a lag of considerably less than an ice age or two.

Fluctuations can be very important, given a pump—and this pump is even simpler than Darwin's successive shaping up of genome variations by a static environment.

PUNCTUATED EQUILIBRIUM arguments are essentially about acceleration and stasis, the extremes in the rate of gradual evolution. This expand-consolidate cycle suggests that the rate of gradual change seen in the central population (the typical source of the fossil record) is markedly affected by sometimes-distant frontier conditions, not merely their severity (e.g., winter culling) but also the slowness of habitat expansion (e.g., ice ages) and of gene pool mixing.

Though the present model emphasizes that repeated inundations of the central gene pool may alone be sufficient to accelerate the otherwise slow pace of gradual evolution associated with large established populations without speciation, loss of the ability to create fertile hybrids between the two populations may have also occurred during some cycles. This might have happened on off-shore islands which were later reconnected to the mainland by falling sea level, or on peninsulas serving as refugia. Though such new species are most vulnerable (as are all specialized small groups) to haphazard extinction, they might have occasionally "taken over" and replaced the previously dominant type.

Still, I have a hard time imagining that there have been *dozens* of such replacement events during the gradual quadrupling of hominid brain size during the last 2.5 million years—particularly when there is such a simple alternative available, where ice-age fluctuations merely pump the periphery and spread around the newly shaped-up subtype. Modern-type *Homo sapiens* (the model year that probably came in with the previous interglacial about 120,000 years ago) could be the exception to the rule, however— big-game hunting and food-preparation technologies might have facilitated a fairly complete takeover, for once, during the last of the two dozen ice ages.

Winter, then, is likely to be of great importance in hominid evolution, once hominids started attempting to live year-round in the temperate zone (which, on current fossil evidence, is between 1.1 and 1.4 million years ago—call it a dozen ice ages). Without the ice ages to expand and contract the habitat size, the evolution of hominids might have been slow going—just as without the daily tides augmented by the moon, it would have been a much slower process for fish to make the transition to land-dwelling.

The fluctuations in hominid-habitable land surface meant that frontier-type genes could be readily spread around the tropics. This provided our ancestors with both the physical advantages of the frontier-type and the cultural advantages developed in lower latitudes where population density was higher and making a living was somewhat easier, allowing for more cultural innovations to be invented and passed around.

THE BALTIC COMES INTO VIEW from the plane's window; the Earth looks thoroughly flattened for as far as one can see. The Baltic is not very deep; it emptied out during the ice ages as sea level dropped. Only 13,000 years ago, Sweden and Norway were a walk from western Europe, as were the British Isles (if you don't count the runoff rivers!).

Poland's landscape bears a striking resemblance to Minnesota on the U.S.-Canadian border, which is also much flattened by glaciers and pockmarked by shallow lakes. Farmers love the good soil in both places, though they complain about the big rocks that the glaciers dropped as they melted back. The Cape Cod fishermen, while cursing such glacial erratics on the shallow continental shelf when they snag their nets and lobster pots, usually stop short of actually moving the rocks, in the way that farmers do when they bend their plow on one.

Getting off the plane in Copenhagen, I noticed a sign that said:

INS
N55 37.6
E 012 39.1
Gate 39

which tells me exactly where I am on the surface of this planet, with an uncertainty of only about a city block. That's the latitude and longitude of this particular gate at Kastrup Airport (we're 55°37.6' north of the equator, and 12°39.1' east of the Greenwich meridian), and it is posted such that the sign is the first thing that a pilot sees when looking out of the cockpit window, as the plane sits at the gate. The pilot punches those numbers into the Inertial Navigation System, so that its computer will know where the flight starts from; by sensing accelerations in the three directions and keeping track of them, a computer can calculate exactly where an airplane is at any moment by the history of the accelerations since the starting point. Punch in the wrong numbers for the starting point, and you'll wind up going to the wrong place if using the INS to run the autopilot. Knowing where you are, and where you're headed, has changed since Neandertal times.

I indulged myself in an evening of sampling the exquisite products of Danish bakeries and breweries, then set off late the next morning in a 747, a nine-hour flight to Seattle that crosses nine time zones—so it stays midday all the way. It reminded me of a wonderful old wristwatch languishing in a drawer back home, since it was the perfect occasion to wear a watch that always stops—for once, it would remain pretty accurate.

[E. D. Cope, the nineteenth-century paleontologist,] first enunciated what he called the "law of the unspecialized," the contention that it was not from the most highly organized and dominant forms of a given geological era that the master type of a succeeding period evolved, but that instead the dominant forms tended to arise from more lowly and generalized animals which were capable of making new adaptations, and which were not narrowly restricted to a given environment. . . . [But] who is to say without foreknowledge of the future which animal is specialized and which is not?

LOREN EISELEY, *The Immense Journey*, 1957

5

OVER THE POLE: SURVEYING THE ICE AGES FROM A SEAT IN HEAVEN

The human psyche has frequently been compared to an iceberg. And in the early days of the polar flight from Copenhagen to California, when planes were smaller and still flew low enough and slow enough for the passenger to see something, there was a wonderful sight along the way. Crossing the Denmark Strait between Iceland and Greenland, you looked down on icebergs floating south. Each was a white jewel glittering in the low northern sun, and were you a passenger viewing the icy mountain from a ship's deck, this would be all that you would see. But from one's window in heaven you saw far more. Painted turquoise by the waters, the immense underwater mass of the iceberg spread all about beneath your eyes. Majestic the frosty mountain of ice might be; but hidden in mighty mystery was the force that supported it. And such is the unconscious mind.

the dramatist ROBERT ARDREY, 1969

Rather than timeless, my "over the pole" flight turned out to be a journey backward in time, as I surveyed the land covered and uncovered by the ice ages. It seems strange to realize that only 150 years ago hardly anybody knew about the ice ages—even scientists still talked in terms of a biblical deluge. The great Swiss (and later American) naturalist, Louis Agassiz (1807–1873), proposed about 1840 that massive ice sheets had pushed their way around Europe, sometime in the not-so-distant past. He also wrote a great work in biology, sorting out the relationships of the fossil fishes to the living species.

Despite this major discovery about evolution in geology, plus the major theoretical feat in classification that paved the way for evolutionary understanding, Agassiz didn't believe in biological change in the Darwinian sense. He was the last creationist who was also a major biologist, and was bitterly opposed to Charles Darwin's interpretation of how species evolved. Perhaps one major heresy per lifetime (extending the span of life on Earth far beyond the biblical scholars' estimate) was all he could manage.

GLACIERS DESCENDING from the north lead most people to think that the center of the ice cap must have been the North Pole (that is, after all, the way it works at the South Pole). It took a while after the discovery of the ice ages before anyone realized that glaciers don't form over open ocean: the pack ice at the North Pole is only a few meters thick (and rapidly getting thinner). As a naval officer sitting next to me on another airplane flight once remarked, "If anyone ever builds a house there, they'll get a surprise if they dig a basement!" (his submarine had punched through the ice, and he had gone walking on top of the world). The bottom of the Arctic Ocean is as deep as the Atlantic. It has features such as Nansen Basin, underwater ridges such as the Nansen Cordillera; both are named for the Norwegian scientist

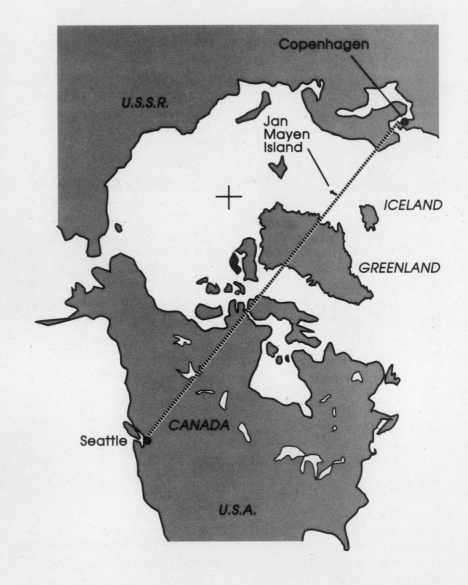

Fridtjof Nansen, one of the first neurobiologists. In 1888, Nansen and the Spanish neurobiologist Santiago Ramón y Cajal simultaneously discovered "the neuron doctrine"; Nansen was later an arctic explorer in 1893 to 1896, still later a diplomat who received the Nobel Peace Prize in 1922.

Although it may snow up on top, the sinking ice changes back into water on the submerged surface of the ice sheet. To build up ice to the thickness of a mountain range, as happens during an ice age, requires a solid foundation such as Greenland. Down at the South Pole, there is a whole continent (9.3 percent of the Earth's land surface) to house glaciers; they have even spread out into some shallow bays and displaced the seawater, e.g., the Ross Ice Shelf. Greenland is about the only such land at high latitudes in the northern hemisphere, although it is smaller than Europe (it usually looks bigger because the high latitudes get stretched on most maps).

When an ice age really gets going, then the Northern Hemisphere has a lot more land on which to house glaciers than the southern. Glaciers often came down to 50° latitude (past London and Vancouver), but to 40° in a few places (such as New York City and Woods Hole). Between 50° and 70° latitude, the Southern Hemisphere has only the tip of South America plus a bit of the Antarctic Peninsula—but the northern has Greenland, northern Europe, the vast expanse of Siberia, and then Canada too. It also has Alaska, but surprisingly the interior of Alaska north of the coastal mountain ranges had few glaciers, probably due to the "rain shadow."

FLYING OVER OSLO, one suddenly notices that the flatland appearance of the Baltic has given way to rock—an ancient eroded landscape, the shallow valleys filled with agriculture. Oslo sits at the head of a long fjord; though at 60° latitude, higher than Scotland, it is warmed by the North Atlantic Current and its harbor usually remains as ice-free as New York City's (at 40° latitude).

A little farther north at 65°, the vegetation is very thin. There is little topsoil in the uplands, except in some of the grooves (only 1 percent of Norway is agricultural, with another 2 percent as grassland). This area has been repeatedly scoured by glaciers,

right down to bedrock. This is not only some of the oldest rock in
Europe, it is some of the earliest rock anywhere on Earth. The
deep grooves are not scrape marks in the manner of the scratches
made by boulders carried along by the advancing glaciers; rather
they are the result of a billion years of erosion of the granite and
gneiss by water runoff.

Snow remains in some of the shadowed grooves, sheltered
from the oblique sunlight at these latitudes, giving this part of
Norway a zebra-striped appearance during some seasons. This is
the 65° latitude (the same as Iceland) that Milutin Milankovitch
used as the reference latitude for his thesis developed in Budapest: elaborating on the 1842 suggestion of the French mathematician Joseph A. Adhémar, Milankovitch proposed that the sunlight
reaching such latitudes controlled the ice ages. He showed that in
the warmest times there was as much sunlight here at 65° as
there is presently at 49° (e.g., Paris). In the coldest periods, 65°
got about as much sunlight as they get today up at 76° (e.g.,
Thule, Greenland—as far north as we'll fly in going "over the
pole" today). So sometimes Iceland has had as much sunlight as
Paris, and sometimes as little as Thule (that hadn't been "intuitively obvious" until the calculations were done).

The winds blow, and the rivers flow, their patterns and
strengths mostly a matter of seasonal sunlight.

THE NORWEGIAN UPLANDS are interrupted by fjords, where
some of the deeper grooves go out to sea. The one to our left has a
steamer ship heading inland, leaving behind a long white wake in
the fjord. A road cuts into the bordering hillside of otherwise
unrelieved rock.

An hour after leaving Copenhagen, we finally depart Europe.
We're now out over the Norwegian Sea, to be exact. We will miss
seeing Iceland, as our route takes us well to the north. We have
reached the latitude of the Arctic Circle; were this midwinter, the
sun would barely be peeking over the southern horizon at noon-
time. Near midsummer, the sun doesn't set, merely skimming the
northern horizon at midnight.

We do see the mid-ocean ridge, where the ocean floor is
spreading apart as new material upwells from the depths of the
Earth. There are some volcanos along that ridgeline: Iceland's are

the best known, but now we see Jan Mayen Island out the right window, its volcano Beeren Berg poking up through the clouds. Its glaciers have receded most of the way back to the uppermost cone; they can't go very far before reaching the sea—except to the south, where the mid-Atlantic ridge has poked up above the waters to form a long spit, like the handle on a frying pan. The island resembles a Hawaiian volcano, arched like a shield or convex lens—except for the top half, whose erect cone sweeps upward like the tip of Japan's Fujiyama.

THE TILT OF THE EARTH'S AXIS of rotation, relative to the plane of its orbit (in the arcane astronomical terminology, "the obliquity of the ecliptic"), changes some over the years. It drifts back and forth between 22° and 24.5°, taking about 41,000 years to make a complete circuit. Currently the tilt is about 23.4° (and declining)—and at that latitude the sun stands overhead on the longest day of the year. We Northern Hemisphere types call this latitude the Tropic of Cancer; it passes just north of Havana, Cuba. At maximum tilt, which last occurred about 9,600 years ago, the sun makes it up to Key West, Florida; at minimum, it only makes it up to the Isle of Pines off the southern coast of Cuba.

This 2.5° may not seem like much (only the difference in latitude between New York and Washington, D.C., or between Geneva and the Mediterranean). But if you live up where the glaciers do, you can get a considerable percentage improvement in the warmth delivered in summertime. The sun climbs a little higher in the sky at midday, stays above the horizon a little longer to make the nights even shorter.

Trying to reason out the physics of all this? A little knowledge of physics can be misleading when it comes to ice ages. The heat exchange involved in freezing and melting a tray of ice cubes is identical—so a change in tilt that produces both hotter summers and cooler winters shouldn't make much difference in ice buildup, right? But that analysis assumes nothing moves—and ice can move. The Atlantic Ocean beneath us is full of icebergs, calved off of Greenland and floating south, the warming job being exported to warmer latitudes than where the snow fell and froze into ice atop Greenland.

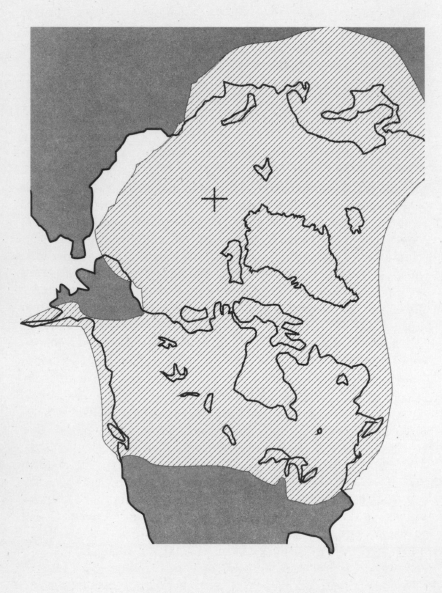

And this is the northernmost extreme of the North Atlantic Current we're flying over. It is nice and warm, flowing up as it does from the tropics. The North Atlantic Current warms up all that cold Arctic air that flows east from Canada, and so Europe gets much more comfortable weather than they get at comparable latitudes in Canada (all of Europe north of the Paris-Prague line is at Canadian latitudes). The North Atlantic Current makes winter in Oslo tolerable even though the sun only stands 7° above the southern horizon at noon. But the North Atlantic Current was shut down during the last ice age, starting up only 14,000 years ago when melting got underway.

I wonder what all those icebergs coming off Greenland during the end of the last Ice Age did to the North Atlantic Current? Certainly there was that period about 11,000 years ago, during the most rapid phase of the meltoff, when Europe paradoxically cooled down. The infamous Younger Dryas. The massive melting of the Canadian ice cap might help explain its thousand-year duration, but there are a series of Dryas-like "cold spikes" all through the last Ice Age, especially during the period of 30,000 to 70,000 years ago. Even if someone should "explain" the Younger Dryas in terms of events unlikely to be repeated in the coming century, there are all those other snaps to explain. Something besides the Milankovitch rhythms and meltoff deluges seems occasionally to cause some centuries-long cold snaps, and they have knowledgeable people worried.

GLACIERS CAN BREAK UP in dramatic ways. When melting gets going, some of the water runoff gets beneath the glacier and thaws the glacier's attachment to terra firma. This allows the glacier to slip sideways—and if the ice is piled very high and heavy (several thousand meters or more is not unusual), it may start to collapse like a house of cards, the edges of the glacier surging outward and breaking up as the center tumbles down. Because the ice surface area exposed to the warm summer air is greatly increased by fragmentation, melting speeds up further.

There is nothing analogous to iceberg deluges and glacial surges in the orderly layer-after-layer buildup of ice during the cooler wintertime. So warmer summers but cooler winters suggests *net melting* of glaciers even if the annual average sunlight doesn't change much. In the models that have been made of this process, a melting rate about four times faster than the buildup rate fits the fluctuations of ocean salinity quite well during the last Ice Age.

But the 41,000-year tilt cycle doesn't, by itself, match up with the 100,000-year period between big meltoffs. What else might increase summertime heating at high northern latitudes? Well, the Earth's orbit isn't circular but elliptical, a bit elongated. That means that our distance to the sun isn't constant: the Earth is closest to the sun ("reaches perihelion") on the third of January. By the fifth of July, we are about 3 percent farther away from the sun. Sunlight's intensity falls off as the square of our distance from the sun; in January, we get about 7 percent more sunlight (averaged over the whole Earth) than in July. If we didn't, northern winters would be even colder these days.

The date on which perihelion occurs is not, however, always the third of January. The date of perihelion drifts because, like other spinning tops, the Earth slowly precesses, its axis tracing out a cone. Since that is independent of the elliptical orbit itself, the Earth's orientation toward the sun at perihelion changes over time. Only 5,500 years ago, perihelion was about the time of the autumn equinox in late September. And 11,000 years ago, it was coincident with the summer solstice in late June—and so the Northern Hemisphere got its maximal heating for the year at the time when its glaciers are most susceptible to melting. The cycle takes between 19,000 and 26,000 years (as tops go, the Earth is rather massive and the precession period quite slow).

Furthermore, the elongation changes as the positions of the other planets pull the Earth into an even more elliptical orbit. Those 7 percent differences in heating increase, considerably exaggerating the summer-winter differences. The maximum eccentricity occurs every 400,000 years, although there is a minor peak at 100,000 years embedded in it (the tilt cycle also has minor peaks, and perihelion date also doesn't advance uniformly).

One of the puzzles about the ice ages is that they recur every 100,000 years, but the eccentricity contribution to arriving sunshine seems too weak to be so important; some geophysicists suspect that the Earth's crust resonates at about 100,000-year periods, it taking that long for the depressed crust to rebound

after sinking under a mountain of ice. Whatever the cause, when
two out of the three astronomical factors (tilt, season of perihelion, eccentricity) are going to have major or minor peaks at about
the same time (as when tilt peaked 9,500 years ago and perihelion
was at the summer solstice 11,000 years ago), northern glaciers
melt back substantially. The glacial maximum was about 20,000 to
30,000 years ago; the meltoff was well under way by 14,000 years
ago and was mostly complete by 9,000 years ago. When only one
of the three astronomical factors is at a peak, there is some
meltback. June perihelion date is best correlated with all of the
minor meltbacks between the major ones.

And so, as the relative mix changes, there is lots of back-and-
forth movement of glaciers between the major meltbacks, aided
and abetted by variations in the sun's nuclear furnace. The augmented summer sunshine not only melted the ice sheets, but it
had some effects at more tropical latitudes as well: the Sahara
was green about 8,000 years ago (the "Pluvial"), thanks to the
way the enhanced monsoons spread into northern Africa, just as
they did on earlier occasions when perihelion was in the northern
summertime.

CROSSING THE COAST OF GREENLAND, one sees fjords
again. The one below the airplane is full of icebergs and broken
sheets of floating ice. Long wide roads of ice, furrowed and
cracked, come down from the Greenland highlands and then end
abruptly in open sea. There are dozens of glaciers emptying into
this labyrinth of fjords on Greenland's east coast; hundreds of
white iceberg tips dot the channels. And this is late in an interglacial period when iceberg birth rates are lowest; one wonders what
this sight would have been like 13,000 years ago when the big
meltoff was getting going and the iceberg factory was running
flat out.

The eroded red rock lining the fjords is old, probably more
than 2.5 billion years (just as is the coast of Norway; back then,
Scandinavia, Greenland, and Canada were all connected, before
the mid-Atlantic rift did its work separating them). Greenland is
part of the Laurentian Shield of Canada, recently revealed to be a
series of microcontinents fused together by some great lava flows
nearly 2 billion years ago. There's not a speck of vegetation to be

seen from 10,000 meters up, though there are surely some lichens clinging to those rocks. But hardly enough to get a soil started.

From my stratospheric perspective, however, I can see a monster of a glacier to the south, staircasing its way down from the highlands, feeding northward out of the prominent mountain range several hundred kilometers away. More familiar locales used to have monster glaciers like that: the one that pushed down out of the north to cover up where Vancouver and Seattle now are, the one that pushed down out of the Alps into the Danube's valley.

Some great blue spots are visible atop those glaciers beneath the plane's wing; they're ponds of summer meltwater. On active glaciers staircasing downhill, a crack will soon open up beneath such a pond and it will drain. The ponds I see are considerably inland from where small blocks of ice are calving off and floating away, so the ponds aren't holes in the ice, of the kind frequented by the surfacing seals that attract both polar bears and Inuit hunters.

I didn't see any coastal settlements, and there aren't many this far north except for some Inuit ruins. The population of Greenland, about that of a large town elsewhere, is mostly along the west coast of Greenland at lower latitudes.

Farther inland, the glaciers give way to smoothed snowfields. Endlessly. Greenland is eerie, a high plateau of ice, everywhere. Tips of mountains barely poke through the ice sheets and snowfields. This makes the mountaintops look like a chain of islands in a white sea; the occasional furrowed glacier showing through the wind-smoothed snowfields looks like an offshore barrier reef producing turbulence. But the highest point in Greenland is on one of those plains of snow; that's where a European scientific team is drilling 3,000 meters down to bedrock and, about 30 kilometers to the west, an American scientific team is drilling a comparison core, part of the effort to be sure about what's real data, and what's just the noise introduced by ice flow over the millennia.

Though it seems frozen and static, the ice is pushing and shoving due to its own weight, eventually working its way down to be born as a multitude of little white icebergs poking up through a real sea. The mountain of ice is as much as 3,410 meters thick. In some places the land beneath it has sunk 365 meters

below sea level (about the same elevation as the Dead Sea),
thanks to the weight of the ice. The glacier could never have
gotten started if the land had originally been below sea level,
another reason why buildup and melting of ice can be so different.

It is still noon as we pass over Greenland. The shadows I see
are about as short as they ever get; usually they are very long,
the mountain peaks casting great shadows for long distances to
the north across the frozen snowfields. The purser says that this
plane turns around in Seattle and immediately flies back to Copenhagen with a new load of passengers, passing over here again
in the early morning hours. At that time, the long shadows will
stretch out toward the south, melting ice around the clock. If you
were to become lost around here, the Boy Scout lore about moss
growing on the north sides of trees wouldn't work: the sun rotates
all around the tree! That presumes, of course, that you could find
a tree—when there isn't even soil yet.

You'd think that Iceland would have been named the "green
land" and Greenland the "ice land," rather than vice versa. The
reversal in names is due to the reversal in regional climate in the
century between their discoveries. When Iceland was first settled
by Vikings about A.D. 860, it was during a cold spell (we now know
from the ice core's oxygen isotopes, which serve as "frozen ther-
mometers"), causing Iceland's fjords to ice up. Erik the Red,
banished from Iceland a century later (a little matter of murder),
explored to the west across the Denmark Straits and discovered
what he called "Greenland"—and we now know that things had
warmed up considerably in that century since Iceland's settlement.

During this warmer period, the Norse explored the northeast
coast of North America, shipping back timber to Greenland. But
it cooled dramatically in the fourteenth century and the fortunes

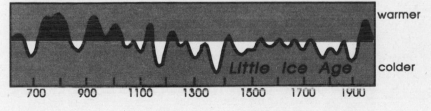

NORTH ATLANTIC TEMPERATURES SINCE A.D. 700

of the Greenland settlers declined. The settlement lasted until about 1540, wiped out by the cooling (and the failure of the settlers, addicted to European styles in clothing, to adopt Eskimo techniques for survival in such climates).

At Greenland's southern tip, something is actually green these days. Along the coastline, there are small trees: occasional willows as high as a person and, in sheltered spots, dwarf birches only half as high. These, and the mosses and berries that cover the ground, probably gave the place its name among the boat-borne visitors lacking our elevated perspective on the ice. Thus the name "Greenland" commemorates a green facade, shielding the mountain of ice farther inland. And a fickle facade at that, varying from century to century with the erratic climate of the North Atlantic.

THE CLOUDS WE ENCOUNTERED over central Greenland now part and I see land below that isn't Greenland because there are no glaciers—it looks scraped clean, the same kind of reddish Canadian Shield as Greenland, but I think it hasn't seen a glacier for many millennia. If this is Canada, then I missed seeing Thule, Greenland, known to the rest of the world mostly for its cold-war radar installations (and as the American "Siberia" to which unpopular Air Force officers were reassigned). Canada's Baffin Island is north of Hudson's Bay, and that must be it below. There is a lot of ice, but exposed sea lanes as well, with pancakes of ice scattered here and there—not icebergs, just flat ice. The Inuit live up here too, the last of the ice-age hunters; indeed, there are more groups in the eastern Canadian Arctic than elsewhere. They can be found from Siberia around to Greenland, following the seals and bears.

Now if this were 1831, the year that the North Magnetic Pole was first located on the Boothia Peninsula, we'd be flying right over it. But it has moved since then, and is now about 1,000 kilometers (about 600 miles) out the right window to the northwest. The North Magnetic Pole is the point toward which all those decelerating charged particles from the solar wind converge to cause the aurora borealis; from space, the aurora looks like a fountain, spewing light—making the Magnetic Pole look considerably more exciting than the Geographical North Pole. No northern lights for us today; they're there 24 hours a day, but it's still noon and we can't see them for all the sunlight that reflects off the thin air to produce a blue sky. We missed the North Pole itself by quite a bit, the distance between Miami and New York City. So this over-the-pole flight might be better described as the almost-over-the-magnetic-pole flight.

If this were 14,000 years ago instead, and I looked out the left window to the south, I would have seen a "mountain range" going all the way to New York City and Cape Cod. The Laurentide ice sheet was truly massive, and so tall that it probably deflected some of the jet stream to more northerly latitudes.

What are Arctic travelers likely to see out the window a few decades from now? Looking into the future with computer simulations, this tundra beneath us may thaw in a big way: northern Canada is likely to warm up more than anywhere else on Earth, as the greenhouse warming progresses. The methane that the thaw releases from the tundra is also likely to make the greenhouse effect even worse.

LAKES SEEM TO BE EVERYWHERE in the Northwest Territories, and we've just passed near Great Slave Lake and our first town since leaving Norway, Yellowknife. Far to the right side must be Great Bear Lake, noted for an ancient volcano tipped on its side, erosion exposing the internal plumbing.

The natives that live up here were also quite successful as emigrants to the United States; the languages spoken by the Apache and Navajo, down south near the Grand Canyon, are closely related to the ones spoken up here, and it appears that the Athabascan-speaking peoples (named for a lake off to our left) hunted and gathered their way down south rather recently—they barely got there in time to be used as slave labor by the sixteenth-century Spanish in building their churches in the Rio Grande valley. This was, of course, a half-century before the Pilgrims arrived in New England in 1620, another fact that my school textbooks somehow omitted.

We haven't seen much of the Precambrian rock protruding through the tundra, but hereabouts ought to be the end of the Canadian Shield. Southwest of here is more recent geology, late-arriving chunks of North America that sailed across the Pacific Ocean during the last 50 million years.

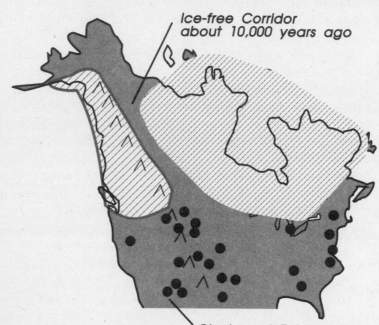

Ice-free Corridor
about 10,000 years ago

Clovis and Folsom sites

THE ICE-FREE CORRIDOR (minus the ice) is seen out the right side, as the Rockies come into view. The pioneers might have been able to walk across the Bering Strait from Asia, but Alaska's northern interior was the end of the line. The rugged coastline, augmented by ice sheets on the continental shelf, probably prevented animals (including humans) from moving south, though there might have been a few small "harbors" along the way if boats were available. And the great ice cap sitting atop Canada would have blocked the alternative inland route. But it was a two-part ice sheet, which is why a corridor was possible.

The Laurentide ice sheet didn't grow down from the Rocky Mountains toward the east—it spread west from Hudson's Bay (drained empty by the fall in sea level) and actually started to push up into the foothills of the Rockies before it met up with the Cordilleran glaciers flowing down the Rockies (eastern Canada then received much more snowfall because the Gulf Stream shifted). From about 30,000 years ago until 14,000 years ago, the two ice masses pushed against each other; then between 14,000 and 12,000 years ago, as both started to melt back somewhat, a corridor opened up from the north coast of Alaska leading down to eastern Montana.

As I said, I tend to imagine this as something like the biblical parting of the Red Sea—a north-south corridor opening up as the ice walls pull back on both the east and west sides. Shortly after the corridor opened, there was a human population explosion in the Americas south of Canada. Besides the relatives of the elephant, there were lions, horses, and camels in North America, back in those days. Many of those species now remain only in Africa; Teddy Roosevelt, early in the century, took a train trip through Africa and called it a "railroad through the Pleistocene," a tour of what America used to be like.

The corridor ran up the eastern front of the Rockies from the southern limit of the glaciers, at about the Alberta-Montana border, to Dawson Creek and Fort Nelson. We must be over Dawson Creek, as I can now see the Alaskan Highway snaking off to the west en route to Whitehorse and eventually Fairbanks. The mountains continue northwest as the Mackenzie Mountains all the way up to the Yukon. No glaciers visible now; just the unfurrowed white patches that are permanent snowfields—the seeds of glaciers.

So the earliest route to the south required first going north, up above the Arctic Circle, almost (unless the Yukon's valley opened up early) all the way up to the North Slope and the Arctic Ocean coastline, reaching the Mackenzie River delta and then turning southeast and traveling down the eastern front of the Mackenzies and Rockies. There were a lot of lakes along the way, formed by moraines of the Laurentide ice sheet: the bulldozing ice snouts actually dammed up some valleys of the Rockies in a manner not unlike modern reservoirs, with an earthen dam of rubble stretched across the exit to the valley except that the rubble was pushed *up* the valley from below by that monster glacier from Hudson's Bay far to the east. Herds of grazing animals probably worked their way down the corridor, following the new grasslands, followed by the hunters.

THE FIRST AMERICAN POPULATION explosion likely came from those hunting bands that found their way down the ice-free corridor. Or maybe it was the second or third, since there is a lot of argument over whether there were some human inhabitants in both North and South America during the last quarter of the last ice age, more than 31,000 years ago. Like the Vikings who explored the Atlantic coastline centuries before the southern European explorers came and stayed (and attracted the even later but more prolific English), so the earliest human occupation of the Americas may have been a multistep affair.

Because the corridor east of the Rockies was open before 30,000 years ago, an earlier Bering Strait emigration from Asia could, conceivably, have initially populated the rest of the Americas. But the door closed on the corridor 30,000 years ago, and didn't reopen until about the time of the Clovis hunters, 11,800 years ago. Of course, the early South American populations presently dated (these numbers are forever being updated, and the radiocarbon dates recalibrated) earlier than 31,000 years might also have arrived by boat from the Pacific islands. Everyone is eagerly awaiting enough bones and cultural artifacts from the early sites to make comparisons to ancient populations of the Asian mainlands that spread into the Pacific islands.

The present-day natives of North and South America seem fairly closely related, just what one might expect from a population explosion based on some initially successful hunting tribes pouring through the ice-free corridor. Whether or not some humans arrived even earlier, the hunters seen starting at about 11,800 years ago were prolific big-game hunters and left their Clovis-style arrowheads and spear points all over the continent, including in the rib cages of some now-extinct species of megafauna. Some groups certainly came later, such as the Arctic-specialized Aleut and the Inuit perhaps 8,000 years ago.

There was, of course, a population contraction in more recent centuries, as the native populations were decimated by the diseases imported via the European and African immigrants. That sort of replacement of one hominid population by another is likely how modern-type *Homo sapiens*, the descendants of the African "Eve" collection of mitochondrial DNA that was around 150,000 years ago, came to dominate the scene. They need not have brutally eliminated *Homo erectus* and "archaic *Homo sapiens*," though there probably were incidents of that sort, just as occurred involving the U.S. Cavalry in the nineteenth century,

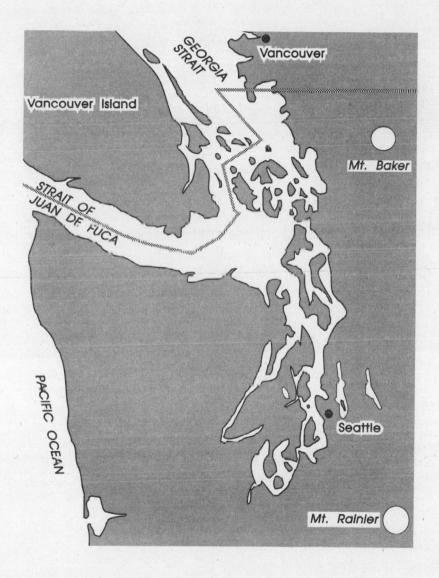

massacring Cheyenne Indian families at Sand Creek. It would suffice to possess an immune system that could cope with a virulent virus that predecessor immune systems could not.

It is difficult, as Richard Leakey points out, to otherwise account for the widespread disappearance of the predecessors (conquest, despite occasional massacres, tends to lead to interbreeding and thus regional retention of some characteristic features). Even without superior technology, the Europeans could have displaced the American Indians—just with the smallpox that Europeans could survive better than the Indians. Anthropologists often argue that waves of settlement shouldn't occur without the newcomers having some advantage such as new-model body styles or advanced culture—but they sometimes forget the pathogens and antibodies that aren't preserved as well as stones and bones.

THE ROCKY MOUNTAINS take a brief respite and we see interior valleys for a few minutes until we cross the Fraser River and we're into the coastal mountains, looking every bit as rugged as the Rockies. I can see why it would be hard to walk down the coast from Alaska: the mountains continue to the coastline; farther north along the Gulf of Alaska, glaciers extend right out to the water's edge, contributing more meltwater to the oceans than any other glaciers in the world, outside Greenland and Antarctica. But then we suddenly pop out of the mountains and are over a real metropolis, complete with a large river delta. It's Vancouver, British Columbia, and that is the Fraser River emptying into the Strait of Georgia.

We are flying right down the strait between the mainland and Vancouver Island to the west. I know we just passed into United States airspace because we are over the San Juan Islands, one of my favorite places; I spotted the Friday Harbor Labs (at least its dock; the buildings blend so well with the natural setting that I can't distinguish them). To the west I can see the Strait of Juan de Fuca, separating Vancouver Island from the Olympic Peninsula, and opening out into the vast Pacific Ocean. The Atlantic for lunch, the Pacific for dinner.

To the south is Puget Sound, not a sound at all (since it is dead-end) but rather a very long bay with only the one narrow exit to the ocean. The world's larger "bays" include the Mediterranean

Sea and the Red Sea. They all have an interesting salt economy—
not of the kind associated with the camel caravans of centuries
past, but a salt economy associated with the bay's gains and losses
of fresh water. The Red Sea is an extreme example: it loses quite
a lot of fresh water by evaporation, but gains essentially none
from rivers (or melting icebergs!). It doesn't dry up into salt flats
because less salty Indian Ocean water is attracted in through the
Strait of Bab al Mandab—and so the Red Sea's salinity has stabilized at about 10 percent higher than the oceans. Puget Sound
has lots of rivers coming down from the mountains to the east,
south, and west; no danger of Red-Sea-style hypersalinity here.
Except, perhaps, if it really turned cold and the winter snows
turned into glaciers rather than runoff.

The Mediterranean gets fresh water from some big rivers
such as the Nile and Rhone, but it also has quite a lot of surface
area for evaporating fresh water. As the Mediterranean starts to
get hypersaline, it attracts ocean water of normal salinity in
through the Strait of Gibraltar. This creates an interesting circulation pattern. Hypersaline water is heavy, and so it sinks to the
bottom of the eastern Mediterranean, the fresher waters from the
rivers and the normal salinity seawater from Gibraltar replacing it
on the surface. The deep salty water tends to escape, creeping
along the bottom and out into the Atlantic, just as the extra salt
flushes out of the bottom of the Red Sea into the Indian Ocean.

During the pluvial period about 8,000 years ago when the
greatly augmented monsoons were watering Africa and turning
the Sahara green, a lot more fresh water was delivered to the
Mediterranean via the Nile (and some large North African rivers
that can no longer be seen, their dry beds filled in with sand). And
the Mediterranean's salty circulation pattern became the exact
reverse (rather like Puget Sound today): the fresher water stayed
on the surface and flowed out to sea, and some deep salty water
was attracted into the bottom of the Strait of Gibraltar. So while
it is a salt economy, it's really all a matter of freshwater runoff
into, and evaporation from, a basin.

While bays illustrate the principles more readily, the same
principles apply to regions of the oceans too, should you have
areas (such as the Northern Atlantic) with more freshwater loss
than gain. This principle was recognized several centuries ago:

But if the water of the ocean, which, on being deprived of a great part of its Heat by cold winds [evaporation], descends to the bottom of the sea, cannot be warmed where it descends, as its specific gravity [density] is greater than that of water at the same depth in warmer latitudes, it will immediately begin to spread on the bottom of the sea, and to flow towards the equator, and this must necessarily produce a current at the surface in an opposite direction.

BENJAMIN THOMPSON (Count Rumford), 1800

Just imagine the North Atlantic Current as the equivalent of that normal salinity surface current flowing into the Mediterranean at Gibraltar, nice and warm. To balance it, you get a deep salty current heading south from Iceland; actually, it flows from the North Atlantic to the tip of Africa, east through the Indian Ocean, around Australia and up into the North Pacific.

It's a somewhat exaggerated version of the Mediterranean's story: the water sinks like a stone around Iceland because it is already hypersaline when it arrives.

Every winter at about the latitude of Iceland, water of relatively high salinity, flowing northward at intermediate depths (perhaps 800 meters), rises as winds sweep the surface wa-

EXTENT OF WINTER ICE IN NORTH ATLANTIC

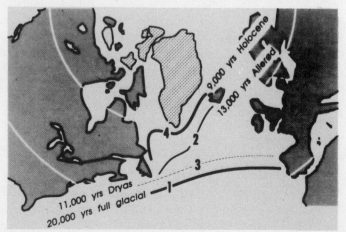

ters aside. Exposed to the chill air, the water releases heat, cooling from perhaps 10 degrees C. to two degrees [50° to 36°F]. The water's high salinity together with the drop in temperature makes it unusually dense, and it sinks again, this time all the way to the ocean bottom. The formation of the North Atlantic deep water, as it is called, gives off a staggering amount of heat. Equal to about 30 percent of the yearly direct input of solar energy to the surface of the northern Atlantic, this bonus accounts for the surprisingly mild winters of Western Europe. (The warming is often mistakenly ascribed to the Gulf Stream, which ends well to the south). . . . [During the ice age, the conveyor was shut down but resumed during the melting; during the Younger Dryas], the conveyor had shut down once again. Deep-water formation had stopped, and so the warm intermediate-depth water that supplies Europe's bonus of heat could no longer flow northward. The chill over this region was dispelled only when the conveyor began running again 1,000 years later. . . . [One theory for the stoppage is that meltwater] poured into the North Atlantic close to the site of deep-water formation. There it reduced the salinity of surface waters (and hence their density) by so much that, in spite of severe winter cooling, they could not sink into the abyss.

WALLACE S. BROECKER and GEORGE H. DENTON, 1990

Cause-and-effect reasoning can be tricky because nonlinear systems often chase their tails. This is a particularly apt description of the North Atlantic Current: it even does a vertical U-turn. The Current—now so cold and hypersaline that it is denser than any layer of underlying water—plunges from the surface to the abyss. There may not be a giant North Atlantic whirlpool or waterfall to gaze down upon, but this "deep water production" is equal in magnitude to 20 times the combined flow of all the rivers of the world. Once the dense water has sunk under its own weight to the sea floor, it flows south—and so attracts even more warm currents north to replace it.

Why did this Current falter? On the model of the Mediterranean in the last Pluvial, the obvious candidates would be all those analogies to the augmented Nile: the salt-free icebergs calving off of Greenland, that fresh water coming out of the St. Lawrence River from eastern Canada's massive ice sheet, and the meltwater from the Scandinavian ice sheet emerging from the Baltic and from Norwegian fjords. The North Atlantic got fresh water from all sides except the south. With sufficient dilution of the ocean surface waters, there wouldn't have been an "attraction" of warm tropical waters northward to replace the hypersaline water that otherwise sinks around Iceland. There may not be any major sources of meltwater left in Canada or Scandinavia, but Greenland has enormous supplies—and its east coast fjords are located close to the current focus of deep water production, south of Iceland. A greenhouse-encouraged glacial surge into the fjords, or the sudden emptying of a meltwater lake, might have effects on climate far out of proportion to their effects on rising sea level.

And remember the "White Earth Catastrophe," where the ice cover prevented rewarming? It could well have happened to the North Atlantic in another sense. As wind and evaporation are essential to the deep-water production, ice cover would limit evaporation and deep-water formation. An iceberg deluge might have shut off the northerly movement of (warm) replacement water, but also (by raising the freezing point of the seawater) allowed winter ice to form much farther south. Indeed, the southern border of the sea-ice islands floating in the wintertime Atlantic descended from Scandinavian to Iberian latitudes (55°N to 35°N) as the Dryas started. This wintertime "cap" on the North Atlantic would have delayed the resumption of the salt conveyor. Ice matters.

WE ARE HEADING SOUTH into the Sound-that-isn't. I just heard someone use the correct French pronunciation of "Puget"— but she was quickly corrected by another European who explained that Americans make it rhyme with "fidget" for some obscure reason. I hope that she hasn't heard about how they pronounce Goethe Street in Chicago.

The Strait of Georgia and Puget Sound were also emptied out by the drop in sea level during an ice age, making this a possible path for a glacier. We are flying right down the route of the glacier that sat atop this area 15,000 years ago, the southernmost "Puget Lobe" of the Coastal-plus-Rockies ice sheet known as the

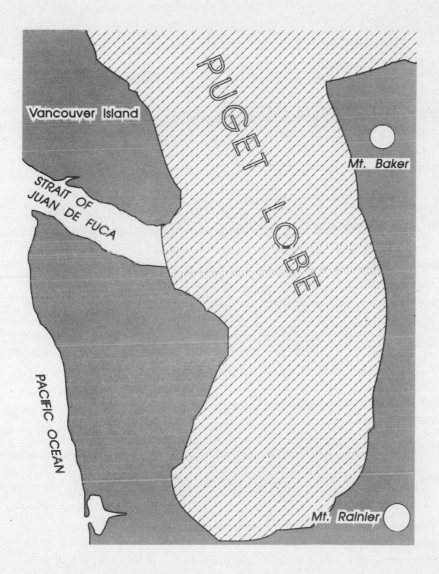

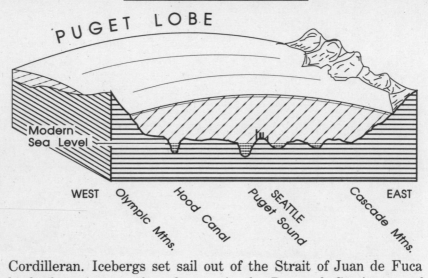

Cordilleran. Icebergs set sail out of the Strait of Juan de Fuca back then, just as they do now in the Denmark Strait east of Greenland. The San Juan Islands were scraped down to 350-million-year-old bedrock. The glacier was a mile high (1,600 meters) here, half the height of Mount Baker, the local volcano over to the east.

The massive tongue plowed down to the south end of Puget Sound, backed up, advanced again, and generally rearranged the land. Whidbey Island, which I see stretched out on the left, is all glacial, sediments deposited by one glacier or another, and carved by the silt-laden runoff from the last meltback. I once encountered some brick fragments on the beach, near the south end of Whidbey, and thought that they were surely of recent human origins, just as are the plastics that have drifted ashore. But maybe not, the geologists tell me: the warm times of the last interglacial, 120,000 years ago, produced a peat bog resting atop an older layer of clay. The peat bog dried up and caught on fire, perhaps due to lightning, and so baked some clay beneath it! As it erodes out of the cliff, the beach becomes littered with red brick fragments.

All the north-south valleys in the Seattle area are probably drainage channels that formed beneath the Puget Lobe. We even got our own fjord out of the deal, Hood Canal snaking along in its fishhook shape out the right window (unlike the Norwegian fjords carved into hard rock, it looks like a runoff channel from the lobe melting).

Below on our left, atop another glacier-shaped landform, is

Paine Field, the birthplace of our airplane—together with all the other Boeing 747s in the world. Some glacial landforms, such as Long Island and Cape Cod, are rather like ancient landfills, plowed into place by the snout of a glacier that then retreated. Actually, those Whidbey Island bluffs were underwater during the meltback; their tops are the sediments that accumulated in the lakes that formed south of the retreating glacier about 13,000 years ago. The land had been sinking slowly under the weight of the ice, but slowly rebounded over the next few thousand years. And so now these postglacial sediments are above sea level; though sea level has risen during the interglacial, these rebounding sediments have risen even more. This did not happen in southern Puget Sound, as it was covered too briefly by glaciers to sink very much. North of Seattle, the rebound has been more than the sea level rise.

The rapid melting about 13,000 years ago left even more dramatic evidence in eastern Washington state: a large lake of meltwater formed east of the Idaho-Montana border, but was held in place only by a dam of ice. When that dam broke, the lake emptied suddenly, a great flood sweeping westward. It carved a broad swath across the state until channeled down the Columbia River along the Washington-Oregon border. It sculpted deep valleys in a matter of days. Similar events must have happened as the eastern Canadian and Greenland ice sheets melted, so that the North Atlantic was episodically flooded with fresh water, disrupting the formation of the deep salty current that had attracted the warm North Atlantic Current northward (and promoting winter ice that "capped" the evaporation needed for resumption of the salt cycle).

Climate change isn't always gradual, and reversals in such salty streams may be among the reasons; still, my physiologist's training makes me worry about the more subtle reasons. All of this salt exchange reminds me of the early days of our physiological understanding of the kidney (the major player in another salt economy, that of our bodies). Since then, we've discovered some of the more subtle regulation, learned how to influence it (and high blood pressure) with medications such as diuretics. Meltwater deluges and ice-capping the salt conveyor may only be part of the story, the equivalent of binge and hangover in the body's salt economy (alcohol dehydrates the body unless a lot of alcohol-free water is also consumed at the same time).

SEATTLE IS OUT THE LEFT WINDOW and I can almost see home. Certainly I can see, in profile, that glacial relic south of the University of Washington known as Capitol Hill. The "Capitol Hill that isn't" was so named a century ago, in hopes of getting the state legislature to locate the Washington state capital there, but Olympia won. I look for its tallest point (about 35 stories uphill from the university) and a towering redwood tree with a perfect conical shape; my favorite "park bench" is just below the redwood. They are in a cemetery not far from home, a place where I often go walking while thinking out some problem.

This white granite bench, you come to realize, is actually a tombstone. Indeed, the most useful of tombstones, inviting the visitor by its very placement to pause for a while. Even on a typical Seattle day, you can see both Puget Sound to the west and Lake Washington to the east. When the clouds part, you see beyond the waters to the Olympic Mountains and the Cascade Mountains, which together formed a north-south channel for the Puget Lobe. On a clear winter day after the leaves have fallen, the bench has a horizon-to-horizon panoramic view, blocked only by that magnificent redwood just south of it.

Deeply chiseled into the edges of the top slab of this bench is a characteristically Seattle epitaph. As you walk around the bench, it reads:

West face: WEST LIES THE SOUND, SOUTH A GREAT TREE
North face: NORTH IS THE UNIVERSITY
East face: EAST THE MIGHTY CASCADES RUN FREE
South face: ALL THESE PLACES WERE LOVED BY ME.

And this unusual tombstone also offers no name, no dates—just an evocative reply to "What shall I build or write / Against the fall of night?"

MOUNT RAINIER now appears majestic in the southern sky as the plane banks over Tacoma to turn back north. This massive white volcano stands about four times as high as the Puget Lobe reached in Seattle (at 1,100 meters' thickness in Seattle, the glacier would have covered a building 260 stories tall). The lowlands south of Tacoma and Olympia are where the glacier stopped

14,000 years ago, though on earlier advances it had gone slightly further before backing up. One can see the deep valleys extending radially outward from Mount Rainier, like spokes from a wheel, carved by Rainier's glaciers before they withdrew. Here and there, the radial valleys meet the north-south valleys (some filled with long lakes such as Lake Washington on Seattle's eastern border) formed by the Puget Lobe.

Not only couldn't anyone make this over-the-pole journey a few decades ago, but it's only in the last century and a half that we've even known the ice ages existed. And the Ice Age still lives here, with nearly a thousand glaciers in this state alone: about 40 glaciers cover Mount Rainier, though some have receded as much as a kilometer in the last century.

The Seattle-Tacoma International Airport is atop still another assortment of glacial till; it's about as tall as Capitol Hill but has been reshaped to look like a mesa. In the process, they uncovered the skeleton of a giant ground sloth, common in the area during the ice ages. Thomas Jefferson was the one who discovered this species of sloth two centuries ago (scientific literacy among Amer ican politicians used to be somewhat better than it is today).

The airport runways now extend to the very edges of the flattened hilltop. And so after the gradual descent on our final approach, the ground suddenly seems to rise up to meet us, like a slow kiss which accelerates.

It is about noon here, the end of a timeless journey spanning the ice ages.

Deeds need time,
even after they are done,
to be seen and heard.
FRIEDRICH NIETZSCHE

6

MOUNT RAINIER: GROWING UP IN A BOOM TIME

But the chief cause of our natural unwillingness to admit that one species has given birth to other . . . is that we are always slow in admitting any great change of which we do not see the intermediate steps. . . . The mind cannot possibly grasp the full meaning of the term of a hundred million years; it cannot add up and perceive the full effects of many slight variations, accumulated during an almost infinite number of generations. . . . It is so easy to hide our ignorance under such expressions as the "plan of creation," "unity of design," &c., and to think that we give an explanation when we only restate a fact.

CHARLES DARWIN, *On the Origin of Species,* 1859

The next several chapters offer a specific set of processes that, in my estimate, might have sufficed to transform an ape into a human. In other words, I'm fairly sure that on some arbitrary earthlike planet somewhere else, they could pump up brain size and intelligence of an ape into something vaguely human. And that they could do it quickly, on the usual evolutionary time scale.

It seems unlikely that they will turn out to be exactly how it happened here on Earth, but they provide a target to aim at. When we finally understand human evolution in some detail, I feel sure that such processes will be involved, among others.

In the Neandertal chapter was a proposal (that expandable periphery) for how to make a minority into a majority, over and over again. But it doesn't, by itself, explain why only prehumans seem to have experienced a lot of change during the ice ages. It leaves hanging the question: Why not the polar bears? Why not the other apes?

At Mount Rainier, I consider some of the developmental processes (most known to every observant parent) that must be modified by evolution. Given boom-and-bust cycles in climate and aided by a culture able to support ever-more-helpless infants, they'll serve to enlarge an ape brain nicely. But it leaves unanswered the question: What about the reorganization of that enlarged brain for our serial-order skills? Brain size isn't everything (in fact, it's mostly bad news).

And so, up on Whidbey Island, I consider an evolutionary cycle of three phases. This cycle seems to be capable of many repetitions to increment brain size; its parts include natural selection balancing acts (one of which involves serial-order skills, one of which has been recently eliminated by cesarean sections), new niches, and modifications of developmental rates. Its sterling virtue is that it doesn't seem to wear out! This reentrant cycle may well be uniquely human, not experienced by any other species.

Then, in the San Juan Islands, I consider the conversions of function our brains have performed in order to acquire plan-ahead consciousness and logic-and-language rules. The concluding chapter at Friday Harbor addresses the next obvious step in that evolution, which has probably become essential for our civilization's survival: Improved think-ahead.

HIDDEN IN OUR SUBCONSCIOUS are some instructions for how to behave in an ice age, a suite of behaviors (what used to be called a "racial memory") for times past. Different environments tend to bring out variations on past developmental programs so as to construct somewhat different bodies and brains, depending on the environment. This can change competition and cooperation, reproductive behaviors such as becoming more or less fussy about selecting mates, as well as height and weight norms.

Genes are always used in combinations, usually a small subset of all the available genes. As each individual matures, the combinations may change (a "gene repertoire," as when fetal hemoglobin is superseded by adult hemoglobin). In modern repertory theaters, some actors are only rarely seen and others are ubiquitous, depending on what plays are being performed in a given theater season. Furthermore, play selection depends on the environment.

So too with selecting a suitable gene repertoire while growing up in the new climate. There is likely a gene repertoire, also used in various warming periods of the past, that promotes a lot of parental corner-cutting in boom times, e.g., doubling up by having more twins, shortening birth spacing, perhaps pushing adolescents out of the nest earlier. Will this boom-time repertoire "speak to us" as the greenhouse effect upsets our climate? Or has it already spoken?

Are such changing repertoires part of the way that prehuman evolution occurred in the ice ages? If we are intelligent enough to cope with this latest climatic challenge, will our brains again evolve? Will human mental abilities, such as our much-valued consciousness, be shaped up "higher?"

TO SAY THE ICE AGES shaped human consciousness is usually meant in a metaphorical way (those consciousness-raising *awareness* connotations of the word). It's another way of saying that our outlook on the world is changeable in ways that were surely "useful" in our hunter-gatherer days: changes, perhaps, in our aggressiveness, our risk-taking to exploit fleeting opportunities, our tendency to promote the interests of our immediate small group (and frequent inability to think beyond that), in our competitive attitudes toward other omnivores (such as bears), and in our predatory attitudes toward herd animals (back before horses became "pets").

Consciousness of the less metaphorical sort must have a genetic basis, being the outcome of a variety of developmental programs orchestrated by the genome. But something so general is unlikely to be resident in some particular stretch of DNA code. We can only understand the evolution of consciousness, I suspect, by understanding the details: the details of how animal planning-ahead is carried out, the details of how really precise judgments and movements are crafted, the details of the developmental programs that shape the neural machinery, the details of the regulatory genes that influence those developmental programs. And, of course, how the gene repertoires are prompted during life: selection must choose among the available variants in the developmental programs, those "plays" that make adults out of fetuses. Those modified programs in turn have to be crafted out of new gene combinations, and remembered by the genes that survive. The genetic basis of consciousness (at least, our more-than-the-apes augmentation thereof) will lie in how our developmental programs differ from those of the apes, how those genes were shaped up by the successive environments that our ancestors conquered.

We can begin to see a combination of regulatory genes—those controlling the rate at which the body grows, and some others controlling how soon sexual maturity develops—that might have something to do with the neural machinery that is so handy for planning ahead. And I can suggest how the environments might have shaped them up.

MOUNT RAINIER is like no other mountain you've ever seen or are likely to see, because it looks about twice as big. It stands alone, a symmetric breast-shaped mountain, its rounded white glaciers and smooth snowfields a proud contrast to the surrounding dark green forests and light blue sky. And it is tall—4,405 meters, 14,410 feet, as high as a 1,200-story skyscraper.

But, apropos discussions of brain size, Mount Rainier serves as a lesson in how it is *relative* size that counts. Standing near Puget Sound only 50 kilometers (30 miles) away, you see it from sea level, not from some mile-high plateau, which is the way that you might see Mount Whitney in California or some of the Colorado peaks that are technically farther above sea level (by less than 0.5 percent). Mount Rainier looks larger, thanks to its isolation and the low elevation of Puget Sound viewpoints.

It can be quite startling, when driving around Puget Sound, to turn a corner and see this improbable volcano suddenly framed in a scenic vista. Sooner or later, you keep driving toward it.

THE LAST OF THE SNOW is melting at Eunice Lake. It is situated about halfway up Mount Rainier, just below tree line, nestled into the second range of minor mountains around the base of that giant volcano. On the hike up from Mowich Lake, one gets wonderful views of Mount Rainier—close enough to be huge, far enough back to see the whole top half of the mountain. Eunice Lake is a delicate alpine setting, flanked by meadows full of wildflowers and a few patches of late-melting snow in August, but in September it has autumn color from all the huckleberry bushes. The growing season isn't long, hereabouts.

Wherever you see an avalanche track, it is emblazoned with crimson. And frequented by hikers (not to mention the occasional bear), looking for the sweet blue berries that grow among the red leaves. Behind the lake is Tolmie Peak, which has colonnades of basalt, rather like the Grand Canyon's tapestries of hexagonal columns at Mile 185 of *The River That Flows Uphill*. Atop one is the fire lookout, and sharp pinnacles extend along the skyline.

THE CLIFFS ECHO, and one of the echos I hear is "lizard . . . lizard . . . in the lake . . . lake." Come now, lizards live on land, not in lakes. Guess again, whoever you are.

Then I hear another little girl's voice saying, "It's a giant tadpole . . . pole . . . pole." Ah, I bet I know what they've found. My zoologist wife discovered them on one of our earlier trips.

I too look into the lake, in the clear shallow water. It's downright distracting, the reflections of the autumn color on the lake's slightly rippled surface: pointillist patches of yellow, green, russet, and dark red. It is like an Impressionist painting, except slight breezes ripple the smooth surface, "smearing the paint" here and there. "Dynamic impressionism," we should call it. Both sound and light play tricks on you, hereabouts.

Finally I get a clear view of some rather improbable things swimming around near the shore. The largest are almost as big as a rolled-up newspaper, but they have four stubby legs. Looking singularly useless, though I suppose that they can "dog-paddle" when the occasion demands.

It's an axolotl, surely the most unusual form of the salamander. The Mexicans consider them quite a delicacy and European scientists have been worrying about them ever since the French explorers of the nineteenth century brought back a few dozen from Mexico.

The reason for all the attention paid to them is that, as the little girl accurately observed, they look like giant tadpoles: axolotls appear permanently youthful. That certainly got the Europeans' attention: mud puddles as the fountain of youth? A way of backing up, reversing aging? (No, but it does demonstrate where the analogy breaks down, between "how species evolve" and "how individuals grow up.")

The typical salamander goes through an aquatic tadpole stage, then crawls out on all fours when its pond starts drying up, loses its gills during metamorphosis, and lives thereafter on land as an adult salamander, returning to the water's edge briefly to lay eggs. But the genus *Ambystoma* is versatile, having acquired during the course of evolution one way of adjusting rapidly to an erratic climate: if the weather forecast is better for life underwater compared to life foraging on land, the tadpole stays in the water, retaining its gills. It does this by using early sexual maturity to lop off the gill-less stage of its developmental program; because sexual maturity may slow down somatic development to a crawl, early puberty can truncate development before implementing undesirable features.

The Mount Rainier axolotls are relatively big; they are probably members of the several genera of salamanders that are permanently larval in morphology, called the perennibrachiate. They *always* keep their gills, no maybe about it. Since their legs don't have to support the body weight, thanks to the buoyancy of water, these "juvenilized" newts can grow to be larger than the land-dwelling version, which has to haul all of its weight around. From a version that backs up on special occasions, the perennibrachiate have become a permanently backed-up version.

> [Ambystoma's] a giant newt who rears in swampy waters,
> As other newts are wont to do, a lot of fishy daughters:
> These Axolotls, having gills, pursue a life aquatic,
> But, when they should transform to newts, are naughty and
>   erratic.
> They change upon compulsion, if the water grows too foul,
> For then they have to use their lungs, and go ashore to prowl:
>
> But when a lake's attractive, nicely aired, and full of food,
> They cling to youth perpetual, and rear a tadpole brood.
> And newts Perennibrachiate have gone from bad to worse:
> They think aquatic life is bliss, terrestrial a curse.
> They do not even contemplate a change to suit the weather,
> But live as tadpoles, breed as tadpoles, tadpoles altogether!
>   WALTER GARSTANG, 1951

ICE-AGE CLIMATES THAT SWITCH back and forth illustrate one reason why "backing up" might be a good thing: suppress the current genes for big bodies when the climate warms up, and go back to the old set of genes that emphasized rapid reproduction instead. Just don't throw away the genes for big bodies as maybe they'll be needed again, many thousands of generations later when the unstable climate cools.

The easy way to back up is simply to abbreviate growing up, stopping before ever implementing a presently undesirable feature. If adults have added-on features that juveniles don't (big fangs, for example, in baboons), then an easy way to get rid of them is to stop growing before ever reaching adulthood. Since sexual maturity tends to slow down body development, early puberty may indefinitely postpone them (though if you live long enough, even slow development during adulthood might eventually implement them). Because there is a lot of heritable variation in the age when puberty strikes, any environmental advantage to the more childlike adults will tend to shift the average age of puberty to earlier years as the centuries pass.

Early puberty thus provides a way of backing up, should the overspecialized features of adulthood prove awkward. While fangs aren't such a big disadvantage, there are contrasting psychological characteristics of juveniles and adults that probably are important. Juveniles play around a lot, thus discovering new ways of doing things. When one is an adult, however, one had best be a good provider and good defender, rather than playing half the time. Adult monkeys are remarkably slow to learn about new foods compared to those juveniles that are always fiddling around. Given a change in climate, the early maturing variants might survive better, simply because they remained more childlike and thus more open to new ways of doing things.

And, as I noted while surveying the Neandertal country of Czechoslovakia, there are also reproductive contests that reward early maturity with more such "genes for juvenilization" in the next generation. The boom times that follow droughts encourage such competitions, and the ice ages institutionalized them in a big way. There is a race to fill up the newly available "job slots" afforded by an environment able to feed more mouths.

One of the fisheries problems in Puget Sound is that the salmon have been experiencing early puberty: instead of taking a few years to mature, some males mature in only one year, and so can be grandfathers before the standard-maturity males become fathers. Such precocious males remain small—and so are more likely to be eaten by predators, presumably one reason why mature males aren't always so small (though, given that fishermen are not allowed to keep undersized fish, human cultural practices may eventually reward salmon genes that promote small size!).

Besides this truncation of the juvenile period, another aspect of growing up quickly has been studied in monkeys: more rapid development during the juvenile period itself. Those baboons that happen to live near the tourist camps in East Africa grow up

In boom times when four offspring survive,
rapid reproduction gives Fast Mom more gene
copies surviving decades later, even though
her contribution is halved with each generation.

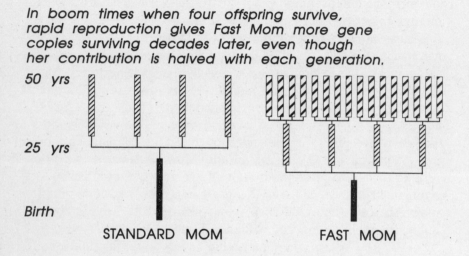

In normal times when population is not expanding,
Fast Mom has no advantage (more grandchildren but
not more gene copies) and her corner-cutting is
likely to reduce offspring survival below standard.

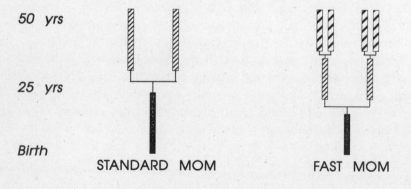

faster; the baboon troops have discovered the garbage dumps, which are considerably more reliable than the usual baboon food sources. The anthropologists Clifford Jolly and Jane Phillips-Conroy compared baboons in the wild with those in breeding colonies, showing that the captive ones consistently erupt their teeth earlier than the wild juveniles.

Jolly cautions against interpreting this solely on the basis of veterinary care and plentiful food (captive primates are usually fed *ad libitum*, while wild ones suffer the ups and downs of the fluctuating availability as the seasons change and the mercurial climate creates scarcity). He suggests that we might want to view this in terms of ultimate causes rather than proximate causes: is there something built into evolutionary processes that might speed up development under some conditions, slow it down under others?

Indeed many animals adjust their reproductive tactics to environmental conditions—and not only the present conditions, such as whether one's stomach is full: some animals "forecast" future conditions and "plan" accordingly. The snowy owl, if its hormonal mechanisms judge that it is going to be a good year for lemmings, will lay a lot of eggs. If the forecast for lemmings is poor, the snowy owl's hypothalamus causes it to lay only several eggs, as lemmings are the favored food for feeding the chicks once they hatch. The snowy owl looks ahead (probably, I suspect, by observing the same environmental clues that the lemmings base their reproductive decisions on, one of which is similar to the Groundhog Day story), and so doesn't produce a lot of expensive eggs whose successors will just starve to death later in the season.

This short-term tactic isn't a violation of the Mama Bear strategy of "keeping up with the Joneses"; the snowy owl still tries to produce as many offspring as possible during her lifetime, but conserves resources so there will be several well-fed offspring rather than a half-dozen weak ones which may all die. Less is more, when the forecast is poor.

AN EPIDEMIC OF EARLY MATURITY in humans has certainly been happening in the last century. Girls used to start having menstrual periods when they were 16–17 years old, but now menarche has nose-dived closer to 12 or even 11 years of age. It can happen within a single generation.

If delaying reproduction is a common response to a forecast featuring substandard prospects, then perhaps speeding up reproduction is a response to a promising forecast—and one way to have more offspring while good conditions last is to hurry up the start of your reproductive period, to "rush the season." Shortened generation time is the more obvious aspect: you can become a grandparent in the time that your neighbor takes to become a parent. Should there be a number of new unoccupied job slots to fill, your descendants will get more of them. Assume that, thanks to booming conditions, everyone gets to produce four offspring that survive to maturity: the neighbor ("Standard Mom") gets four offspring into the next generation, but Fast Mom's rushing the season yields 16 in the same time (assuming the characteristic is heritable). Early maturity also allows more pregnancies in a mother's lifetime, at least if the standard lifetime isn't also shortened by the speedup: the speedy mothers might have six surviving offspring, each of whom also produces six—and so Fast Mom has 36 grandchildren in the same time as Standard Mom's four children. In short order, the population characteristics are skewed toward the speedy ones. Lacking the boom-time expansion, the population characteristics change little.

But why not always have a longer reproductive span, e.g., routinely start childbearing at age 12 rather than 18? At least in mammals, early pregnancies tend to be associated with more problems, such as low birth weight. If there isn't going to be enough extra food for a gestating fetus, the prospective mother is better off putting on some weight herself, getting better prepared, rather than building a baby. She will need to be able to nourish the baby off her own fat supply, should famine strike.

All of this seems to be part of the evolutionary diversity that we call the r-K spectrum. It concerns parental strategies: r and K are just somewhat abstract variables in an equation used by population ecologists (I'd rename it the q-Q spectrum, since the emphasis shifts from quantity to Quality). Animals that lay great quantities of eggs (such as mosquitos) but invest nothing in caring for them or raising the juveniles are called r-selected; just remember "lay them and leave them" if you prefer. Other animals (primates are good examples) have relatively few single (not twin or triplet) pregnancies, carefully gestate the fetus during early development and nurture it after birth, often for years. They are called K-selected, mostly because such a strategy is associated with conditions where the species is operating close to the carrying capacity of the environment: they are exploiting the resources about as fully as possible, and so the extra advantages associated with quality become important. The ultimate version of K-selection so far (though it is due to cultural evolution, not biological) is when parents put their offspring through not only college but postgraduate education as well.

Some K-selected animals, however, will vary their strategy as the climate fluctuates: let the prospects improve and they will r shift, not all the way to the mosquito's lay-them-and-leave-them strategy but certainly cutting a lot of corners, producing extra offspring because it looks as if there will be room for them. When times are good (or when they can predict that the climate is improving), they go on a reproductive binge.

They may start having more twins, despite the hazards of crowding *in utero* on development (the pediatricians say that twins have a harder time, both during gestation and afterward). Sheep ranchers have discovered that they can increase the number of twins born, just by feeding the ewes a high-caloric diet for a few weeks before mating season. Both ovaries let loose an ovum: the ewe fires with both barrels into the uterus.

In addition to doubling up, parents may devote less care to each offspring in other ways as well, as the offspring may be able to manage on their own with such improving environmental conditions. Instead such parents have as many offspring as they can by starting early and repeating just as quickly as possible. When prospects turn sour, they may K-shift back toward the more conservative strategy of sinking one's bets on a few well-placed shots. When your species is already exploiting the environment near the limits of its carrying capacity (which includes food availability but also nesting sites and such), play it safe by waiting until you are better prepared, then raise only a few offspring and devote a lot of care to them.

If this also applies to humans, then two questions immediately arise: How is the "boom-time" r-shift implemented? (Is sexual maturity sped up, or is juvenile growth rate, or perhaps both?) And what triggers it, what aspects of the environment are "read" for the forecast? If we are ever to replace this corner-cutting "Quantity is Better than Quality" philosophy of nature and effectively combat its fatalistic "Life is Cheap" corollary, we need to understand what drives it (the "hangover" that follows a reproductive "binge" is better known as a population crash).

What's natural isn't always good, as David Hume pointed out two centuries ago, but the Pope still holds to the "Naturalist Fallacy." One wonders how many other "natural" reproductive behaviors the Church would care to endorse?

> *Every man is to be respected as an absolute end in himself;*
> *and it is a crime against the dignity that belongs to him as a*
> *human being, to use him as a means for some external*
> *purpose.*
>
> IMMANUEL KANT, *Metaphysics of Morals*

BEHIND EUNICE LAKE IS TOLMIE PEAK, and there is a fire lookout tower atop it, just two stories high, enough to look over the tops of the stubby trees growing around it. Tolmie Peak rises several hundred meters above Eunice, sheltering the lake from the north winds of winter. From the top of Tolmie, there is a better view of Mount Rainier—and of the Olympic Mountains to the west facing the Cascades across Puget Sound. One sees the other Washington State volcanos to the north, even Mount Baker up on the Canadian border. Looking south just to the right of Mount Rainier, I can see a much-diminished Mount St. Helens, plus even more volcanic peaks across the Columbia River into Oregon. There's nothing quite like seeing a long-familiar mountain, now missing its top, to make you realize that the natural world can change abruptly.

This string of volcanos in the Northwest, mostly in a band about the same distance in from the coastline, is due to what happens to the bottom of the Pacific Ocean as it is recycled. The ocean floor slowly creeps east from where it is formed in the mid-Pacific upwellings. When it reaches the west coast of North America about 100 million years later, it dives under the continent to rejoin the molten magma of the Earth's core. This "subduction" process is associated with volcanos of the type we have in the Northwest, sitting atop the zone where the ocean floor is folded back into the hot interior, a series of escape valves for the excess steam pressure.

If islands are carried along with the sea floor conveyor system, they may be appended to the west coast rather than subducted down to Hades: all of North America west of the Rocky Mountain chain seems to be a hodgepodge of different rocks from different places (the firm granite in the Cascade Mountains is very different than the unreliable granite of the Olympics, as mountain climbers around here soon learn). Of course, adding coastal mountains poking up into the clouds attracts lots more rainfall to the coast while producing a "rain shadow" inland. The islands that are subducted probably cause giant earthquakes hereabouts, as they snag and then pop free. The ceaseless motion of the sea floor and the continents means that plants and animals are constantly having to adapt to changing conditions.

Tolmie Peak also has a hummingbird, performing the usual disappearing act—now you see it, now you don't. Hummingbirds haven't yet made an evolutionary adaptation to the false alarms caused by the bright jackets favored by hikers, and usually come over to inspect the big flower. Bees make the same mistake; to keep them from swarming around my head, I once had to take off a bright neck scarf and throw it aside. They followed it. It makes me worry that we humans have such senseless attractions too, following things for reasons we don't understand. And following to excess some of the "natural" attractors we do understand, such as sugars and fats: my colleague David Barash points out a number of supernormal releasers in *The Hare and the Tortoise* and Annie Dillard discusses supernormal attractors in *The Writing Life* (not to be confused with the strange attractors of chaos!).

WHAT ASPECT OF THE ENVIRONMENT is "read" to predict boom times ahead? In the days before market surveys, shoe manufacturers contemplating expanding their factory probably used secondary indicators such as the strength of the baby-carriage business. Since even owls can forecast, r-shifting is surely an unconscious business; owls don't go out and take a market survey, a census of owls and lemmings, divide, apply a safety factor, and reset their factory. If it is like other things biological, r-shifting probably operates on secondary indicators such as light and humidity and social crowding.

But speeding up juvenile growth rates suggests that *even children might be "judging" the future market for babies.* What might they be judging? Much has been made of the deleterious effects of overcrowding on reproduction (e.g., aborted pregnancies) —but a lesser degree of crowding might work the other way. Cliff Jolly suggests that the number of other children—how many playmates a child has to choose among—could serve as a secondary indicator that the resources were improving, enough so that people can successfully live at somewhat higher population densities. These are mechanisms below the level of consciousness that nonetheless have the same effects as conscious ones—such as "keeping up with the Joneses" in terms of family size, e.g., the Israelis worry about the neighboring Arabs outnumbering them and encourage large families. Economic conditions are the more familiar birthrate determinants in industrialized societies; what we are here concerned with are preeconomic life-styles, and what might lead to corner-cutting.

More babies encouraging even more babies sounds like a positive feedback loop which would become unstable, given the aggression that comes with overcrowding. We might not design such a system ourselves, knowing about control systems and harmful oscillations, but maybe our reproductive system wasn't well designed.

Another possibility for the mechanism of early human maturity is that lighting conditions could be serving as an indicator. The length of daylight is one cue used by birds in determining how many eggs to lay; for example, the European robin raises a clutch of three or four at Mediterranean latitudes, but a clutch of six in Sweden where the summer days are longer (since robins forage for food only during the day, the amount that they can collect during a working day determines how many offspring they can raise). Lighting affects growth rate too: farmers have long known that one way to speed up growth in farm animals is to leave the barn lights on at night. Is there a human equivalent of this? (Many humans now tend to rely on artificial lighting during the evening, getting 16 hours per day of light, year-round).

ACCELERATED MATURITY isn't merely a speedup in the time scale: to the extent that the maturation of the reproductive organs gets ahead of the speedup of general somatic development, you get a juvenilization of adult body styles. Since puberty tends to send signals that slow down somatic development, such individuals tend to be smaller than average (rather like those precocious salmon, though the axolotls demonstrate how other factors may cause the juvenilized version to be larger instead). For example, girls with early menarche are typically (though not always) short. Some tall girls have gotten in a few years' more growth before puberty slowed body growth.

Facial characteristics are also likely to be affected, since the lower face and jaw get in a lot of late growth when not terminated by early puberty. Though the brain itself is about full-grown by age seven, the skull adds thickness and the sinuses fill out in later childhood; one might expect early puberty to affect them too. General robustness is likely affected, once the more gracile adolescent build becomes the new adult standard.

There is a lot of hidden change too: the brain *size* may change little after age seven, but much still happens internally. If not already myelinated, some axons will gain insulation during later childhood and adolescence. And synapses are being edited all through childhood, the elimination rate decelerating at puberty. Juvenile brains have many more interconnections between nerve cells than adults; a third to a half of all cortical synapses are lost during childhood, the peak occurring about eight months after birth and it's all downhill thereafter. Should those extra connections be crucial for some task (I suggest that they're very useful for throwing), early puberty might help out, saving some synapses from being disconnected.

IF *r-K* STRATEGIES regulate growing up, then surely they are involved in the making of a new species. What modifications make us grow up to be humans, rather than chimpanzees? Might some of the evolutionary changes in the hominid lineage be explained by early maturation too?

Juvenilization has apparently played a large role in the evolution of humans from the apes, just as it played a large role in the evolution of apes from Old World monkeys, just as it played a large role in evolving the vertebrates from the invertebrates known as ascidians. Backing up from overspecialization, then evolving some new specialization, backing up a bit from that, and striking out in a new direction once more—we've done a lot of that, and at major turning points in our evolutionary history. The French have a phrase, *reculer pour mieux sauter* ("step back to leap better"), that epitomizes a crucial evolutionary principle.

This does not mean, of course, that humans are merely infant monkeys, or that the whole human genome was present in the ascidian, just waiting for repeated juvenilizations to come along (keeping us all from finally growing up to be sand dollars!). Animal development isn't one-dimensional (like our usual train of reasoning).

ADULT DOMESTIC ANIMALS are paedomorphic (literally, "child-shaped"), exhibiting a lot of juvenile characteristics: flatter faces, smaller teeth, and more behavioral plasticity than their wild predecessors. While most of this is probably the early puberty of a boom time (being fed regularly), there might also be some selective survival: there is a lot of natural variation in the time of sexual maturity, and humans could have selected those wild animals that were more juvenilized. Since juvenile animals solicit attention, juvenilized adults are the ones more likely to hang out around humans and get fed. But that's probably not the route used for human juvenilization. Human juvenilized appearance ("neoteny") might, of course, have occurred because of natural selection for its usefulness. In particular, sexual selection might have done it: the novelist David Brin suggests that prehuman females competed for the attentions of those variant males most likely to be nurturing of their offspring (in our African ape relatives, males have no special relationship with their own offspring). And as part of this competition, juvenile-appearing females preferentially attracted the nurturing males; together they made a good team, getting more offspring to maturity because of two adults to share the work load. And so juvenilized appearance *per se* could have been under natural selection in females (that's where it is most pronounced), and not just a hauled-along secondary consequence of boom-time opportunism or some other advantage of juvenilization (of which, more later).

But consider the boom-time argument a little further. Just within the species span of *Homo sapiens*—and almost-modern-looking people seem to extend back through most of the last Ice Age to the last interglaciation 120,000 years ago—there have been a number of changes in the "carrying capacity" of the human environment (think of it as one of those "maximum occupancy" signs erected by the fire marshal). First came the Ice Age itself, but that changes so slowly it would be hard to detect an improving trend. Even during the rapid meltback phase, the average rate of uncovering new land was only 0.4 percent per century. The rapid warmings (such as the Allerød event 13,000 years ago, or the end of the Younger Dryas at 10,720 years ago) might, however, have caused a few generations to experience rapid change.

But boom times aren't caused only by changes in the natural environment. There have been some technological improvements during the last Ice Age that have markedly changed human prospects. As each was introduced, it might have permitted boom times until the new niche filled up.

○ First was probably the invention of big-game hunting. The attachment of spear points to shafts goes back to the penultimate Ice Age. Following herds of big game around and exploiting them for meat is probably what carried *Homo sapiens* into every reach of the temperate zone. Loren Eiseley used to say that meat provided the energy that took man around the world. While opportunistically eating meat is very old, eating big game *regularly* may have been one of the innovations of the more recent ice ages. Boats were also invented sometime during the last glaciation, greatly improving the prospects of coastal peoples by allowing offshore fishing.

○ Second was cooking, which allows many kinds of flora and fauna to be eaten that cannot be consumed raw in any quantities. That too seems to date back to within the last glaciation, not as an initial invention but as a widespread and improving technology that left behind more and more charcoal and burnt hearthstones for archaeologists to find.

○ And food preparation got fancier with the introduction of baskets and especially pottery, again expanding the range of foodstuffs that could be exploited.

○ Finally, with the melt-off 12,000 years ago, we start to get agriculture—which, combined with all the improvements that followed, is said to have increased the human population a thousandfold.

With the adoption of each of these technologies, it would be just as if the hunter-gatherers' environment had improved: just as more rain brings better foraging, so an improving food technology may have repeatedly stimulated an r-shift in human ontogeny (not to mention economic inflation!). It depends on what is actually sensed unconsciously by growing children, but it would not be surprising to find boom-time reproductive strategies coming to the fore on each of those occasions when technology expanded the food that could be captured, prepared, and digested.

TOOTH SIZE REDUCTION has been a big puzzle to the physical anthropologists: during the last Ice Age, as I mentioned earlier, human tooth size slowly and steadily decreased, late ice-age teeth being 10 percent smaller than the standard earlier in the last Ice Age. C. Loring Brace says that a steady decline occurred between 60,000 years ago and the great melt-off 10,000 years ago—but thereafter the reduction sped up even more, perhaps due to the agricultural technologies that developed. This worldwide decline in tooth size became more pronounced in each region as pottery was introduced. The domestication of animals also reduced their tooth size (just compare your dog's dentition to a wolf's!).

Thus the anthropologists are asking: Are small teeth an adaptive response (Are large teeth a disadvantage? Are smaller teeth better for something?) or the result of the removal of selective pressures that were keeping average tooth size large (maybe the rougher food from before cooking and fancier food preparation was selecting against those variants with smaller teeth—but with easier foods, the tooth size returned to its inborn value). I would suggest yet a third alternative: maybe small teeth are just another manifestation of more rapid maturity, that the boom-time juvenilization has struck again! Juveniles have smaller teeth, just as they have flatter faces, and larger brain/body ratios.

Note that early maturity is comprised of several processes: somatic growth rates (as seen in tooth eruption speedups upon domestication of wild animals) and also the speedup in sexual maturity. You can have one acceleration without the other, e.g., a speedup in sexual maturity without a speedup in somatic growth (the medical use of the term *precocious puberty* tends to refer to six-year-olds with pubic hair, but I am talking about downshifting the adolescent growth spurt by several years). The two rates are regulated by somewhat different hormonal systems, *melatonin* from the pineal being important for sexual maturity and *growth hormone* from the pituitary being important for somatic growth, among many others. But some hormonal systems affect both somatic and sexual developmental rates, as in the common effect of *testosterone* on muscle building and maturation of secondary sexual characteristics (and, of course, testosterone affects the primary sexual differentiation of the month-old fetus—the prime reason why potentially pregnant women should *never* use muscle-building steroids that can mimic testosterone's actions, as masculinization of a female fetus can result even before pregnancy is detected).

The relative speedup of sexual development, compared to somatic, is the common cause of juvenilized appearance (at least, in the days before eye-enhancing cosmetics and for-appearances-only dieting!). If both sexual and somatic rates were equally accelerated, presumably the adult form wouldn't change. But smaller teeth, low birth weight, twinning, and less robust long bone development suggests that corners are being cut—and that sexual development might have sped up even more than somatic. The situation is not unlike a boom-time economy where quality control slips: there is so much demand for the product that no one is being choosy about the product's durability.

In addition to the progressive reduction in tooth size during the last Ice Age, has there been an increasing flattening of the face? Is it all due to one boom time after another (big game, cooking, pottery-related food preparation—and then agriculture)? Even the ice-age meltback itself is potentially a boom-time event, and there have been lots of those during the 2.5 million-year period of encephalization. Could boom-time physiology alone have pumped up brain size, simply through the reproductive contests during expansionistic times?

Or has natural selection also worked on one or another aspect of early maturity as well? Perhaps all those synapses that are being eliminated during late childhood turn out to be handy for something in the context of the hunter-gatherer life-styles, so that early puberty serves to conserve them. That's been my proposal for what happened even earlier, in the 2.4 million years preceding the last Ice Age and modern-style *Homo sapiens*, though it may not apply to the most recent glaciation. Repeated juvenilizations may serve to enlarge relative brain size, but they won't necessarily reorganize the brain at the same time, to give us those serial-order skills that we have in such great abundance.

[A woman must store a minimum] amount of body fat in order to begin and maintain normal menstrual cycles. Activities that reduce fat below the threshold, such as serious dieting and intensive exercise, can delay the age of menarche . . . to as late as 20 years. Such a loss can also "silently" halt ovulation . . . in someone who menstruates every month. . . . [This] helped to explain [why] American girls now begin to menstruate when they are 12.6 years old; a century ago the age was 15.5 years [and that is about when athletic girls now begin their periods]. [Roger] Revelle and I postulate that the earlier menarche is explained by the fact that children now become bigger sooner because they are better nourished and have less average disease.

the reproductive biologist ROSE E. FRISCH, 1988

HIKING BACK DOWN THE TRAIL, I almost ran into a young deer on the trail—we both jumped in surprise, and the doe leaped nimbly uphill and then eyed me while munching on the greenery again. It looks like one of this year's, almost grown, trying to find enough food to get it through its first winter. A mild winter will mean a boom time for deer next year, because winter and wolves are what keep the deer population from expanding exponentially.

Body fat certainly makes a big difference in when teenaged girls start to ovulate. That raises a lot of questions: How much of that accelerated ovulation is inheritance, how much can be manipulated by diet and exercise? And, of course, how much does early ovulation affect general body development thereafter—especially the brain? We've always thought of the prenatal period as the particularly important period for shaping brain development, but cortical pruning and labile menarche together raise the possibility that the early adolescent period might also be an important one for biasing adult brains one way or another.

I got to thinking more about human boom times, trying to summarize it all in my head. Culturally, I know what is meant: people save less, borrow more, open more risky small businesses, cut corners on quality because demand is so high that buyers aren't fussy, and generally become less concerned about the future. We get inflation, a bullish stock market, and a party atmosphere—at least in comparison to the downside of the business cycle.

That's the psychology of boom times. Not much is really known about boom-time physiology, especially in humans. We do know that the apes are very K selected (perhaps too much so) because of their long birth spacing (nearly five years and no twins). Humans are near the K-extreme: we have relatively few offspring and devote a lot of postnatal care to each one, but still manage to reduce birth spacing to four years (down to two years in agricultural societies, with bottle feeding reducing it even further). And we manage twins on occasion, something apes do not.

But what might shifting away from this average position involve? Assume for the moment that this r-shifting is due to "selfish" genes, doing their usual behind-the-scenes manipulation in an effort to produce more grandchildren carrying the gene—use that for a moment rather than our usual humane concerns about infant mortality and overpopulation. To the selfish gene, the name of the game is not simply a matter of having more children than average—if they die in childhood at a higher-than-average rate because of lack of parental attention or not enough food to go around, one will not end up with more grandchildren than average.

Since half of all children do not survive childhood (except in certain parts of the modern world), the calculating gene has to, in effect, weigh the potential of a child dying before reproducing itself—and compare it to the chances of getting by on less parental care, while the parent tries raising yet another infant. Mothers who simply have additional children do so at some risk to the existing children; the statistics show that all children in a big family grow up (gain height and weight) more slowly, perhaps because of not as much food per child, perhaps from a more complicated effect of the r-shift mechanisms.

In an improving environment, the calculating gene might well decide to decrease birth spacing: if the environment is easy, maybe the existing children will make it anyway while Mom is busy with another pregnancy and another infant. One way of implementing such a hurry-up-while-the-getting's-good strategy is to stop breast-feeding early, so as to build up maternal body fat once again and thereby resume monthly ovulation. Or the selfish genes might decide to try for twins or triplets, a somewhat risky business because of *in utero* crowding and less individual atten- tion while the children are growing up.

And a calculating gene in a child's body might make reproductive decisions too, speeding or slowing somatic development and sexual development. The number of offspring per mother is also a func- tion of her reproductive span, starting several years after puberty and ending with menopause. Maximizing one's offspring is not simply a matter of becoming pregnant as young as possible, as babies born to young mothers have low birth weight and higher mortality; the new mother is more inexperienced than if she had watched child- rearing techniques a little longer before trying it herself.

Even selfish genes cannot take a "So what if I lose the first one?" attitude toward a teenage pregnancy. The mother loses something permanently by trying early: Since early menarche tends to cut short the mother's growth, she won't have the bodily resources to devote to her later offspring that she would other- wise have by waiting until the usual year to become fertile. But if the environment was obviously improving, a child's selfish genes wanting to maximize her number of grandchildren might "decide" to reach puberty sooner and let the babies take their chances.

Selfish genes being what they are, any tendency to shift reproductive strategies toward exploiting a boom-time environ- ment would result in more such genes in the subsequent genera- tion (provided the gamble paid off), compared to genes reflecting a static strategy that maintains parental investment per offspring regardless of the environmental quality. Both groups will get more grandchildren since the booming environment will somewhat reduce childhood mortality, but the shifting-strategy group could easily get twice as many grandchildren before the next downturn—and so increase their proportion in the population with each boom-and-bust cycle.

SOME HUMAN MOTHERS consciously choose to have a dozen children. But if a related strategy (rushing the season via early puberty and growth speedups) can be implemented *even by children as they grow up*, perhaps we'd better rethink our assumptions and search for a more widespread "cause" than many independent rational choices. What is it about the booming environment that is sensed for the boom-time cue by the selfish genes? What hormonal systems implement the shift?

Implementation first—maybe it will provide a clue as to what is being sensed to trigger it. Let me start by simply making a list of all those possible ways of *cutting corners* to increase grandchild production rates. For the mother, it could involve early weaning and encouraging early mating by her offspring via sexually permissive advice. She could also cut corners by double ovulations or other means of having twins. For the child mother-to-be, it would involve "rushing the season," hurrying up sexual maturity so as to get in several extra pregnancies.

Now mothers are not usually thought to be able to dictate the characteristics of offspring, but if selfish genes are at work using indirect means, what else might increase the number of grandchildren? Shifting the sex ratio toward more males than females—since females are almost guaranteed a minimum number of offspring and so are the conservative strategy, males (who can in effect have multiple pregnancies going at the same time in different mothers) are a risky investment that pays off best in boom times.

Inherited personality traits might shift too, not just reproductive traits. For example, about 15 percent of modern infants fall into the extremes of very shy and very bold, when exploring a novel situation. Might *r*-shifting increase the number of bold infants, so as to better exploit a more benign environment? In rats, there is even a brain structure difference between the shy and bold rats: the very timid ones have markedly larger right cerebral hemispheres compared to their left sides. The very bold rats tend to have somewhat larger left hemispheres; the average rat (like the average human) has a somewhat larger right hemisphere. Is this heritable? Have humans followed this pattern during boom times of the past? Have human hemispheric asymmetries changed in the last century, concomitant with the earlier puberty—might r-shifting be affecting fetal brain development? Between the physical anthropologists studying old graveyards that construction crews accidentally discover, and the neuroradiologists studying modern human brains with the various imaging techniques, we might actually be able to answer such questions.

Social behaviors might shift too. Males might shift toward even more of a "love them and leave them" strategy to spread their genes around as widely as possible, abetted by a relaxation of the usual female tendency to be choosy about selecting a good provider. If maximizing grandchildren is the name of the gene-propagation game, and not the quality of the grandchildren, these are all ways of cutting corners to increase production rate. But, at least for humans, they're not "fate."

Our learning biases and emotional responses . . . are not random or manufactured from thin air; they are the products of the unbroken process of evolution by natural selection that extends across the whole of history, into our prehuman past, and millions of years before that. This is why even a seemingly "purely cultural" phenomenon, such as an arms race, may be most effectively dealt with from a perspective that includes a thorough understanding of our history of natural selection. . . . Moths fly to their deaths around electric lights; this maladaptive response to an environmental novelty is understandable . . . only by knowing the nocturnal behavior of moths prior to the introduction of electric lights.

RICHARD D. ALEXANDER, 1987

SOCIAL COMMENTATORS have been remarking on developments in our culture that involve quantity rather than quality of offspring, though I think that we must be careful in establishing links, lest the overenthusiastic inflict another eugenics monster on us.

I have a hard time believing that all such changes can be accounted for by a hidden biological strategy like r-shifting—some are surely just cultural phenomena or selective recall about the "good old days" instead—but culture isn't going to account for everything on the boom-time corner-cutting list. Boom-time r-shifts is a hypothesis that needs testing if we are to get control of the situation and encourage quality as the preferred strategy. The human cultural version of K-shifting is "quality, not quantity"— and that's very different from mere birth control. If we wait for biology to do the K shifting for us, there will likely be a dramatic crash in human population that accompanies it—potentially including Neandertal-like problems, a return of the life that is "nasty, brutish, and short."

What price success? Heretofore, we have seen it as a big boom-and-bust cycle, our ice-age genes remaking our world into an overcrowded, famine-ridden place, likely to be followed by a population crash. People often discount dire predictions, believing that (as often in the past) some new invention will come along and change the whole situation. But the price of ignoring boom-time shifts in human reproductive strategies may also be some undesirable shifts in human characteristics *during* the boom itself: corner-cutting on quality. Whatever the pleasures of becoming the first 28-year-old grandparent on your block, they may not outweigh the immediate losses associated with the decrease in parental competence and attention per child.

Our ice-age selfish genes may not have been concerned with the quality of life, but they did provide us with an amazing ability, never seen before in evolution, to look ahead and correct our course.

[Jorge Luis Borges' *Labyrinths*] *exploits the paradox of making the future present through foreknowledge. As the god simultaneously sees the world's fate and possibly deflects it, so do our perceptions of the inevitable and the possible sometimes alter the very soil from which the future springs. This is one of the reasons I have argued so vehemently against the doctrine of biological fate. Beliefs may fulfill themselves not by virtue of their truth but by virtue of their fixity, and we are only too ready to disavow responsibility for what we perceive as biologically imposed.*

the ethologist SUSAN OYAMA, 1985

7

WHIDBEY ISLAND: RATCHETING UP BRAIN SIZE

We like to imagine that preindustrial peoples endured (and endure) less stress than we do—that, although they may have lacked physical amenities, they spent peaceful days weaving interesting fabrics and singing folk songs. But the psychic stresses of the simple life are, in fact, far greater than those experienced by the most harried modern executive. It is one thing to fret over a tax return or a real estate deal, and quite another to bury one's children, to wonder if a fall's harvest will last the winter, or to watch one's home wash away in a flood.

To grow up surrounded by scarcity and ignorance and constant loss—whether in an African village or a twentieth-century urban slum—is to learn that misery is usually a consequence of forces beyond one's control and, by extension, that individual effort counts for naught. And there is ample evidence that such a sense of helplessness is often associated with apathy, depression, and death—whether in laboratory animals or prisoners of war. . . . Modernization, through such mechanisms as fire departments, building codes, social insurance, and emergency medical care, has cushioned most of us against physical, psychic, and economic disaster. But, more importantly, it has created circumstances in which few of us feel utterly powerless to control our lives. We now take for granted that we are, in large part, the masters of our own destinies, and that in itself leaves us better equipped to fight off disease.

LEONARD A. SAGAN, 1988

Since Washington's capital is really in Olympia rather than atop Seattle's misnamed hill, state legislators will be held responsible for environmental policy in a way that few others can be: If they allow pollution of the oceans and atmosphere in such a way that excess clouds reflect sunlight back out into space (and so cool the Earth), then the glacier will plow its way down Puget Sound again and loom outside their windows. If instead they allow warming pollution that melts the polar ice caps via the greenhouse effect, then the capitol dome will be submerged underwater by the rising sea level (perhaps it will have to move to Capitol Hill after all—we're a potential refugia for public servants!).

Juneau, capital of Alaska, is even more exposed, what with the large Mendenhall Glacier already on the outskirts of the port town. Washington, D.C., in comparison, is only exposed to rises in the sea level—unless, of course, the body politic fouls up in a really big way and causes an all-time-record glaciation that makes it well past New York City.

THE NATURE OF EXPLANATION is, as Darwin noted, particularly troublesome in evolutionary and ecological matters. Our approximations to explanation are often inadequate: contemplating an ancestor's skull, a physical anthropologist may label a feature (for example, the "brow ridge"), suggest a function for it, and then pass on to contemplate another piece of the puzzle. For some purposes such an "explanation" suffices (living as I do in Seattle, I like Grover Krantz's joke that brow ridges function as a visor for keeping rain out of the eyes!).

But often the more serious version of this one-feature-at-a-time explanatory exercise isn't very enlightening. There are parts, process, and product—and it is often difficult to understand function without appreciating the transforming processes involved. In the case of our own evolution during the ice ages, about all we know are a few of the parts (the stones and bones, and a stand-in for our ancestor: the "average ape"), and the end product (us). The *process* is what transforms the parts into the product.

Around a state capital such as Olympia, everyone knows about the "legislative process" (it transforms problems and public opinion into laws and budgets). And they're not likely to confuse the process with the law itself, nor with the various constituent pressures that interact to transform the first draft of a piece of legislation into the much-amended statute that finally takes effect as the law of the land.

Personally, I always associate the legislative process with cold winter mornings and fog-shrouded freeways in the predawn light (the Washington State Legislature convenes in January). To lobby the legislators or testify at committee hearings involves long drives in the dark, sipping coffee and eating what was available at the bakery en route, while you plot tactics. The legislative process involves lots of quick conversations with busy people, trading information. Different interests may be "balanced" when the committee marks up a proposal, amending it into something quite different than the way it started out. Even if it passes one house of the legislature, it has to go through the same committee process again in the other house of a bicameral legislature, where a different set of pressures come to bear, where it competes for attention with other matters. The proposal often has to go through the cycle twice, as one house will amend the bill in a way that requires the other house's consent. What emerges from the legislature still has to get past the governor. At least in Olympia, only about 17 percent of the bills that start ever manage to finish; the rest die along the way.

The evolutionary process is a lot like that: many pressures to balance, multiple times through some subsidiary loops, with overall progress dependent on opportunities afforded by the failures or stalemates of unassociated proposals.

Have we merely labeled evolution, or have we explored it as a process? We have certainly identified some of the parts: the primate brain and some of the primate behaviors which were likely to be modified or augmented. We have identified some of the product: our fourfold larger brain, our plan-ahead intelligence,

our versatile language, and a variety of other features. And
regarding process, we have attempted to identify what influences the rate of evolution: mutations vs. permutations, waves
of selection, conversions of function, isolation in refugia or
other islands, new niche expansions when the rules are off,
etc. These give us some glimpses of the processes that were
surely involved in the transformation of an apelike species into
humans.

But, when you compare it all to the legislative process, you
see that we haven't really discussed human evolutionary process
in any specific way, in the sense of playing off one pressure
against another, or the multiple loops before an advance is made.
To be specific, you have to get behind the facade of a "big brain
gene" and ask what developmental programs were altered, and
when. What conversions of function took place? What was the
new niche in each of the "model years?" Can the process be repeated for additional progress, or must you have a series of
different selective pressures, one after the other, to keep making
progress? Was there backsliding, or was it prevented by some
feature of the pumping process?

ON THE SHORES OF PUGET SOUND, Mount Rainier appears
in the south, the Olympic Mountains to the west, the Cascades to
the east. The long beaches are swept clean by the tides, with their
piles of driftwood at the high water line. The Sound's tidal excur-
sion is twice as large as on the Pacific Coast beaches outside the
Strait of Juan de Fuca.

You'd think that it would be half, not twice. Tides become
smaller and smaller as one passes Copenhagen and goes farther
into the Baltic. Similarly when going along the Spanish coast to
the east of the Strait of Gibraltar. So why are tides *bigger* inside
Puget Sound than they are outside?

This paradox confounds the student who has forgotten about
resonance. Puget Sound itself is a nice size for water to slosh back
and forth within, and at a rate that the coastal tidal rhythm can
reinforce. Just as you want to push on a playground swing at a
rate which corresponds to its natural pendulum "ticking" rate, so
a basin with a natural slosh interval of 13 hours will be most
effectively driven by the Pacific Coast's 13-hour interval between

high tides. The sloshing water is the swing, the next coastal tide is the periodic push.

And so within Puget Sound, the tidal range is enough to cover and uncover a typical one-story house—six times as large as the tidal range in Hawaii, which wouldn't even come up to the bottom of the windows. A good low tide uncovers a lot of beach around here. Thanks to how water sloshes around the ocean basins, both the Atlantic and Pacific coasts of the United States have high tides twice every day (the shallow Gulf of Mexico has to get by on once-each-day highs).

Today ocean-going ships plow their way through the waters of Puget Sound, having come through the Strait of Juan de Fuca bound for the ports of Seattle or Tacoma. Amidst the reflections of the sun off the windswept waters, there are sailboats. Fishing boats loll offshore. Here on Whidbey Island, halfway between Seattle and the San Juan Islands, are many summer homes. But there are still long stretches of beach without adjacent habitations. Most of them are protected by high bluffs, a dozen stories of cascading sand and clay (and, in places where the ancient peat bog burned and baked the slightly-more-ancient clay layer, red brick!).

There are places where the high bluffs protect from the winds of winter, and there the original fishermen often lived, starting sometime after the glacier retreated to Canada. Small fishing villages grew up in such spots, close to the beaches with their plentiful supplies of shellfish and firewood. The tidal range is why the beaches of Puget Sound have been so attractive to humans, as the shellfish were regularly exposed, free for the taking.

Drinking water drips out of a nearby cliff for much of the year, groundwater left over from the rains of winter. Only after a dry summer would they have had to walk some distance down the beach to the nearest creek. These American natives may not have set up camp by the creek—because the sheltering cliffs had been eroded down by the water runoff, the beach would have been exposed to the winter winds out of the north. But for drinking and cooking, the seeps in the bluff were quite adequate most of the time; for washing, there was always plenty of salt water.

In fact, the fresh water supply was a little too adequate on occasion. The Puget Sound region is sometimes soaked by the rains of winter; as the ground becomes sodden with water, the

flow in such seeps becomes quite a stream. All the movement of
water within the bluff lubricates its sand and silt so that it can
move around and work its way downhill a little, closer to the
seashore. Every few generations, the fishing village would get an
unpleasant surprise: a whole section of the bluff would collapse
during a heavy rain, the mudslide inundating the village. If the
people were not alert, they could lose their lives as well as their
possessions. They likely dug around in the cold mud trying to
locate lost possessions, but many were missed. How long did it
take for people to realize that dwellings should be located some
distance from the water source? How long did this caution take to
become part of the cultural heritage that was reliably passed on to
future generations?

Fishing villages didn't last very long anyway, because a severe winter storm coinciding with high tide would, once a century
or so, sweep into the village and wash it out to sea, leaving
nothing for their owners to recover. And nothing for the archaeologists of the twentieth century—who have, however, found some
old mudslides and excavated them. Mudslides tend to do more
damage than the layer of ash that buried Pompeii, but they do
provide the archaeologist with a blurred snapshot in time of a
Stone Age hunter-gatherer band of the kind that specialized in
fishing. Most of the villages preserved by the mudslides are not
much older than the European rediscovery of the Americas five
centuries ago—but that is, at least, before metal hooks and outboard motors modified the traditional Stone Age ways of the
coastal Indians.

Under the mudslides, of course, one also discovers that not
all survived: Human bones are also found.

MADONNA-AND-CHILD was a favorite subject of Renaissance
painters. Here one sees a madonna and child that isn't a work of
art.

Human bones had been eroding out of a headland, a few more
found on the beach every winter after a high tide had lapped
against the shoreline. The local Indian tribe asked the archaeologists to excavate the area so that the bones of their presumed
ancestors could be properly reburied a safe distance away from
the shoreline.

In the process of excavating a skeleton, my archaeologist friend discovered another skeleton nestled within its pelvis. A pregnant woman and her unborn child. A reminder that pregnancy is still hazardous in most of the world.

WE TEND TO TAKE OUR BIG BRAINS for granted. Even those with a working knowledge of evolution often make the mistake of assuming that big brains would naturally evolve by slow increments: we assume that a bigger brain is a smarter brain. And since a smarter brain is surely a better brain, then it is not surprising that, analogous to compound interest, we should have bootstrapped ourselves up to a much bigger brain. After all, some people naturally have somewhat bigger heads than others, so all it takes is some natural selection for the obviously useful variant.

There is something very wrong with this commonplace explanation: it ignores the enormous natural selection *against* bigger heads. Maybe bigger brains are indeed better for something, but it would have been bought at an enormous price, extorted over and over again at each little increment along the way to a brain four times larger than that of our presumed ancestors, the australopithecines.

Actually, it isn't clear that bigger brains are even necessary; an ape-sized brain reorganized to facilitate language and plan-ahead might work equally well. Yet the truly horrendous problem with bigger-heads-are-better should have been obvious long before anyone got around to noticing that someone's hat size didn't correlate with how smart he was: big heads cause a lot of trouble at childbirth. Big heads not only kill themselves but, moreover, others carrying similar gene combinations: their mothers. Thus all potential siblings (and occasionally some of the still-dependent prior children of that mother as well), many likely to carry those same gene combinations, will also be eliminated from the surviving gene pool.

It is hard to imagine any form of natural selection that is more powerfully negative; modern genetic diseases such as hemophilia pale by comparison. Big heads are a candidate for the worst genetic disease of all time. By all rights, *any straightforward tendency toward bigger heads should have been promptly squelched.*

Those who nonetheless argue bigger-is-smarter-is-better should realize that a small increment in intelligence would have had to be overwhelmingly better even to establish a somewhat larger brain. The next increment would have had to be overwhelmingly better than the previous miracle, and so on. While perhaps anything is possible given a long enough time and compound interest, bigger-brain cleverness per se seems unlikely as a source for the fastest encephalization on record, fourfold in a mere 2.5 million years.

It makes you wonder how bigger-brains-are-better ever became established in the first place as the dominant explanation for human evolution. If women had been the scientists doing the theorizing, I suspect that we would have long ago abandoned the notion and gone in search of a better idea.

Big heads, however, nonetheless happened. And so there is presumably some way around this problem. Something else must have been under frequent selection pressure, with big heads as an unwanted side effect that was dragged along. This suggests that big heads were achieved by some decoupled backdoor route, rather than via straightforward selection for variants in brain size. And indeed big heads come as part of a package, a panoply of linked features called *juvenilization* (or *paedomorphosis* or, in even older literature, *fetalization*) that has been a repeated theme of vertebrate evolution.

BIG HEADS, RELATIVE TO BODY SIZE, are most readily achieved by exactly the same process used by those salamanders at Mount Rainier: early puberty. We know that brain size, as such, isn't the determinant of cleverness, since elephants and dolphins aren't the leaders in that department. Furthermore, among modern humans a large brain is no sign of genius; despite centuries of looking for a correlation, geniuses keep coming in a variety of head sizes.

Brain size considerations remind me of seeing Mount Rainier from sea level: it's the relative size that counts, given that brain size tends to scale up with adult body size across mammals. But despite our realization that we need to normalize brain size in some manner, there is really no rational reason for talking about the brain/body ratio: losing some weight around your waist, and thereby increasing your brain/body ratio, might be a wise move but it won't make you smarter more generally. And if women are smarter than men, it probably isn't because of their larger brain/ body ratio (that they typically owe to earlier sexual maturity than men, and to their lower levels of testosterone).

So it is hard to imagine why brain size would be under natural selection for its advantages—especially when the disadvantages of an increased brain/body ratio are so immediate and so horrendous. *For it is the bigger head relative to the smaller body that gets us into so much trouble*: If hip size had increased commensurately, no birth canal bottleneck would have developed.

Yet it. is precisely brain/body ratio that increases with juvenilization. And so an adult woman has to give birth with (by the standards of earlier generations) the narrow-hipped body of an adolescent girl. True, hip size in women does increase with childbearing; true, short adult women cannot find something that fits in the children's section of a clothing store, thanks to the hip size disproportion. But whatever the hip size compensation has been, it has been insufficient: it cannot explain the fourfold larger brain of modern humans compared to apes and the australopithecines. So if the boom-time physiology of the ice ages produced juvenilizations, selection against big heads would surely have followed.

WOULD THAT REVERSE the trend that produced juvenilization? There might have been some other way of compensating, of having your cake and eating it too. Back-and-forth need not imply maneuvering along a one-dimensional track; when there are many degrees of freedom in a developmental system, an advance on one track may be partly compensated by a retreat on another. It's similar to the way a cook can raise the oven temperature but shorten baking time; time and temperature are two of the major themes the chef varies (along with ingredients and the order of mixing) in looking for better versions of a dish.

What are the typical "variations on a theme" in human development that might have been involved? Variation in head size is not, as such, a major theme. The major themes are robust-to-gracile, short-to-tall, time of puberty, rate of somatic development, plus various behavioral traits such as bold/cautious, etc. And so it is useful to discuss such prominent themes, rather than postulate random changes in this or that.

○ Body size varies and short-average-tall is also partially heritable.

○ Early in this century, the pioneer anthropologist Franz Boas noted that there was a considerable variation in the rate (slow, average, fast) at which infants and children add on to height and weight; he called it the "tempo of growth."

○ Another heritable variant, not merely part of somatic development, is the time of sexual maturity: mothers with early menarche tend to have daughters who reach sexual maturity early too.

These themes are somewhat interdependent (time of puberty affects height, for example) but let us discuss them as if heritable genes (note the plural) for *stature* existed, as if *somatic development rate* genes existed, and as if *sexual development rate* genes were separate too. And that nutrition influenced them all.

Now suppose early puberty had happened to an early hominid for whatever reason (boom-time physiology, or some advantage of juvenilized adults such as behavioral plasticity, or even throwing skill). What next?

A single phenotypic trait—height, for example—may be influenced by a number of different genes; conversely, a single gene [whose alternative versions are called alleles] may influence the development of various traits. Furthermore, a particular favorable value of a trait may be attained, by different members of a species, through different allele combinations. We cannot assume in a human population that all persons of a given height have the same combination of alleles for controlling height. There may be a substantial number of alternative genetic patterns that, holding environment constant, would produce people of the same height.

HERBERT A. SIMON, 1983

WE'RE NOT SHORTER on average than at least one adolescent specimen of *Homo erectus* dated to 1.6 million years ago: he was 168 centimeters tall (known in several idiosyncratic countries as

5'6") and, had he survived to adulthood, would probably have reached 180 centimeters (5'11"). You might expect that we would be considerably shorter, since early puberty tends to reduce body size.

So it seems likely that stature has reenlarged via some other gene affecting stature, just as those juvenilized axolotls become larger than the land-loving salamanders. If repeated juvenilizations have occurred in the hominid lineage, we would all be miniature pygmies if some reenlargement trend had not supervened. While many of the influences on stature—such as the improved diet and fewer childhood diseases of industrialized countries in the last century—only affect the phenotype (body style) and not the genotype (the genes carried by that body and passed on to offspring), stature is nonetheless relatively heritable.

Natural selection likely operated on these variants in the genotype, e.g., bigger bodies for better throwing distances, better nursing of babies during involuntary fasting, better abilities to undertake long migrations to distant patches of food, or better protection from predators. Competition between individuals can presumably enlarge the average species stature, just as harem mating systems and male competition have caused male gorillas to become twice as large as females. And in the context of the temperate zone where someone was occasionally trapped out in a blizzard, the reduced surface-to-volume ratio that goes along with bigger bodies would have increased the survival time in freezing conditions because of lengthening the time it takes to reach a life-threatening internal temperature (body size is indeed larger at high latitudes). Bigger females have bigger birth canals. For these and other reasons, bigger bodies are sometimes better, despite costing more to build and operate.

Rather as a baker might have tried raising the oven temperature but shortening the baking time, we now have a population whose body style (and genome, because natural selection has been operating) is somewhat juvenilized compared to their ancestral population, but whose body size has reenlarged via another genetic route. What now?

Man, with his remarkable brain, developed the use of fire, but, even apart from considerations of brain power, as F. W. Went has pointed out, only a creature of man's size could

*effectively control that fire. It happens that a small campfire
is the smallest fire that is reliable and controllable. A still
smaller flame is too easily snuffed out and a larger one too
easily gets out of control. Prometheus was just large enough
to feed the flame and keep from getting burnt.*

the architect PETER K. STEVENS, 1974

THE BIRTH CANAL BOTTLENECK comes next because, without further changes, bigger-headed fetuses are going to start getting stuck during childbirth (if they hadn't already had trouble at the smaller stature). This in turn will start selection operating on another common variation-on-a-theme, somatic developmental rate—just due to their genes, some children gain height and weight more slowly than others.

We knew that some more changes were going to be necessary because juvenilization by itself tends to suggest a shorter childhood — indeed, its truncation by early sexual maturity. But the monkey-to-ape and ape-to-human transitions show exactly the opposite: a lengthening of childhood. This paradox is resolved if we assume that a slowing of general body development (selected from that variation-on-a-theme that Boas observed) has been superimposed on juvenilization, moving the earlier menarche back out to its original year and even beyond. It's the *relative* rates of somatic and sexual development that control childhood's tempo and the resulting adult shape, just as it is the relative rate of growth in the north and south sides of a flower stem that cause it to bend south toward more sunshine.

The main reason to believe that slowing has actually happened is that slowed development is more general than just childhood. Most life phase durations (conception-to-birth, birth-to-weaning, weaning-to-menarche, adult span) have been nearly doubled in going from monkey to ape. And nearly doubled again in going from ape to human. Though human gestation would at first appear to constitute an exception (it is only several weeks longer than in apes), this doubling rule seems to apply there too: human infants do not attain the same developmental landmarks as newborn apes until many months after birth, for a total internal-plus-external "gestation time" about twice that of chimpanzees.

This halving of the rate of the somatic developmental clock throughout pre- and postnatal life also needs explaining; I'm surely not the first to suggest that it was the solution to the childbirth problem presented by that big head that came along with juvenilization. If there had been a way of slowing only prenatal development without concomitant slowing of postnatal development, it might have done the job too—but the more generalized slowing may have been the only variant available.

Because juvenilization makes the adult head relatively larger and the adult pelvis relatively smaller, repeated juvenilizations will eventually run into trouble when the baby's head can no longer get through the pelvic outlet. The gene combinations that result in early puberty and normal somatic developmental rates will then be edited out, unfortunately via maternal mortality rather than merely unsuccessful fetuses (but therefore at a much faster rate, because of the kin selection practiced by the unsuccessful fetus). The same would be true for faster-than-average somatic development genes. The gene combinations of precocity

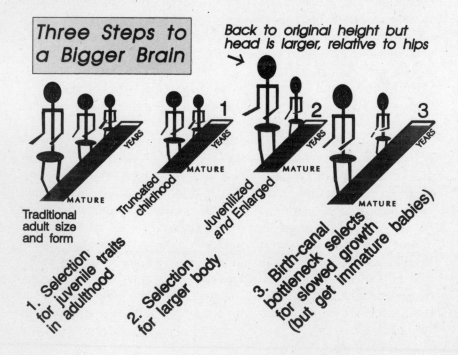

Three Steps to a Bigger Brain

Back to original height but head is larger, relative to hips

Traditional adult size and form

Truncated childhood

Juvenilized and Enlarged

1. Selection for juvenile traits in adulthood

2. Selection for larger body

3. Birth-canal bottleneck selects for slowed growth (but get immature babies)

MATURE

YEARS

1   2   3

and slowed somatic developmental rates will get by, provided parturition is not equally delayed.

So long as the surviving mother can cope with raising a relatively fragile premature infant, the gene pool would soon come to be dominated by the genes for slower-than-average somatic development. *This escape route for big baby heads would seem to require slowed somatic development superimposed upon the accelerated sexual maturity;* our longer life spans after birth may be largely a side effect of the slowing of somatic development needed to work around the birth canal bottleneck.

Thus we get the sequence of 1) juvenilization via faster-than-average sexual development, 2) re-enlarged stature via other taller-than-average genes, and 3) slower-than-average somatic developmental rate. And because of the carryover of slowed development into postnatal life, the usual time scale is stretched; the number of years that it takes to get to puberty may have moved back out beyond what it was before the changes started to take place. Body size is also potentially back to the norm. Only head size is still increased, along with a few other uncorrected side effects such as reduced tooth size, flatter faces, and other such juvenile features.

Eureka? Only if the three-part cycle can be repeated quite a few times. And body style doesn't backslide.

Heredity is particulate, but development is unitary. Everything in the organism is the result of the interactions of all genes, subject to the environment to which they are exposed.
the evolutionary biologist
THEODOSIUS DOBZHANSKY, 1961

WALKING ALONG THE WHIDBEY BEACHES, one cannot help but be impressed by cycles. The twice-a-day tides. The twice-a-month extreme tides at new and full moons caused by the moon, Earth, and sun approximately lining up and so exaggerating the pull on the oceans. There are even greater extremes every 170 days when the moon is threatening an eclipse because of being very near the Earth-sun line and pulling in the same line as the sun. And if the sun is at its closest (perihelion) and the moon is also at the minimum in its elliptical orbit at such a time (perigee), the low and high tides reach their true extremes (that's fairly rare, but the moon at perigee coincident with new or full moon happens every 9.3 years).

I assume that the coastal Indians noticed the relation between moon phases and the tides; they might even have made the connection between eclipses and extreme low tides (and, instead of fearing eclipses, considered them a portent of good clamming prospects, what with all that uncovered food).

All this is not quite as obvious as the cycles of the seasons due to the tilt in the Earth's axis. The severity of winter and summer also varies, due to all those orbital parameters that cause the ice-age cycles—but that is also on too long a time scale for anyone to notice without generation-spanning recordkeeping (such as the weather records of the last century).

There are also cycles we don't understand (though chaos theory is helping), such as why the local shellfish undergo a population crash every so often—or why "red tides" occur and the shellfish become poisonous (there is a potent neurotoxin from a dinoflagellate, *Gonyaulax tamarensis*, which produces paralysis in humans; *Gonyaulax* thrives in low salinity, such as near river mouths). Given how the natives of that fishing village probably relied on shellfish, those would have been hard times, making fishing skills extremely important until the clams become safe to eat again. The local salmon are easier to catch in rivers than here—but they too have their cycles; the salmon returning to local rivers increase every few years and then drop back.

A cycle implies that the process can be repeated, that it doesn't run out of steam (pendulums swing back up after reaching the bottom of their arc because their potential energy has all been converted into kinetic energy; they stop and reverse when all the energy of motion has been reconverted into potential energy). The shellfish and the salmon are probably locked into some sort of back-and-forth, boom-and-bust relationship with their food sources or their parasites and predators, seen more easily in the ups and downs of the Arctic lynx and hare populations (and modeled by those same equations that gave us r and K terminology; just remember that hare populations can oscillate even without lynxes around!).

Can this evolutionary process of juvenilization-reenlargement-slowing become a repeating cycle? Is it like a college course that can be repeated for additional credit? Or has it run out of steam after the three phases, like most inventions in evolution—run to the end of its growth curve, with no further progress possible? The classic example of a limited growth curve is hairlessness: when something such as swimming success starts selecting for variants with less body hair, there is a limit beyond which further selection cannot operate (as you can only become so naked).

Can our slightly juvenilized (but reenlarged and slower-growing) hominid, with its slightly larger-than-ape brain and its slightly flatter face and slightly smaller teeth, be subjected to yet another round of selection exactly like the first one? Can boom-time physiology (or some specific advantage of a juvenilized body style) select for juvenilization again? Can the resulting population then reenlarge? Will the birth canal bottleneck then again select for slower-than-average somatic development rate genes?

WELL, WHY NOT? If any one of the selection pressures is removed, the cycle won't repeat. If any one of the three processes runs out of growth curve, it'll stall. If anything is invented that can break the cycle—such as cesarean sections or really big hips—it should stop. Otherwise, it ought to cycle until the disadvantages balance out the advantages. There might be counterpressures (if you are a hyper-robust australopithecine and need big teeth for processing plant food, this counterpressure might have prevented further rounds of juvenilization). Something, for example, happened after a similar juvenilization transition from the Old World monkeys to the apes: they seem to have stabilized for 30 million years rather than repeating the cycle of juvenilization and slowing.

Might body size have counterpressures? There are situations (islands with dwarf elephants, for example) where small body size is common. But, at least in the temperate zones, our typical adult stature seems better than a pygmylike stature; while bigger-is-better may not extend to 250 centimeters' stature, it may apply in the 100–200 centimeter range if one judges from the latitude data on aboriginal populations—and so another juvenilization episode would again reposition stature on the lower half of its growth curve, ready to reenlarge again seemingly forever. The ever-more-helpless infant may well have required some prerequisites: the kangaroo's pouch may suffice for its helpless infant, but we probably adapted with the aid of bipedal locomotion for infant carrying and the two-parent family for provisioning mother and child.

So we are left with whether there were even earlier sexual maturity gene versions around (apparently so, judging from the heritability of early menarche). So what is the juvenilization advantage that comes under selection? Whatever that feature is, it must have had a very long growth curve—where more and more was always better and better—for it to have been used repeatedly during the last 2.5 million years. That's a big order. What's so good about juvenilization that has such characteristics?

Reproductive races in boom times might work, if repositioning by slowed somatic development suffices. But it really ought to backslide readily in hard times. I've got another candidate for why juvenilization was so useful, one with a spectacular growth curve. It is just what I'd recommend to an ambitious ape, wanting the brain capacity for language.

The scientist [J.B.S.] Haldane,
brooding upon the future,
has speculated that we will even further
prolong our childhood and retard maturity
if brain advance continues. . . .
[But ultramodern man has] happened already.
Back there in the past, ten thousand years ago.
The man of the future,
with the [even bigger] brain,
and the small teeth. . . .
Those who contend that
because of present human cranial size,
and the limitations of the human pelvis,
man's brain is no longer capable
of further expansion, are mistaken.
Cranial capacities of almost a third more
than the modern average have been attained
among the Boskop people [of southern Africa]
and even in rare individuals among other,
less [juvenilized] races.
                    LOREN EISELEY, *The Immense Journey*, 1957

8

HAND-AX HEAVEN: THE AMBITIOUS APE'S GUIDE TO A BIGGER BRAIN

Progress in science is achieved in two ways: through new discoveries, such as x-rays, the structure of DNA, and gene splicing, and through the development of new concepts, such as the theories of relativity, of the expanding universe, of plate tectonics, and of common descent. Among all the new scientific concepts, perhaps none has been as revolutionary in its impact on our thinking as Darwin's theory of natural selection.

the evolutionary theorist ERNST MAYR, 1988

Fidalgo Island is the northern sister to Whidbey, but considerably more mountainous than glacial till ought to be: Mount Erie is a hundred rocky stories tall, and would have made an excellent easy-to-climb lookout for the Indians. Its view is of the Skagit River delta to the southeast, where great flocks of migrating birds winter, over to the mountainous Olympic Peninsula in the southwest, the San Juan Archipelago and Vancouver Island to the west—and of course the volcanic Mount Baker to the north and Cascade Mountains stretching to the east. You can almost see out to the Pacific Ocean from atop Mount Erie, survey the entire domain of those Indians who lived around here. There were megafauna hereabouts, probably hunted during the meltback by newly arrived Indians. Looking southwest over to the Olympic Peninsula, I can see the area where a mastodon skeleton was found.

Did the hunters use this viewpoint to spot pods of whales cruising around? Hunting whales might have been their variant of big-game hunting, once the mammoth and mastodon disappeared from the glacial grasslands about 10,000 years ago. The whale hunt would have demanded even more organization and cooperation and planning ahead than the mammoth hunts, what with keeping those hollow logs in seaworthy condition.

Individually digging up clams and snagging salmon in streams would have sufficed much of the time. But inventing boats would have meant a boom time, just as surely as if the climate had dramatically improved.

BOOM-TIME PSYCHOLOGY is somewhat familiar to us, as I mentioned earlier (bullish stock market speculation, decline in savings, increases in borrowing, more risk-taking everywhere—even higher hemlines and more daring décolletage in women's fashions). Boom-time reproductive physiology is more obscure.

Until we know what the boom time's proximate mechanisms are—what aspect of the environment that even children are sensing, what hormones they use to implement the change—and what that mechanism's disadvantages might be, we won't be able to adequately evaluate the proposition that boom times alone could work the ratchet to yield ever-larger brains and ever-smaller teeth. The mere fact that the succession of boom times started 2.5 million years ago with the ice-age melt-off cycles, and that this nicely overlaps the period of hominid encephalization, speaks in its favor.

In evolutionary arguments, it is no longer enough to demonstrate that something could have done the job, given enough time. By compound-interest reasoning, *any* slight advantage can eventually do the job. There are usually multiple ways to do the job, and the one that gets there first on the fast track tends to preempt the niche. The speed of the cycle is always important—and especially with this proposed encephalization cycle, simply because the fourfold increase in hominid brain size in only 2.5 million years is "almost unbelievably fast" (in the words of Ernst Mayr) by the standards of natural selection. We need fast tracks, even if slow tracks might have sufficed.

This rapidity provides an important constraint on proposed explanations for what happened since the australopithecines: most proposals for how hominid encephalization evolved are too leisurely to explain the Great Encephalization. Spanning the same period as the fourfold encephalization is the evidence for the ice ages, for prolific toolmaking, and for hominid hunting. Might toolmaking or hunting do the trick?

Tool use is, of course, shared with quite a number of animals, including the birds. The fancier types of toolmaking during the ice ages are mostly associated with hammering techniques—but hammering isn't unique to hominids either. Female chimp nut-cracking involves surprisingly sophisticated skills in positioning and grading of delicate blows; one wonders how much early hominids needed to improve on our common heritage in order to produce the early toolkits that sufficed until the hand ax.

It is also hard to see what the growth curve for toolmaking was like during the relevant period. Remember that the brain size of *Homo erectus* doubled during a period when the dominant toolkit persisted without major improvements, a period of a dozen ice ages starting 1.5 million years ago; this is hardly suggestive of man-the-toolmaker being the driving force behind hominid evolution during this period.

So what about hunting?

MANY SKILLS ARE IMPORTANT for human hunting: detecting the prey, outsmarting and outmaneuvering it, and killing it while avoiding injury. Many other human attributes facilitate our hunting endeavors: our social organization, reproductive strategies, and communications skills.

But, carnivores are clearly experts at outsmarting and maneuvering. Snatching the defenseless young hiding in the underbrush, or outrunning small mammals, is also practiced by both baboons and chimpanzees. Both hunt cooperatively, baboons chasing gazelles into the arms of a fellow baboon, chimps moving to guard escape routes and attempting to draw off adult pigs so that other chimps can snatch their young. What used to be thought of as uniquely human hunting skills are often shared with other animals—animals that haven't experienced rapid brain enlargement.

What then are the uniquely human aspects of hunting, and what role did they play in hominid brain evolution? Clearly, hominids could have adapted chimplike maneuvers to chase competing scavengers away from dead meat; it probably did not require a bigger brain to make this small modification to ape behavior. But, though I love to look at all those microscopic marks on teeth and bones, I tend to question scavenging as an important evolutionary path: the food chain would limit prehumans to populations similar to those of the existing top predator, if they made their living that way. That's not usually the way to a new niche or population boom.

Projectile predation seems to be a form of hunting not practiced by other mammals in competition for the same resources: this "action at a distance" hunting is a very important invention. It reduces the chance of injury to the hunter, keeps one out of range of horn and hoof. From an evolutionary standpoint, throwing is not a one-step invention: it has aspects such as accuracy and length of throw that may be improved, time and again, for additional advantages, generating a long growth curve. The type of throw, the distance of the throw, the weight thrown, the accuracy of the throw, the suitability of the object thrown—all can be improved again and again.

Chimpanzees certainly throw, but the thrown object (usually a branch, sometimes a rock) is primarily used as a threat to chase off leopards or intimidate fellow chimps in dominance displays. The accuracy of the threat throw is largely irrelevant, so long as it threatens to generate a blink reflex by its high angular velocity. Chimps throw both underarm and overhand, using much the same postures and motions that human children utilize; only the occasional chimp attains a reputation among human observers as a thrower.

While they obviously have the neural and musculoskeletal machinery for the basic throws, chimps may not have the precision-timing neural circuits needed for accurate launch at distant small targets. No one has ever measured chimpanzee throwing accuracy, to the best of my knowledge. Were chimps even half as accurate as humans, however, I think we would have heard about it: they'd be the terror of Africa, and (given how they love meat) they'd be eating meat every day.

Minimal accuracy (a "side of the barn throw" in baseball phraseology) might have limited hominids to throwing at large nearby targets—but there weren't very many blind mammoths. So how did we get started? What bootstrapped hominid hunting? What might we recommend to an ambitious ape? One clue, in my opinion, is the earliest fancy tool.

ABOUT THE EARLIEST STONE TOOL of fancy design was the Acheulean hand ax. It's almost as fancy as the arrowhead (first seen during the last Ice Age but mostly in the 10,000 years since the melt-off). The Acheulean hand ax is far, far older: it was the most prominent feature of the Acheulean toolkit made by *Homo erectus* between 1.5 and 0.3 million years ago. It is found everywhere from the tip of Africa to Europe to South Asia, made of whatever local rocks were handy.

There is only one problem: for more than a century, no one could seem to figure out what the Acheulean hand ax was especially good for. For archaeologists, it has been like one of those "What is it?" exhibits in the children's room at a museum, where

A PLEISTOCENE CHIMERA

Why did *Homo erectus*
give the misnamed "hand ax"
the head of an arrow
but the body of a discus?

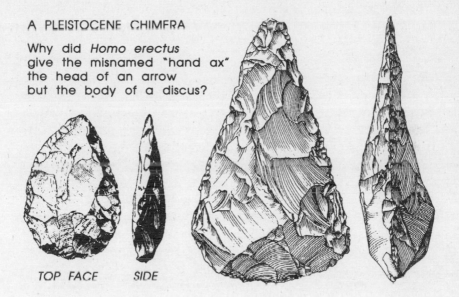

TOP FACE   SIDE

the children attempt to guess what the covered pan on a pole was once used for. To preheat beds with coals from the fire is not a modern problem, what with other forms of heating; I'm not sure that our guesses about hand ax usefulness are much better than the children's guesses about the pan on a pole.

Labeling the Acheulean creation a "hand ax" was certainly a major error, though the name has stuck anyway for various reasons. The sharpened edges of the typical hand ax continue all around its perimeter, and so would do a lot of damage to any hand that attempted to use a hand ax for chopping: it would, so to speak, bite the hand that held it.

The archaeologists' fallback position is that perhaps it was used for separating meat from skin and bone. But a flesher is hardly an important item in a toolkit, since split cobbles work so well for the purpose already. A hand ax (especially one with a broken edge) could certainly do double duty as a flesher, but some other function must account for its singular features:

1) it is bilaterally symmetric,
2) usually has a point,
3) usually has a sharpened edge all the way around, and
4) it is also usually flattened, something like a discus.

The exceptions are interesting. There are some with blunt back ends, just as there are some (called Acheulean cleavers) without a point. But they may simply be broken versions of the classic shape; that's the default position to take concerning such variants until they are shown otherwise.

Surely we can do better than the position taken by some frustrated archaeologists: that it was a ceremonial item, functionless in the everyday sense of the word. "Form for form's sake" certainly exists, but it is subject to fads and fashions—the Acheulean hand ax would have to be the all-time-record fad, extending over Africa and Eurasia for more than a million years! What use requires all of those four features, a use that would inhibit further variations in the usual manner, so that the design would remain stable for a very long time? It must be nearly perfect for some important task to achieve such an all-time record for design stability.

Because its shape is reminiscent of the spear point and arrowhead, there was an early suggestion (H. G. Wells mentions it in his 1899 book, *Tales of Space and Time*) that the hand ax was thrown at animals while hunting. This suggestion floundered because the back end of the hand ax is so unsuitable for attachment to a spear (hafting didn't appear until well after hand-ax days): the rear edge of a classic hand ax is carefully rounded and sharpened. Throwing it without a shaft seems a bit silly too: how would one keep the point oriented forward in flight? Any explanation for the function of the hand ax needs to explain that *point*, those *all-around edges*, that *symmetry*, that *flattening*.

This unsatisfactory state of affairs lasted until an intrepid undergraduate at the University of Massachusetts made a fiberglass replica of a big Acheulean hand ax and gave it to some varsity discus throwers to experiment with. Eileen O'Brien took her cue from a 1965 suggestion by a South African anthropologist, M.D.W. Jeffreys: that the smaller hand axes could be thrown with spin, perhaps into a flock of birds. The replica indeed spun well; that flattened shape and bilateral symmetry are very useful for setting a spin. O'Brien and her two athletic friends discovered a totally unsuspected aerodynamic property of their hand-ax replica: in mid-flight, it would turn on edge and land that way. Indeed, the hand ax would usually slice into the ground and bury its point. Now, as you probably recall from your own experience, having the Frisbee turn edge-on shortly after launch is something that happens to all inexperienced Frisbee throwers—*but those experienced discus-throwers couldn't keep it from happening*. It seemed to come with the shape.

And the tendency to land edge-on matches up with a previously puzzling aspect of the archaeology: hand axes are often found in dried-up ponds and lakes and creeks, sometimes standing on edge! This strongly suggests that hand axes were indeed thrown at animals visiting the waterhole to drink—that hominids were practicing an old carnivore trick, lying in wait at the only waterhole.

O'Brien's experiments were a major advance, but they left many questions unanswered: Waterhole predation ought to work with any old handy rock; the painstaking preparation of this rock seems excessive. Why the sharpened edges all around? If spin is nice, why not just use a flat slab of rock, broken to be symmetrical? The answer implicit in these experiments was that a "spinning ax" could do a lot more damage than a rock: by landing on edge (especially a sharpened edge), all of the force is concentrated on a thin edge. But why the point?

THERE THE MATTER RESTED for nearly a decade; I had to puzzle over it for four years before I stumbled upon an interesting clue. It seemed to me that the hand axes were not being thrown at individual animals but at whole herds. Teaching introductory biology for the first time while writing *The River That Flows Uphill* had reminded me of why animals cluster into herds or schools: to protect against predators.

As herd size increases, there are more individuals on the periphery of the herd exposed to predators—but the average animal is safer. The *percentage* of the herd on the periphery will drop as the herd size increases. That's why there is "safety in numbers." For a small herd, half are exposed on the periphery; tenfold larger, and most of the herd is protected inside that vulnerable outer ring. To a physiologist, this is just another surface-to-volume ratio problem of the kind familiar from thermoregulation, from why an animal needs a circulatory system to move oxygen around, if larger than the size where diffusion suffices.

But lobbing a rock up over, and thus into, a herd gets around this restriction of only the peripheral ones being vulnerable; *you circumvent a two-dimensional design with a lob into the third dimension!* Furthermore, herds cluster ever more tightly together when feeling threatened—which would only make matters better for the hunter lobbing rocks into their midst, as fewer rocks would fall between animals. Even when you miss, it's easier next time!

You aim at the herd, not any one individual animal: it is a "side of the barn" throw rather than a precision throw. And knowing what I did about how hard it was to throw with precision, I thought that lobbing into herds was likely to be a good entry-level technique for the beginning hunter. Invention in behavior tends not to be the "light bulb" flashing on, the bright idea after contemplation—it tends to be an old way of doing things, converted to a somewhat similar task, one that turns out to hit upon something valuable. After this invention, adaptations streamline the behavior and eventually the body style itself. Chimps can probably throw well enough to hit a herd, though probably not with sufficient consistency to hit an isolated animal from any distance (and no second chances: the animal runs away after the first launch).

There is just one problem with hitting a herd animal in this way: most lobbed rocks that strike it would hit its back and bounce off—an unlikely way to kill an animal. On the rare occasions when a rock hit the animal on its head or spine, it might have conveniently collapsed—but otherwise the hunters would likely be left with an angry animal running away, with a good head start on the pursuers. Even if knocked down, the animal could likely have gotten up and run away before pursuers arrived.

Ah, but when I thought about it some more, I realized that if the animal should be knocked down, it might be further injured by its fellow herd animals—they would stampede when the hunters launched. Even if the herd didn't trample the injured animal, they would delay it getting back on its feet. This might give the hunters time to run up and club the animal, or perhaps throw stones from up close at its head.

I was especially impressed with this scenario when I realized that there was a perfect transition from known behaviors of chimpanzees: while chimps do throw rocks, my primatologist friends tell me, they particularly like to throw big tree branches after flailing them around furiously. Such a branch, lobbed into a herd lapping up the lake at sunset, would land just as the herd was wheeling around and starting to run away—so it would often trip an animal or two, expose them to trampling by the rest of the herd, delay them enough so that the hunters could corner them and polish them off. If chimps lived among herds of grazing animals, the more patient chimps could easily practice such a technique. If they ran out of branches, they would probably throw their other favorite projectile, big rocks.

If that's the way hominids got started hunting, how did they ever arrive at a fancy scheme such as making Acheulean hand axes? What is it about flattened bilateral symmetry, a point, and sharpened edges all around? So I decided to fiddle around with throwing hand axes.

I TOO FINALLY ENLISTED THE AID of an experienced discus thrower, Gareth Anderson, and we repeated the O'Brien experiments with five crude hand axes from southern Algeria and a fiberglass replica of a fancy flattened one. They all exhibited the same aerodynamic peculiarity as the giant replica that O'Brien tested: they tended to land on edge, even if thrown horizontally like a Frisbee.

Gareth and I had picked a well-worn soccer field for this experiment; it had close-cropped grass and many worn spots, and the ground had been softened up by a Seattle drizzle the day before. So when a hand ax landed and then bounced away, we could see the gouge it left behind. Gareth would retrieve the hand ax and bring it back to fit into the hole in the ground, trying to figure out its orientation when it landed. And because of packed dirt adhering to the hand ax, we could usually see the place along the perimeter of the hand ax that hit the ground first—and it was no preferred place. Since the hand ax was spinning, it rotated after impact and the point eventually poked into the ground. Sometimes the point would snag the ground and impale the hand ax, just as in the O'Brien experiments. Thus the point helps stop the hand ax—meaning that, in the case of an animal target, it would cause the animal to stagger much more than when the rock merely bounced free.

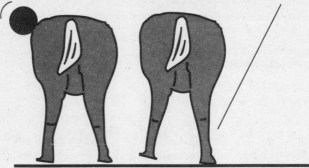

1. Momentum transfer causes rightward movement unless countered

2. Protect against toppling by quickly extending right legs

Withdrawal flexion of both hind legs overrides the reflex extension of right legs

Animal either sits down or falls to right

Even if little momentum, incision pain causes flexion reflex

So if the soccer field were instead the back of a zebra or gazelle, the projectile would no longer bounce off their backs like a rock would—but rather transfer most of its forward momentum to the animal. The animal might not be able to right itself in time, before collapsing, due to an interesting neurological peculiarity: injury to the back in a four-legged animal causes the legs to flex, as when an animal scrapes its back on an overhanging tree branch or rock and the hindquarters hunch down to free the skin from the sharp obstruction. To keep from collapsing sideways after a hand-ax impact on its near side or its back, the animal needs to *extend* its legs on the far side—but the back injury from the sharpened edge of the hand ax would tend to make it *flex* the hind limbs instead. Thus the reflex protection against toppling would be countermanded.

And that's when the pointed front end of the hand ax finally began to make some sense. It would spin around and tend to bury itself in the skin (or snag a roll of skin pushed up by the forward motion of the hand ax landing). This would not only transfer much of the hand ax's forward momentum to the animal—but it would yank on the just-incised skin.

A clean cut of the skin is not necessarily painful if you're busy with something else, as I discovered myself one night as a child playing hide-and-seek after dark: I got a big cut on an ankle (from the nearly buried stump of a newly sawed off bush) that I didn't notice until my mother complained at me ten minutes later, for tracking something red into the house and across the carpet. One of the things that amazes medical students during their first duty in the hospital emergency room is how many patients with a bad cut or scrape (and even broken bones) will claim that it doesn't hurt (someone finally compiled some statistics: 37 percent claim no pain for several hours after injury, though almost everyone hurts a half-day later).

But what is guaranteed painful is to manipulate the cut skin edges (just ask a surgeon: they can often continue operating after local anesthesia wears off, so long as they don't touch the skin edges; when they start to place stitches is when the patient requests a booster dose). The spinning hand ax, incising the skin and then snagging its point to yank on the new incision, ought to produce a powerful withdrawal reflex that lowers the hindquarters. Even a small hand ax might cause enough sharp pain to make a big animal suddenly collapse. If the animal were standing alone, it might still get up in time to run away from the approaching hunters—but with a herd stampeding past, just being knocked down might prove fatal.

And so lobbing branches and then rocks into herds visiting waterholes looks like a good way to make the transition from chimpanzeelike behaviors to hominid hunting—*without improving the brain's timing abilities at all*. That's the basic invention for hunting. Making a "spinning-snagging ax" (as we ought to rename the hand ax, though I suspect that "killer Frisbee" will win out!) probably doubled and tripled the yield, permitted hominids to graduate from small gazelles (for whom a thrown rock might have sufficed) to the larger herd animals such as zebra. To make further improvements beyond that, you have to improve throwing accuracy so that you can hit small herds or single animals.

Note that the lobbing technique won't work against anything except targets that are tightly packed together, at least not until accuracy improves quite a lot. That's why I don't think that this invention was important for aggression *within* a hominid species. Yes, a tendency toward mayhem probably existed in our common ancestor (newly installed silverback male gorillas practice infanticide, and chimps savagely beat up "enemy" chimps), and yes, accurate throwing would have allowed intermediate prehumans additional ways of committing mayhem. Attacking one another is definitely *a* potential way of shaping up prehumans to be bigger and better fighters—which, judging from the history of warfare, may well have played some role at some point in the ape-to-human transition. *But the shift from gathering-snatching-scavenging to successful waterhole hunting was not a major step along that path*; it was instead a major step in food acquisition that would *not* work well against fellow hominids (unless as tightly packed as a herd!). And this invention was probably of "new niche" proportions, the sort of thing that can create a new species and spread them around the continents.

What might any of these aspects of side-of-the-barn throwing have to do with juvenilization? Certainly they might produce boom-time conditions as they increased the hominid population size that could be supported. But I think that precision throwing came later, and that it has a much better tie with juvenilization.

PRECISION THROWING is what children work up to as they develop their throwing skills, starting with the high-chair food fling, developing into the kindergartner's unaimed sidearm lob, and gradually progressing to the overhand direct trajectory that can reliably hit a small target, a technique mastered by elementary-school-aged children.

At Laetoli, Tanzania, Mary Leakey found rocks that appear to have been carried in from outcrops a good hike away; these 2 million-year-old manuports (from "hand-carried") would seem suitable for threat throwing, as in warding off scavengers from a kill or butchery site. But it is also obvious that, at some point long before baseball, our ancestors began throwing apple-sized stones with accuracy. Barbara Isaac has surveyed museum collections, finding various examples of rocks that might qualify as ancient throwing artifacts, smoothed and with thumb grips, etc. While they could have been merely used for threat throws (they aren't heavy enough for side-of-the-barn throws into waterhole herds), they tend to suggest precision aimed throwing, something closer to the modern style where one "gets set," launches with care, and practices the technique with small variations.

Precision aim has a much better growth curve than does the waterhole lob. Hitting the head of the prey is an obvious improvement. Maintaining accuracy while standing farther away is important, not only because of the "approach distance" of prey animals (the distance at which they decide you've come close enough and move away), but because throwing twice as far (using a relatively flat trajectory rather than a high-angle lob) means throwing about twice as fast. This creates a bonus: the projectile arrives with as much as four times the kinetic energy (or "stopping power"), enabling ever larger animals to be felled with precision throwing techniques.

There are growth curves in materials as well as technique: graduating to the spear, boomerang, and other throwing sticks such as the knobkerrie. But both faster throws and more accurate throws are always better and better, *provided that the brain can cope with the more precise timing requirements for letting loose of the projectile*. Both of these timing-dependent throwing aspects make considerable demands on brain reorganization, as most brains are incapable of fancy timing.

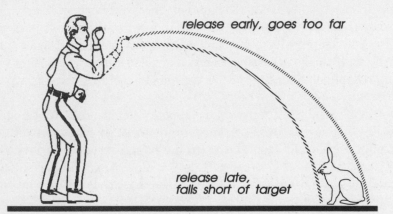

release early, goes too far

*release late,
falls short of target*

*11 msec launch window at 4 meters
narrows to 1.4 msec at 8 meters;
requires 64 times as many neurons.*

THERE IS A BOTTLENECK that needs to be overcome in order
to throw with more-than-an-ape's accuracy. A crucial skill is accurately timing the moment when the hunter lets loose of the projectile.
Release too soon and the rock lobs too high, lands behind the target.
Release too late, and it hits the ground in front of the target. The
"launch window" is the range of useful release times; it shrinks to
submillisecond values for reasonable throws to rabbit-sized targets.

     The only known way of achieving such one-millisecond-in-a-
thousand timing precision with jittery neurons (individually no
better than about ten-milliseconds-per-hundred) is to assign many
timing neurons to the same task. The heart has the same problem:
individual heart cells don't discharge anywhere as rhythmically as
a heart; only when hundreds are massed together does the regular
beat emerge. Applied to making timing more predictable for throwing, you have to wonder where the extra cells come from: this
averaging technique is extremely "cell hungry." It is not something to be implemented merely by quadrupling the traditional
brain area for muscle sequencing, the premotor cortex. Nor by
tripling everyone's favorite candidate for a precision delay-line
timing device, the cerebellum. We are talking of *hundred-* and
thousandfold increases in the numbers of brain sequencing circuits that need to be temporarily synchronized.

It reminds me of expanding the choir to include the whole audience, when singing the Hallelujah Chorus. I suggest that the only practical way for the brain to achieve such numbers is temporarily to synchronize large areas of cerebral cortex, utilizing the widespread intracortical connections between the various areas. Neurons, especially those outside the traditional sensory cortical "receiving areas," do not seem committed to single functions; they enjoy widespread inputs from multiple sensory modalities. This generalized wiring suggests that neurons can be "borrowed" from their primary task (if, indeed, they have one). In such a manner, "getting set" to throw may serve to assign many neurons to a choral-like parallel assembly; after they function briefly in tandem, to determine the moment of projectile release, most are presumably unhitched from this temporary duty and return to their regular assignments. The Darwin Machine outlined in Chapter 2 would provide a simple way of sorting through the different throwing options while ending up with many clones, handy for the choral performance needed for precise timing.

DOES PRECISION have anything to do with juvenilization? The answer is a conditional yes, based on such "Law of Large Numbers" arguments. Because primate neocortex exhibits a tendency to eliminate some of its widespread interconnections during postnatal development, there is a progressive reduction in synaptic connections with age, a carving process that Daniel Dennett and J. Z. Young suggested a quarter-century ago. In addition to detaching synapses, reduced connectivity also occurs by neuron death in some cortical regions; a monkey's motor cortex loses a third of its neurons during infancy and the juvenile period (though very few during adulthood).

Some individuals have a tendency to mature early; they might incidentally slow down these two carving processes, conserve widespread connections into adulthood. They might be better throwers, everything else being equal, able to recruit more cerebral assistants on the occasions when a lot of helpers were temporarily needed. Our big heads may be only an epiphenomenon of a developmental solution to the temporary synchronization requirement for accurate throwing, as our ancestors juvenilized to retain the more widespread intracortical connections of juvenile animals

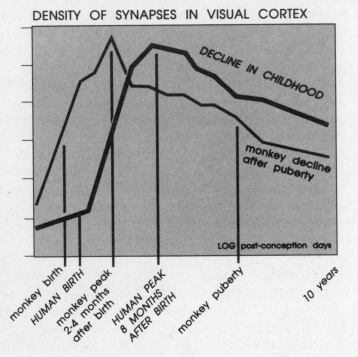

DENSITY OF SYNAPSES IN VISUAL CORTEX

into adulthood (or, more likely, juvenilized during a boom time for the usual reproductive race, but didn't drift back later because throwing success kept the more juvenilized versions well fed as the climate worsened).

Happily, neocortical pruning has the requisite long "growth curve" that the proximate mechanism would need if the three-part cycle is to be repeatedly used. The synaptic reduction curve peaks at eight months after birth in the current model of *Homo sapiens*, so further juvenilization in the future might allow ever larger assemblies for precision purposes.

Obviously, that's not all there is to throwing (or infants might be the best baseball pitchers! Everything else often isn't equal). One trade-off is in motor skills, which are a prominent part of childhood development; all of the precise timing in the world won't do any good if the muscles downstream of the controller aren't up to carrying out the commands. Or the cortical commands go to more muscles than they should for precise movements; each corticospinal neuron makes connections to many levels of the spinal cord and thus many muscles, and these too are edited during postnatal development (though probably on a different time schedule than within-the-cortex connections).

WHAT THIS WORLD NEEDS is a beach with discus-shaped rocks—which these islands seem to lack, though I keep looking. Sunbaked and windblown, I've been musing that the different kinds of waterfront correspond to the ages of humankind.

Homo habilis (and probably the australopithecines as well) would have loved a shingle beach such as the ones on Cape Cod, with all those nicely smoothed throwing rocks that fit the hand, so handy for the Darwinian toolmaking technique as well.

For *Homo erectus* we need the discus-covered waterfront, the sort of place where you find good "skipping stones" these days. There were some lakes in the Sahara (well, at least during some Pluvial period in *Homo erectus* days) whose beaches were likely paved with genuine Acheulean hand axes. Apparently hand axes were lost in the mud, and sank even deeper as the worms churned the bottom sediments. As the lake expanded, the shoreline moved back—and so new regions accumulated lost hand axes as well. After a while most of the lake bottom was paved with lost hand axes! Let the lake dry up and some surface dirt erode away, and you have exposed a sea of hand axes.

Some sand dunes in southern Algeria have recently shifted and exposed exactly such ancient lake beds as my scenario hypothesizes: my archaeologist friend said that the whole lake bed appeared to be covered with hand axes. Presumably our ancestors could have mined such lake beds for ready-made hand axes— they would have considered it Hand-Ax Heaven! For more recent inhabitants of the Sahara, those newly exposed tools for the taking would have been the Pleistocene equivalent of our oil wells and coal mines. Buried wealth, and long before fossil fuels.

The waterfront symbolizing *Homo sapiens* is riprapped, covered with broken concrete and imported boulders, symbolizing both our abilities to look ahead to trouble during next winter's storms (but not far enough to build well back from the shore, for that once-in-a-lifetime storm). And symbolizing our tendency to pave over nature with manhandled stones, rendering the beautiful into the ersatz.

For the biocomputer age to come, *Silico sapiens* and such, what else but the golden sands where silicon and human skin already lie in close contact?

THROWING LOOKS LIKE A FAST TRACK to a bigger brain, given that more precision is always better and that each increment in precision timing always requires a doubling of the number of neurons synchronized together. Throwing has a nice relation to juvenilized brains, given the possibility of juvenilization conserving connections that would otherwise be broken. Finally, temperate zone hunting is under enormous selection pressure—and as "pumping the periphery" suggests, the ice ages are likely to have spread the temperate zone genes around the low latitudes within several ice-age cycles even if hunting wasn't important in the tropics.

In temperate climates, winter selects for hunting skills. Lacking food storage techniques (which conflict with the need to move around, e.g., to follow the herds), meat becomes the major source of calories and salt for a few months. A hunter's offspring could starve if he or she missed the target: winter means that gathering cannot serve as a backup for a few months each year. Only grass remains nutritious in any quantities throughout the winter, thus accounting for the popularity of grazing; eating the muscles created (at less than 10 percent efficiency) by that grass is a popular way of making a living in wintertime.

Winters are important for a fast-track evolutionary reason: they happen once a year, producing annual waves of selection that shape up the species to better fit the environmental opportunities and hazards. If the three-phase postulate and the throwing-recruitment analysis should both prove correct, it gives us a fast-track ratchet for pumping up brain size.

In comparison, the tropical savannah seems a most unlikely setting for rapid evolution, even if it does provide optimal conditions for fossil deposition (like the hand axes, the margin of an expanding lake provides an excellent setup for preservation of skeletons) and recovery (the Rift Valley has been splitting apart recently and exposing old layers). One must ask if the Rift is not

analogous to the streetlight in that old joke about why the tipsy
fellow was crawling around looking for a lost item under the
streetlight (no, that wasn't where he lost it, but the light was
better there). The Rift has been very useful for answering What
and When questions, e.g., about a fourfold encephalization in a
mere 2.5 million years, since it provides minimum dates for important features. But we are skating on thin ice when we assume the
Rift will also answer those Where, Why, and How questions.
There may have been faster tracks elsewhere (with spread back
into Africa), and the temperate zone is a likely candidate at some
point.

HOW DOES THIS ARGUMENT CIRCUMVENT the previous
objection to big heads per se? Juvenilization *plus* slowing allows
for a significant fraction of the population to escape the birth canal
bottleneck. And there is a degree of decoupling between the
features under positive and negative selection pressures:

1) Selection for juvenilization via generation-time shortening
   or hunting success happens first, and primarily on the
   frontiers.
2) Selection for slowed somatic development then occurs, and
   not just on the frontier but throughout the population
   (since the ice advance causes frontier-type genes to perme-
   ate the tropics).
3) Frontier hunting selects for the fast half of the sexual
   maturity variants; the birth canal bottleneck selects for
   the slow half of the somatic development rate variants,
   *and the frontier survivors are the fraction of that sub-
   population having both traits*. And they are the ones that
   get all the extra babies, the next time that the ice sheets
   melt, the ones who are exposed to yearly episodes of
   winter.

WITH SO MANY of the pieces of this jigsaw puzzle still missing,
it is difficult to be confident of any proposed scenario. The evolution of humans has only happened once; almost everything that
happened along the way can therefore be argued to be important
for shaping our present capabilities. That's one of the reasons why
fast-track arguments are so important in sorting through possibili-

ties. The groupings of the pieces are becoming clearer (thanks to both hard-earned new data and reevaluations of traditional data), and the proposed links between hunting, big brains, and the juvenilization family of traits suggest plausible solutions to one part of the puzzle.

Now if only the lessons of hand-ax heaven were known in earlier centuries: One of the reasons that the cannon was so effective when first introduced was because opposing generals were fond of infantry formations that clustered soldiers together. They make rather easy targets, even for the inexpert gunner—a lesson that I suspect was first learned several million years ago with herds visiting waterholes.

The need is not really for more brains, the need is for a gentler, a more tolerant people than those who won for us against the ice, the tiger, and the bear. The hand that hefted the ax, out of some blind allegiance to the past, fondles the machine gun as lovingly. It is a habit man will have to break to survive, but the roots go very deep.

LOREN EISELEY, *The Immense Journey*, 1957

9

SAN JUAN FERRY: DOES CONSCIOUSNESS EMERGE FROM CORTICAL CONSENSUS?

History, with its flickering lamp, stumbles along the trail of the past, trying to reconstruct its scenes, to revive its echos, and kindle with pale flames the passions of former days.
WINSTON CHURCHILL

Under way at last, the ferry-boat pulls away from the giant parking lot on Fidalgo Island and sets off for the San Juan Islands. For several hours, it will wend its way through a dozen islands, stopping about four times. Sometimes it then continues on across the international boundary in Haro Strait to Vancouver Island, landing just north of Victoria, British Columbia.

I've caught the early-morning ferry. In the wintertime, everyone aboard would be either a truck driver or a resident of the islands: farmers, fishermen, carpenters, and the people who have retired to homes in the islands. They would cluster in the ferry's little coffee shop and take up conversations left over from last week's meeting in the grocery store. On a midday ferry in the summertime, the overwhelming impression is of excited tourists setting out on a minicruise, their blasé children milling around until captured by an indoor coin-eating video game. But the early-morning ferry in autumn-winter-spring has a distinct homely quality to it, worth getting up early for. The east-west ferry route crosses much of the width of the glacier that came down from Canada into Puget Sound, scraping these islands clean (of course, they weren't islands then but hills in a broad valley, since sea level was more than a hundred meters lower during an ice age).

Particularly in the winter when the islands are poorly defined in mist, you lean over the ferry's railing with a cup of hot coffee. You watch for the belated sunrise, seeing the patchy fog roll back revealing the rosy-white mountains and the evergreen islands, hearing the salmon jump and the crow complain. And listening to your own thoughts. It is very easy to feel oneself detached, a passenger on a meandering ark, who has been granted a privileged glimpse of a corner of the universe.

You just have to remember what Richard Feynman cautioned, about the problems inherent in a beginner trying to guess the rules of chess—while watching the moves on only one small corner of the board.

IF THERE IS PURPOSE IN THE UNIVERSE, it is remarkably elusive. If things were arranged for human habitation and happiness, it's being kept a secret from us, hard though we look.

The physicists and astronomers have certainly looked hard for a way out of a nasty bind. On the Universe's time scale of billions of years, the distant future seems to have two unpalatable choices: either the Universe will continue to expand until it becomes cold and motionless, or its expansion will reverse and eventually the universe will compress itself back into 10^{-42} centimeters. Neither Cold Death nor Heat Death seems compatible with human life—or even the maintenance of information, any history that might aid a subsequent life-form in a successor Universe.

One can only look upon this situation as one of those evolutionary stimuli to "do or die," even more dramatic than the need to develop hunting skills to get through the winter: either figure a

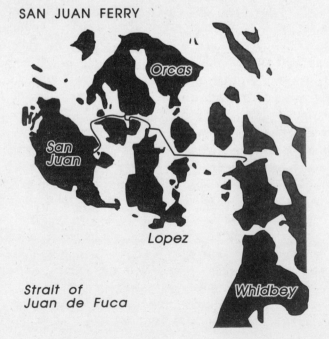

SAN JUAN FERRY

Orcas

San Juan

Lopez

Strait of
Juan de Fuca

Whidbey

way around the obvious laws of nature, or you'll be erased and the Universe restarted (and even the reexpansion is uncertain) with a clean slate. The Big Crunch Imperative. For which the Greenhouse Imperative is (quite literally) the warmup.

Given how we've gotten into the greenhouse mess, it might help if we understood ourselves a little better. How we work. Why we overdo things when it comes to reproduction. Where we came from. We might even discover some "purpose" along the way.

TRYING TO GUESS THE RULES of ape-to-human evolution is, it would appear, a problem that extends far beyond the boundaries of stones-and-bones anthropology. There are a lot of half-glimpsed bases along the way that a theory has to touch, poorly defined though they may be. While surely only "a corner of the chessboard," it's all we've got.

One strategy is to identify common variations on a heritable theme that can be exploited, and by what. We have to trace that back to what happens during pre- and postnatal development, and how the gene repertoires alter. We have to spread this successful variant ape around the world, meaning that we have to identify exploitable resources, counterpressures, bottlenecks, new niches, and all the rest.

And, since more than one "model year" is likely to be involved, repeat all this dozens of times, taking into account the niche expansions and the modifications to the environment that have occurred in the meantime, the growth curves of each item of natural selection or reproductive quirk, and so on. In analogy to how Puget Sound enhances the Pacific tides, we have to ask whether or not there was some "resonance" in evolutionary processes that the ice ages' rhythms exaggerated, by "pushing" at about the right repetition rate (not that we've found any resonance candidates yet).

THE JUVENILIZATION for purely reproductive advantage in temperate zone boom times will rapidly be shaped up for its adaptive value. It is, after all, the winter-adapted populations that get the extra babies in the boom times associated with meltbacks. And winter happens once a year, producing a rapid selection for the juvenilized body styles that can, incidentally, feed themselves in winter.

Boom-time juvenilization is all well and good, but by itself seems insufficient. The three-phase juvenilization-reenlargement-slowing cycle is much better. It demonstrates how, with a little unwanted help from the birth canal bottleneck, the fluctuating climate could have pumped up brain size by repeated juveniliza-tions. This could explain the relatively big head and a number of other juvenile features of modern adults (that flat face, those small teeth, etc.). So far, so good—especially for the features preserved in fossils that can be studied by the paleoanthropologists.

But by comparing humans to apes, we see a number of other features that were surely changed during that seven million years— and some of them are features that no juvenilization cycle is likely to produce. Repetitions of juvenilization-reenlargement-slowing could produce a big brain but, had nothing else happened, it might have had the internal organization of an ape brain. Humans have more cerebral cortex, relative to deep brain structures, than does a juvenile ape. Humans have considerably more serial-sequential propensities than do the other primates: that too isn't a juvenile ape feature, simply enlarged.

Juvenilization explains a lot, but not everything. And so we construct "Juvenilization Plus" theories.

FIRST STOP IS LOPEZ ISLAND, and the currents are a little tricky here. The ferry approaches the landing from an odd angle, balancing out the tide and the winds, and glides right into the portal. A dozen passengers walk off the boat carrying luggage and parcels, several bicyclists follow, and then two dozen cars bump their way down the ramp (it's high tide). A few people walk aboard, followed by several cars, which are going from Lopez to one of the other islands.

These cars back onto the ferry, because there is no room to turn around on deck. The last car aboard will become the first car off (what the computer programmers like to call a "last-in-first-out" buffer, similar to a pile of plates in a kitchen cabinet). Their drivers perform this task with nonchalance, as if accustomed to backing up a long driveway. Living in the islands develops some skills more than others.

The whistle blows. The lines are cast off. We back out into the channel, sliding past several sailboats. Waves are exchanged, the people on the sailboats otherwise warming their hands on coffee cups as they too start the day.

AT LEAST ON THE SURFACE, the hominid brain started reorganizing itself away from the ape standard more than two million years ago. That's the conclusion of Dean Falk; she studies the imprint that the brain leaves on the inside of skulls. The blood vessels and the cortical infoldings can often be seen, and each species has its own characteristic pattern. The australopithecines have an apelike pattern of folds—then, at two million years, one starts to see a more humanlike pattern develop in the frontal lobe.

By itself, this doesn't imply that function was changing—the simultaneous enlargement of the brain starting just before two million years ago might have forced the cerebral cortex to fold somewhat differently during fetal development, and this might be without functional consequence. Indeed, some hyper-hardnosed skeptics point out, the uses of those frontal lobe areas for speech and plan-ahead might have waited until 5,000 years ago, just in time for the invention of writing to preserve them—but I'd bet it all started closer to two million years ago. To assume that form evolved entirely before function strikes me as a "Sistine Chapel solution"—Michelangelo's God finally providing the spark of speech to a fully shaped Adam. And besides, function tends to evolve before form follows, using makeshift arrangements until efficiency shapes up a better form than the original.

THE NEXT STOP, only a short time later, is Shaw Island, with a ferry dock much smaller than the others and part-time employees not wearing the ferry system's uniform. Indeed, a nun comes out to lower the drawbridge onto the ferry deck, turning the winch by hand.

She is incongruous, a medieval figure operating hand-powered technology that matches the tides to a rumbling ark, shaking its way into the portal. But this isn't the River Styx, she's not Charon, and Shaw Island is far closer to heaven than to Hades.

The Hallelujah Chorus keeps running through my head. It's such a good example of how the experts can temporarily borrow some nonexperts, as when the audience joins in. And temporal precision for throwing occasionally needs all the helpers it can get, a massive chorus whose timing becomes far more precise than that of even the experts. Unlike other examples of temporal precision such as sound localization, throwing is one-shot: you cannot average over a hundred repeats of a waveform to get your timing (the target tends to run away after your first attempt). You have to use a hundred timers in parallel instead. If, of course, you can muster them for the occasion—if you have some borrowable brain.

Was there some specific natural selection (beyond that for juvenilization more generally) for more cerebral cortex, for more serial-sequential brain circuitry? Especially the kind that can be converted into a Darwin Machine? Throwing accuracy is certainly demanding enough on the brain *and* has the long growth curve of niche-expanding proportions. While bigger is better, the real test is whether a brain can be functionally reorganized during "get set," so as to borrow all of those Hallelujah Chorus helpers. Juvenilization per se might have provided some advantages in that direction, given all those synapses saved from pruning, but perhaps there were variants in brain wiring that were better at this recruitment task, and so throwing success helped them survive and raise offspring even after the fickle climate reverted and boom times no longer encouraged precocious variants.

A somewhat similar, though less detailed, "Juvenilization Plus" argument can be made for language, its usefulness selecting those variants in brain wiring that facilitated organizing our ideas, communicating them to others. It's not clear what demands this makes on the brain, or what its niche-expanding properties are, or if there is a decent growth curve involving many redoublings. But there were certainly some aspects of speech that appear to have been under considerable selection sometime in the past.

Compared to other primates, as I noted earlier, our larynx is located low in the neck. It starts out in the higher position but, during the baby's second year, descends several vertebral segments in the neck, elongating the vocal tract. This has some implications for the efficiency of speech: a longer vocal tract enables the larynx's rather crude sounds to be shaped up into the fancy phonemes we use. Vowels, in particular, become better differentiated as the vocal tract lengthens.

This lengthening brings with it, however, a big disadvantage: our tendency to choke on food or fluids that "go down the wrong way," winding up in the lungs rather than the stomach. All other mammals (and human infants less than a year old) have an anatomical arrangement in the throat that generally avoids this—but apparently the advantages of a lowered larynx have outweighed such common disadvantages as choking on food and aspiration pneumonia.

And if the throat was under such natural selection for improving speech, you have to figure that the brain too was under some pressures in the same direction. Again, juvenilization won't provide for the vocal tract lengthening: it's not a feature of juvenile apes that can be retained by precocious puberty.

THE THREE-PHASE BOOTSTRAPPING CYCLE (and whatever ancillary natural selection there was for brain reorganization) may "explain" our hunting prowess, our changes in body style, our big brains, and how we humans might have spread around the world so successfully. It doesn't speak directly to the rest of our uniquely human collection of serial-sequential abilities. What about music and dancing? What about our elaborate language abilities? What about intelligence of the plan-ahead variety, particularly our ethics? The speech-shaping argument can be extrapolated to more-and-better circuitry for grammatical language. Another possibility (not mutually exclusive) is that some other serial-order task, such as versatile hammering, produced the Darwin Machine capabilities.

However, as I elaborated in *The Cerebral Symphony*, I think that these particular examples of uniquely human abilities were major beneficiaries, not major movers in their own right—that each of those abilities represents a spare-time use of the same neural machinery that we occasionally use for accurate throwing. Call it a conversion of function if you like. Or an emergent property. Or just a gift (each was something largely unearned, at least initially).

However important throwing and bootstrapping cycles may be in their origins, these secondary uses have to be examined in their own right. Secondary doesn't mean "less significant"—

sometimes the by-products are more important than the products,
as Havelock Ellis used to say. In serial-order behaviors, you have
to string together one thing after another: hand-arm muscle command sequences, but also oral-facial-laryngeal command sequences,
or what-shall-I-do-next plans, or musical notes, or the body-leg-
foot movement cycles of dance. Furthermore, you have to string
them together into *unique* sequences, not specified by the genes
in the preprogrammed manner of walking, chewing, swimming,
and breathing movement sequences. These aren't simple chain-of-
beads strings either (though such are handy for illustrating the
generations of a Darwin Machine) but rather linked events on
many "channels," more like the roll for a player piano.

But using this elaborate sequencing machinery for secondary
uses need not always exploit its channel capacity; just chaining
simple schemas seems powerful, though prepositions and embedded clauses might exercise more of that sequencer machinery
(much as diagramming a sentence tends to fill in the blackboard
below the one-line sentence).

If we develop rules about chaining, we can greatly expand
the power of words: syntax helps us identify actors and the
acted-upon, spot an embedded clause, deduce whether a string of
words is a statement or a query, about those present or in another
time or place. With chaining rules so good that one thing reliably
entails another, we can sometimes make novel chains with great
explanatory power—like the ones we call "mathematics" or "logic,"
which so impressed the ancient Greek philosophers and served as
a focus for learned culture long afterward. It's easy to see why
they were so impressed, but remember too what their enthusiasm
served to blind them to: variations, and the competition between
them. And the fuzzy logic associated with approximations. Less
reliable, but more creative.

FROM SEQUENCING TO LANGUAGE is not all just spare-
time use: that's one of the implications of the descent of the
larynx. What was so useful about speech or language that was
powerful enough to overcome the considerable disadvantage of
choking so often?

Remember that natural selection isn't always about predators, pathogens, and food-finding. It is also about reproduction,

and mate selection often has some peculiarities that are reflected
in our anatomy and physiology. Nicholas Humphrey and Richard
Dawkins, in a BBC radio program, discussed the possible role of
sexual selection in evolving language. And I recently tried out my
version of the idea on a group concerned with the evolution of
language and intelligence. While this will likely remain an alien
idea in anthropology and linguistics for some time (it does conflict
with the Puritan Ethic, though not with Darwinism), you can see
how female standards for male abilities could have bootstrapped
the prehuman language abilities. Just as female birds seem to
have favored elaborate songs by males (not to mention long and
shiny feathers) when choosing a mate, so prehuman females might
have promoted a fancier form of language, shaping up preadapta-
tions such as throwing sequencers into something more specific
for grammar.

All a female need do is to favor males with language performance at least as good as her own. Women have higher verbal
IQs—but why? The answer probably lies in developmental modifications by testosterone, augmented by the possession of a Y
chromosome (which only males have). Should a woman suffer
brain damage, she is far less likely to develop aphasia, suggesting
a better-organized language cortex. Testosterone does some odd
things to brain lateralizations during childhood; *even with equal
genes for language*, adult males may be substandard to females
because of such developmental degradation. Furthermore, males
are more likely to suffer brain damage during a difficult delivery;
this too makes their brain organization more variable.

Suppose that 10 percent of the males were substandard to
nearly all females. So females selecting for the top 90 percent of
the genome in language ability will serve to bootstrap language to
even fancier levels in the next generation for both males and
females. Males might degrade that inheritance a little during
development, but they'd be better as adults than the previous
generations—and their daughters certainly ought to be better,
lacking the testosterone degradation.

That's a possible mechanism (and surely there are others as
well), but how fast might the various mechanisms be? Female
choice in mates has been greatly augmented by concealed ovulation sometime during hominid evolution, thus providing more

opportunities for sexual selection than seen in the other apes. The chimpanzees provide examples of how this might work: some males are particularly adept at detecting the onset of estrus in a female, and also adept at persuading the female to "go off into the bushes" with them ("to consort" is the official term in primatology) for several days. Such males are likely to achieve many more successful pregnancies than the unsuspecting or antisocial males left behind in the main group. The suppression of estrus behaviors might serve to evolve sociable males that consort frequently (no longer knowing when ovulation occurs, males have to keep trying all the time, which means remaining socially acceptable as a companion). Communications skills are important in chimpanzees for promoting a consortship; surely they are also important in prolonging it, persuading the female not to return to the main group for a while longer, preferably not until pregnant.

Environmental selection is important, but it isn't the only way. And sexual selection, if we judge from the birds, often goes to extremes (magpie tail length, peacock tail iridescence) before the disadvantages counterbalance; prehuman sexual selection might be a quicker way to evolve language from a throwing-like preadaptation than would language's usefulness for finding food, avoiding predators, etc. Of course, once we had it, grammatical language would be useful in those ways as well.

JUST ACROSS THE CHANNEL from Shaw Island is the ferry dock for Orcas Island. And there is a lot of traffic for Orcas, a large and mountainous island with several fjordlike channels that divide the island up into north-south lobes at the foot of Mount Constitution.

Another leftover from the ice ages? Certainly the peak itself was well covered by the Puget Lobe: the ice was probably twice as high as Mount Constitution.

To be able to imagine this whole area covered by ice is surely a uniquely human ability among the animals of the world. Most animals have associative memories, but few seem likely to connect them in a string, like frames of a movie film. A dog could probably learn each different car in that line of vehicles waiting to board the ferry, but would it remember the order in which they drove up the ramp?

OUR CONSCIOUSNESS OF THE PAST often has an aspect of connectedness: we remember episodes, novel events connected by a stream of time. Replaying this "tape" of the past is notoriously unreliable (as when we confuse one visit to the grocery store with another) but other animals may have even less episodic memory: they learn new objects, new people, new places (just as we also learn new words), but their abilities to recall complete episodes could be limited.

Episodic memory is something which we may have acquired with our other exaggerated serial-order abilities, such as language and throwing. So animal consciousness might lack much of our narrative richness, and it might correspondingly lack our scenario-spinning (it needs episodic memories against which to judge candidates for novel scenarios).

There are certainly aspects of human consciousness that seem particularly serial: spinning scenarios that attempt to explain the past, forecast the future. We tend to see ourselves as poised at a choice between alternative futures, thanks to this ability to project the past and present into a foreseen future.

But consciousness is also noticing things, focussing one's attention on the present. When I use my right hemisphere to survey this scenery, I am mostly scanning, ignoring the details in favor of grand spatial relationships. Forests here, shining sea there, the ferry beneath me, the warm wind whistling past: I am simultaneously conscious of them all. At other times, I focus on particular objects and try to identify them, as when I concentrate on that sea gull, trying to use the color of the feet as a means of distinguishing between two common forms of gull hereabouts. This object identification, or word-finding, activity is a left-hemisphere aspect of focussed awareness.

Making decisions is often conscious, at least when dealing with *novel* courses of action that first require a little Darwin Machine massaging (Chapter 2), to eliminate the nonsense that randomness throws up and thereby evolve a plan of quality, safe to carry out. But we also decide in the sensory sphere, as when we entertain the notion that there are several species of gull and split the old "sea gull" category into two or three schemas. Darwin Machines can also lump schemas together, see if the components make sense (apples and oranges lumped into fruit); here the order of the schemas in the sequencer track is presumably ignored, with the sequencer merely acting as a versatile associative memory, capable of categorizing and contrasting collections of schemas.

Darwin Machines may not be absolutely necessary for most of the aspects of consciousness, but they seem likely to greatly augment such conscious activities of their proud possessor. And they seem capable of solving the "seat of the soul" problem that fascinated Descartes: just where is this "chief executive" located within our brains? The inability of the neurologist to find a region of brain that is essential for consciousness has not caused the problem to disappear: each of us has the strong impression that we focus, decide, and move according to the central direction which we apply to our personal world. Yes, there are involuntary movements. Yes, there are subliminal perceptions. But they don't make the "illusion of centrality" go away. If there isn't a single anatomical site for this narrator of consciousness, how might various areas conspire to act "as if unitary?"

As the Darwin Machine's population of sequences evolves, one string of schemas tends to dominate, becomes the most common sequence. It may be a string of schemas whose order is unimportant: that evergreen forest, that shining sea, and the ferryboat deck. Or the order may be relevant, as when I shape up a grammatical sentence in my mind, preparing to remark on the feet of the gull poised alongside the ferry, hovering in the breeze. If it is a command sequence for throwing, orchestrating those 88 muscles needed for projectile predation, ordering is absolutely essential.

The success of a particular sequence in cloning itself implies that it may occupy substantial areas of cerebral cortex at the same time. It won't be like a series of little bird shapes, repeated over and over as on a wallpaper pattern or Escher design. It will probably be a spatial pattern of neuron activity rather like those nonsensical-appearing bar codes on product packages. There is a different one on each different product in the grocery store, adequate to evoke the product name and price, print them out on the cash-register receipt. Or the cortical representation could be a temporal pattern (what you get when scanning a bar code), repeating in many places like a chorus. Just imagine a string of nonidentical products, lined up on the checkout counter, producing a string of wordlike representations, constituting a candidate sentence or novel category. Or a string of identical products, analogous to one word that speaks loudly to you.

Cloned many times, that *string* of word representations may occupy a lot of my brain, once I've focussed on the gull identification problem long enough to decide what to say. Just imagine the bar codes for five products, strung together—but cloned hundreds of times, repeating like a wallpaper pattern throughout regions of association cortex. It is this *cortical consensus* which may constitute "conscious awareness," what I'll describe if anyone should ask me what I'm thinking about.

There is no known stuff in the brain that corresponds to attentional resource. . . . Rather, there are different ways of using the finite neural network. When wide areas of the network are involved in one mental operation . . . other operations are deprived of the necessary cerebral functional space. . . . In other words, multi-purpose cerebral computing space can be used either for a wide-ranging but shallow encoding, or for a single but difficult mental operation.
the neuropsychologist MARCEL KINSBOURNE, 1988

Similarly a plan of action, when finally shaped up by Darwinian processes into a thing of quality, all ready to let loose on my muscles, should also have many widespread clones. In both sensory and movement aspects of consciousness, both right- and left-hemisphere modes of noticing the present, both recalling names and recalling serial-ordered episodes of the past, Darwin Machine reasoning leads us to suspect that no one cortical area is crucial. Certainly no one antibody molecule is crucial for the immune response, nor is any one biological individual crucial for a new species: the new group is distinguished by the preponderance of a new type of individual, not any particular one.

The "center of it all" turns out to be a widespread cortical committee of near-clones, in this view. Is consciousness the dominant harmony of the association areas, arising from near unanimity in a population of Darwin Machines, able to "speak loudly enough" to govern?

Let me forestall an obvious bit of phrase-making: "The har-mony of the hemispheres" isn't quite right, because the clone need not take over an entire hemisphere, much less both of them. Just how large a consensus is needed to dominate probably depends on competing Darwin Machines (one imagines the sequencers as par-titioned into various islandlike subpopulations, each evolving quasi-independently) and how strong a consensus they have been able to reach about other things (which we otherwise know only as the subconscious). The access of a particular sequencer population to language processes is probably also important; left prefrontal association areas might have better access than right parietal association areas, for example. Surely, however, a takeover of conscious awareness need not imply a cloning of all association cortex.

The cortical consensus is particularly attractive as an expla-nation for consciousness because it allows for specialized cortical areas (in the Hallelujah Chorus analogy, the expert choir) without having them exclusively committed to one task (borrowable as a helper by another expert). It allows for a center of consciousness without a physical hub, vulnerable to pinpoint damage by a bro-ken blood vessel. It allows for focussing on the present in both left- and right-hemisphere styles. It allows for novel courses of action, for decisions, for both thought without action and reaction without thought. And it has a natural home for subconscious processes, a route whereby they can sometimes come to dominate.

Not a bad start, that—considering that we've probably ex-plored only a fraction of the "chessboard" of mental activities.

THE FERRY IS MOSTLY EMPTY now, our load lightened. But more than a dozen cars drive up the ramp onto the ferry, bound from Orcas to Friday Harbor. They didn't have to back up be-cause there is now room for a car to drive to the rear of the ferry and turn a half-circle, join the rear of a line of Friday-Harbor-bound cars, pointing the right way. A little working room helps to avoid awkward maneuvers, allow for first-in-first-out queues to form naturally.

Serial-sequential behaviors are important in the list of uniquely human happenings, but we wouldn't be human without quite a few others, such as the concealed ovulation that contributes to our mating system, our unusual attraction to swimming and shore-lines, and similar modifications from the standard ape that must be separately accounted for. Throwing (or whatever it was that selected for the augmented serial-order machinery, conceivably language's usefulness) may have bought us a lot, but not everything.

Is the picture of hominid evolution sketched in the preceding chapters correct? Almost surely not, at least in some details—and probably in some major feature. First of all, I worry that we could presently have insufficient parts with which to construct a sufficient theory; I didn't have all that much choice.

○ The throwing theory is about the only detailed explanation that has been attempted so far, regarding how a uniquely human skill might have rapidly changed the brain; other factors which might be equally important, such as language and toolmaking skills, are harder to relate to brain size and reorganization requirements at our present state of knowledge.

○ Juvenilization-neoteny-paedomorphosis seems to be the only broad-scale summary of relevant developmental changes that we have to work with—and certainly the only one easily related to climate fluctuations.

○ And the r-K spectrum is about the only good summary of ecological opportunism and how it interacts with such developmental changes.

While I can relate them to hominid brain changes via that three-phase pump, I'd feel more confident if I'd had more choice of available subprocesses.

Secondly, reading the history of science tends to promote caution, if not humility. One sees all the perfectly reasonable proposals that turned out to be wrong. But one also sees how they set up targets, both to challenge and to mimic-with-variations. I suppose that what I am really trying to do is to improve the standards of what constitutes a serious proposal for hominid evolutionary mechanisms. And doing this by illustrating the many viewpoints that must be brought to bear: the ethology of niche busting behaviors, their neurophysiological mechanisms and the developmental modifications that affect them, the ecology of the new model and how it is influenced by climatic changes, and so forth.

It isn't just brain size: these evolutionary resources have also got to explain brain reorganization as well. Not to mention such emergents as our peculiar consciousness.

Man is the only being that knows death; all others become old, but with a consciousness wholly limited to the moment, which must seem to them eternal. They see death, not knowing anything about it.

OSWALD SPENGLER, *The Decline of the West*, 1926

10

FRIDAY HARBOR: HAS INTELLIGENT LIFE EVOLVED YET?

Nature evolved our sense of purpose blindly, but now we have it. That sense of purpose has given us dominion over the biosphere. We, who were not created, have become creators. We are ignorant and fallible, and like any other animal our minds work best in the short term and the bodily scale. We do not think clearly in megatons or picture generations much beyond our grandchildren. Nonetheless, the earth has become our garden; it behooves us to cultivate it with wisdom.

the ethologist ALISON JOLLY, 1988

The ferry slips through a narrow channel separating Shaw and Crane Island, sailing westward out into San Juan Channel; Orcas Island is now behind us. San Juan Island itself comes into view, a large wooded island with the mountains of Vancouver Island in the background. A dozen sailboats wander about the broad expanse of San Juan Channel, and a commercial fishing boat chugs along. Turn right here, and you'll soon cross the international boundary into Canadian waters. We turn left and lose the view of the mountains.

Indians used to live among these islands, mostly fishing but also hunting and gathering. Indian villages hereabouts tend to disappear over the centuries, as they're usually fishing villages like the one on Whidbey Island that is eroding out of a headland; once a century, a fierce winter storm is likely to sweep such a village away, unless it has been buried in the interim by a landslide.

And outsiders who write history and take photographs of the Indians have only been around here for a little over a century. They did, fortunately, record the words of Chief Seattle (for whom the city is named), who in 1854 was reported to have said:

The air is precious to the red man, for all things share the same breath—the beast, the tree, the man, they all share the same breath. The white man does not seem to notice the air he breathes. Like a man dying for many days, he is numb to the stench. . . .

What is man without the beasts? If all the beasts were gone, man would die from a great loneliness of spirit. For whatever happens to the beasts soon happens to man. All things are interconnected.

This we know. The earth does not belong to man, man belongs to the earth. This we know. All things are connected like the blood which unites one family. All things are connected.

The biologists and climatologists have finally discovered just how true that is, but we're having trouble selling the stewardship idea to the rest of the world.

American settlement here did not involve great wars with the displaced Indians, so far as I know. Of course, European settlers usually unknowingly spread smallpox to the immunologically defenseless Indians. Since their microbes preceded them, Europeans competed with much-weakened tribes. (Perhaps, in revenge for smallpox, the Indians gave the Europeans tobacco?)

The San Juan Islands are a special place, even in the history of warfare. They are largely inside the United States, though the archipelago extends through Canadian waters alongside Vancouver Island and on up north into the Gulf Islands. The international boundary represents one of the sterling examples of how to resolve international disputes. In the middle of the nineteenth century, when settlers were just starting to farm the islands, both the Americans and the British claimed the islands since nationals of both countries were living here. A dispute over a farmer's pig caused settlers to take sides and this led both the British and the American governments to send some troops here. They never fought each other. They merely established garrisons, the English on the north end of San Juan Island on the shores of a pleasant bay, and the Americans on a windswept ridge near Cattle Point at the south end. The English planted an orchard around their little camp; the American soldiers got the view of the Olympic Mountains and the Strait of Juan de Fuca. It is not recorded who won the sporting contests that they organized between the troops during the 12-year occupation.

Eventually the dispute was submitted to arbitration: Kaiser Wilhelm of Germany drew the international boundary line in 1872, which survives to this day. The so-called Pig War could serve as a model to other nations about how bloodlessly to settle disputes.

FROM A FORESTED SHORELINE of nature preserve (with Mount Baker having reappeared on the left side), suddenly one turns right to see a town ahead. "Friday Harbor," announces the disembodied voice. *"Friday Harbor,"* it repeats in that "time to wake up" tone of voice that streetcar conductors use to announce the end of the line.

All along the right shore are the University of Washington's Friday Harbor Laboratories. My wife did the research for her Ph.D. thesis here, and I've lots of experience visiting. I look back into the forest along the shoreline at the apartments nestled into the rocks. I well remember the spring of 1980, while we were up for a weekend, sleeping in one of the mobile homes hidden even farther back, under the trees. We had gotten used to the sound of pine cones falling on the metal roof during the night. But after daybreak, we were awakened by a boom that shook the room. An earthquake? (We had once had our bed shaken in the middle of the night by a small earthquake while at Friday Harbor.) But this was too noisy for an earthquake: I leapt out of bed, convinced that someone had backed a car into the side of the mobile home.

As I stood in the doorway contemplating the complete lack of candidate cars, several more booms shook the place. But the ground seemed stable and the trees didn't sway. My wife, as puzzled as I was but busy trying out possible explanations, wondered aloud if someone was firing the cannon that they use to start the boat races. I didn't think that the racing committee had recently acquired the guns from a battleship: that was an awfully deep-throated boom. The previous year on sabbatical in Jerusalem, I had developed an ear for judging the sound of explosions—most of which turned out to be dynamite explosions for digging basements in the rocky ground, not terrorist bombs. This sounded more like an ammunition dump going up.

While hurriedly getting dressed, I got on the shortwave radio network (the local amateur radio community has situated a repeater atop Mount Constitution over on Orcas Island, and so even the little hand-held radio in my briefcase could reach long distances) and asked if anyone else had heard the explosions—yes, indeed, people in Victoria had heard them, and in Bellingham too. And then a distinctly Canadian voice came on; he reported talking to an amateur radio operator in Portland, Oregon, who had looked out his window. And observed that Mount St. Helens had blown its top.

Mount St. Helens is 280 kilometers (175 miles) from Friday Harbor, near Washington State's southern boundary just as San Juan Island is at its northwest extreme. Could we see the eruption? It seemed unlikely, but we drove to the south end of San

Juan Island; from Cattle Point there is often a clear view south into Puget Sound. On the drive down, we stole glimpses of Mount Baker, just to our east—no ominous steam plumes, fortunately.

Looking south from Cattle Point, the overcast seemed featureless. Then, between two layers of clouds in the south, we saw a mushroom cloud rising, just when the radio reported another big eruption. It was three times as high off the horizon as the highest mountain peaks; we almost missed seeing it because we were looking lower with the binoculars. That ash was clearly being injected into the stratosphere. The morning blast was 500 times greater than the atomic bomb exploded at Hiroshima (but was small stuff compared to the prehistoric eruptions at places like Oregon's Crater Lake or California's Mono Lake region).

That same spring at Friday Harbor, the throwing theory occurred to me while I was throwing stones at the beach, trying to find excuses for why I was so inaccurate. Its progeny, the Darwin Machine and the cortical consensus, have not been associated with any ominous rumbles or thunderclaps, so far.

Well, a friend reminds me, at least if you don't count California's 7.1-rated earthquake in 1989. I spoke to a group of computer designers at a summer camp, located in an interesting place: on the San Andreas fault in the mountains between San Jose and Santa Cruz. And on a similarly risk-taking topic: how to build a "conscious" computer using Darwin Machine principles. The earthquake was centered only a few miles away—but it came three days after my talk. If God was trying to tell me something, her reflexes were a little slow.

WE DON'T NEED AN OCCASION to visit Friday Harbor but this time there is one, not Darwin Machines but a gathering of the friends of the late Graham Hoyle at one of Graham's favorite places, the Friday Harbor Laboratories.

Graham, professor of biology at the University of Oregon at the time of his death, firmly believed in studying the nervous system from the vantage of behavior, but also digging deeply into the electrical mechanisms of nerve and muscle. He solved the problem of how insects seemingly manage to violate the sodium-in, potassium-out rule of all nerve cells. He also was probably the first to discover the role of potassium currents in modulating neural excitability during learning, now a hot research area.

Trained in the British tradition of vigorous academic debate, Graham often made those trained in more polite traditions (if you can't say something nice, don't say anything at all) a bit uneasy. Graham could always be counted on, at a scientific meeting, to stand up and ask a pointed question, often softened with self-deprecating humor. Many of us learned to love him; neuroscience meetings just aren't the same anymore, without Graham.

The ferryboat cruises past the Labs on the way into Friday Harbor, the only town on San Juan Island, the second-largest of the San Juan archipelago. Here one can see what wasn't evident from that over-the-ice-ages flight from Copenhagen. Though much of the shoreline of the harbor is becoming developed (and the Port of Friday Harbor is always pile-driving to create an endless maze of pleasure-boat moorages obstructing the old harbor), the north shore is largely a nature preserve. In one small part of this preserve is situated the university's research station, a collection of buildings nestled into the rocks and trees by a sensitive and skillful architect, and a wooden pier extending out into the harbor.

There are a few boats moored on the pier, plus a commercial sized fishing boat. The motorboats are for collecting animals and algae. The rowboats are available for transportation into town, whenever researchers or students develop an irresistible longing for beer or ice cream. But the days of leaving the rowboat on the town beach are long since gone: no beach remains. These days, you have to consult a map of the maze just to discover the three places where one is allowed to park a rowboat temporarily; if you forget to check the map before departing the Labs, you could row forever around the Port of Friday Harbor's moorage maze, seeking a temporary haven.

More frequently, the rowboats are used just to get a little exercise: Graham always used to end a long afternoon at the microscope by launching a rowboat and vigorously rowing across the harbor to Brown Island and back.

THERE IS A DEER nibbling away at some greenery outside the library. I am sitting on the balcony of the library, enjoying the view of the water and Mount Baker—and am taken by surprise by

the sound of the deer behind me in the trees. One of the charms of
working here is that you can look up from peering into a microscope or book, glance out the window to rest your eyes, and find a
pair of big brown eyes watching you.

Or a pair of little black eyes. One has to keep the doors to the
labs closed, as whole families of raccoons will come in and help
themselves to all that live food swimming around in the seawater
tanks; they are particularly fond of small crabs. It is a similar
fondness for shoreline creatures that probably led some other land
mammals back into offshore waters, reinventing some aquatic
specializations. When I see these raccoons out on the shore at low
tide, poking their paws into the tide pools, I think of seals and
aquatic apes.

But deer aren't quite as adventuresome as our raccoons—
deer swim between islands occasionally, as the ferryboat crews
can attest (that's probably how the Irish elk arrived in Ireland
during the Allerød warming of Europe—only to be killed off
1,500 years later by the Younger Dryas cold spike), but deer
aren't fishing along the way. Swimming is probably a once-in-a-
lifetime thing for most deer; without natural selection for daily
foraging in the water, the deer aren't likely to develop aquatic
adaptations very soon.

The Fernald Building at Friday Harbor Labs is a modern
two-story wood-and-glass structure tucked into a rocky recess in
the waterfront, blending with its natural surroundings in a way
that few architects ever attain. I once started describing this
building to architecture professor Robert Small as the modern
building I most admired in the world—and he confessed that he
had helped design it back in the fifties, as an assistant to Ralph
Anderson. The library on the upper floor is an idyllic place to
work. Its carrels run around the windows, big plate-glass walls on
the two sides that face the harbor. An exterior walkway balcony
runs all around the building's upper floor, and on the harbor side
there is a long bench as part of the balcony. So one moves back
and forth from library desk to the long park bench in the course of
a day of reading and writing.

And if one wishes to stretch one's legs a little more, the
balcony walkway leads off the west end onto a great craggy bluff
of bedrock scraped clean by the Puget Lobe and more recently

filled in with pads of moss, some soil, and some grass in those natural depressions that tend to hold the rainwater. Multicolored lichens cover the exposed rocks like a patchwork quilt. One sees Mount Baker sitting on the eastern horizon beyond the harbor entrance. The sea gulls often hover over the bluff, flying into a breeze.

Once a great blue heron stood offshore of the bluff for a long time, admired by me but being pestered by the gulls—until it finally let out a series of loud complaints and flew away in disgust, settling down again in the little cove of the nature preserve, its feathers still ruffled. Birds have learned that size isn't everything; they often "mob" birds that are much larger than they are. I once saw a lone crow mob a bald eagle, chasing the U.S.'s emblematic bird for several minutes—reminding me, alas, of the way that the U.S. Congress had once again been frightened away from a rational discussion of population policy by a vocal minority opposed to birth control devices.

Humans have been around here only since the last Ice Age; Western civilization's tenure is a mere 1 percent postscript to a long succession of Indian tribes. We scientists are intruding on the deer and raccoons that meander among the trees and buildings, the rabbits that (at least this year) render lawn mowers superfluous hereabouts. The birds remind us that small dinosaurs are still with us; the giant Puget Sound octopus reminds us of an entirely different evolutionary route to cleverness.

But our civilization is a startling postscript, if simply because of the accelerated time scale on which our cultural evolution operates—and our tendency to remake the land on a scale approaching that of the volcanos and glaciers. We're also likely remaking the weather on a slightly slower time scale—my guess is that we just haven't noticed the disruptions yet.

THE HOYLE MEMORIAL SYMPOSIUM broke up at five o'clock this afternoon, so that its participants could go out for a row, just as Graham always did at that hour. There was even a rowboat race, though not as far as Brown Island (they settled for a buoy in the harbor).

Some people, contemplating evolution and where it is going, suggest that the next stage of evolution is a giant group mind, using the same Darwinian principles of shaping up variations on a theme, but with individual humans being the contributors to the larger "organism." Some suggest the economy as a model, having a life of its own. I usually reply that every scientific meeting that I attend seems especially like a superorganism—the group mind has already been invented! There is something about meetings of only a few dozen people at Friday Harbor; they seem to resonate somehow.

Science as a whole is much more than any one of its contributors can fathom; it seems to have a life of its own. Lots of variations occur in the individual minds of its contributors, are shaped up there, and are usually shaped up further by checking against nature in experiments. But it is not a finished work, for when a scientist presents a talk on the work at a meeting like this, a lot more shaping up (or throwing out) goes on, since the other scientists have different information in their heads. New variations on a theme occur (sometimes you can even see a wave of them pass through the audience, as various people start to raise their hands to interject comments), and so the concepts get further shaped and refined. Though science is the best example I know, any subject with a marketplace for ideas—art, literature, technology—works this way too.

Yet in this candidate for a supermind, there is no decision-making apparatus equivalent to clone dominance in a Darwin Machine, nor is there a "super-individual" that lives or dies *as a whole* depending on how good its collective judgments are. A concept, viruslike, enters into a race for reproduction instead, perhaps being amplified by copying—almost like a cancer metastasizing in other scientists' heads (Richard Dawkins in *The Selfish Gene* usefully defined "memes," contributions to culture to be mimicked). There it either grows by additional contributions, or it lingers, or it dies out—perhaps to be rediscovered 20 years later in another country when the environment for it is more likely to lead to copying. For better or worse, science is so international these days (thanks to easier travel and better communications linking us together) that national fads are declining, and there is less likely to be a protected niche for a new idea, so that it has a chance to develop before being overexposed to the competition for attention.

Earth system scientists have predicted that, as a direct con-
sequence of increased carbon dioxide levels and the resultant
greenhouse effect, storms will become more numerous in the
coming decades, and they will be far more severe, with winds
in excess of two hundred miles per hour (high atmospheric
temperatures will accelerate evaporation, which will speed
up atmospheric convection currents). Droughts will become
common in the middle latitudes; rivers in the American
Southwest, for example, may shrink by as much as forty to
seventy-five percent, all but obliterating agriculture. And
polar ice will begin melting, causing sea levels to rise by as
much as two hundred feet and submerging such highly popu-
lated coastal areas as Hong Kong, New York, and Rio de
Janeiro. The specter raised by such changes, at least in the
minds of some scientists, is that man constitutes a threat to
the global processes that, until now, have maintained the
conditions necessary for life.

EDWIN DOBB, senior editor of *The Sciences*, 1989

WHEN SCIENTISTS GET TOGETHER to hash out recommen-
dations on something such as the greenhouse effect or abrupt
climate change, they usually retreat to a conference site—and
marine labs such as Woods Hole or Friday Harbor are a favorite
of the biologists and oceanographers. Someday these very meeting rooms are likely to see a critical meeting in the history of the
world, where new knowledge is evaluated, scientific opinion solid-
ifies, and policy-makers pose questions.

Will new knowledge save us, or will the boom-time breeders,
the know-nothings, and the life-is-a-big-party types bring us down
after all? Since no one is in charge here (or rather everyone is in
charge and time may be too short for educating enough of us), one
is led to hope against hope for a new stewardship force in nature
that will protect the planet from the inappropriate ice-age psychology and reproductive physiology of five billion humans, the
same way that the Gaia system is said to buffer the atmospheric
oxygen to keep it in the life-giving range.

Plato's solution to such problems would have been a dictator-
ship of the enlightened, but we've seen what usually happens with
rule by the few, even if they start off well-educated and well-

motivated. The political arena has its hazards, to be sure: special interests using highly selected data to confuse and confound the nonscientist, for example. We've recently seen how someone can ignore millennia of data, concentrating on only the last 30 years, ignore the proxy climate indicators and just concentrate on weather bureau temperature records, ignore the worldwide data and concentrate on only the U.S., to make a headline-grabbing case for "don't worry." The fluctuating nature of the underlying processes makes it inevitable that countertrend periods will exist, as well as periods of confusing data—especially when those data are taken in isolation. While we always have to assume that our data are incomplete and new data could arrive tomorrow that would cause us to reconsider, both scientific and political perspectives need to be worldwide, long-term, and sensitive to whole ecosystems.

Most of the climate-change imperatives are identical to those required by depletion of fossil fuels and by famine-producing overpopulation trends; we'd need to do most of them even if the greenhouse factors disappeared somehow. Promoting political wisdom in a positive sense in this area is not easy to do. You can see the dilemmas in the greenhouse debates starting to take place, trying to define the choices to be made down the road. And we're not even yet discussing long dikes or high technology, just which research opportunities we will choose to emphasize with our limited scientific budgets.

The need to invest in massive studies of the ocean-atmosphere-ice systems, and in the large computers needed to simulate their modes of operation, seems particularly obvious. But the studies of human physiology and psychology are perhaps as important, insofar as they affect our ability to modify overpollution and overpopulation tendencies.

And some such areas have been neglected in a way that will reflect very poorly on us, one of these days. In reproductive physiology the emphasis has been on proximate mechanisms of fertility. Despite the decades of awareness about the population explosion and the repeated examples of the cruel famines that follow runaway population growth, the real action these days is *in vitro* fertilization—augmenting fertility by solving infertility problems.

Why is that? Though worthy of a humane society's concern and certainly making a few couples happier, it's probably not what a survey would identify as a high priority among the world's problems. Rather, we see an example of "that's where the money is," what we can expect more generally if basic research is further "privatized"; public research money has been very thin and unreliable, and a major source of single-issue private funding can redirect a whole area of basic research. The U.S. government, in particular, has often been unwilling to support most basic and applied research in human reproduction—and has routinely turned away requests by other countries for aid in reducing birth rates with known techniques.

We can, if we choose to so convince our elected officials, greatly expand our support of research and education about birth control—and research on understanding ultimate causation, such as those boom-time shifts that, without higher education and careers for women, induce urban children to hurry up and become 28-year-old grandparents. Understanding boom-time psychology and physiology might provide us with some ways of stabilizing the world's runaway growth—and implementing a "quality not quantity" ideal.

Life must move forward,
but it can only be understood backward.
                                        SØREN KIERKEGAARD (1813–1855)

A WALK ON THE EDGE OF THE UNIVERSE is how I used to think of my nocturnal wanderings, when I'd stroll out the top of a breakwater projecting one block into Lake Michigan. I'd be surrounded by water, set off from the business of the Northwestern University campus, with the night sky overhead and the waves lapping underneath, the breezes whistling past my ears.

That was back in the Sputnik days of the late fifties, when only one artificial satellite at a time circled the Earth, and I'd always watch for a slowly moving star. I was of the generation that had gathered on rooftops with binoculars, in the cold of the early winter mornings of 1958. And tried to imagine a lonely dog orbiting overhead, the first animal to leave the Earth. Later I discovered that breakwaters were nicer than the freshman dormitory roof. One could pace, to the rhythm of the waves.

Walking on water while contemplating the heavens, complete with a human addition. Exhilarating stuff, as was what I was learning every day. After several years, in spite of having dutifully read "a little learning is a dangerous thing," I decided that the only two truly fundamental scientific endeavors were cosmology and brain research, those inquiries into how we came to be. I picked brains. Without those breakwaters, I might now be an electrical engineer.

But instead I'm a neurobiologist caught up with evolutionary problems, now taking another nocturnal stroll, this time along the breakwaters at the Friday Harbor Labs. They are three concrete floats, each about 30 paces long, that are anchored offshore from the main pier and which protect the plants and animals. Not from the occasional winter storms, as you might initially suspect, but rather from the everyday wakes of the passing ferryboats, seaplanes, and speedboats. A series of gangplanks connects the main pier to the breakwaters, and one can walk more than a city block before turning around and retracing one's steps, still surrounded by the open skies, intimate with the talking waves that lap against the floating path.

THE EMERGING VIEW OF HUMANITY is hardly a Garden of Eden. It implies that we humans pretty much invented ourselves, imperfections and all, and are still inventing ourselves. It implies that we are responsible for ourselves and our planet, that we can no longer blunder about like an energetically curious child poking around inside a clock with a screwdriver, confident that everything will be made right by an all-capable parent.

Our ability to modify our environment has gotten considerably ahead of our ability—or at least our resolve—to look ahead. It took us a little while to understand what fossil fuels do to the atmosphere and what DDT does to bird shells, yet we go right ahead introducing new chemicals in bulk quantities without the slightest idea of what they will do to the natural ecosystems on which our descendants will rely.

All of this rapid change during our lives has led to a boom-time psychology and physiology that entices us to exploit the opportunities of the moment rather than investing for the future. This opportunistic aspect of our basic biological heritage, shaped by the ice-age population explosions, is winning out over the predicting-the-future abilities that might avoid the bust that usually follows the r-shifting boom.

One sometimes hears "the world would be better off if we were all still hunter-gatherers," that civilizations haven't really been worth it after all. There is something to be said for that viewpoint, at least as it pertains to the *average* civilization, as the physiologist Jared Diamond noted:

Archaeologists studying the rise of farming have reconstructed a crucial stage at which we made the worst mistake in human history. Forced to choose between limiting population or trying to increase food production, we chose the latter and ended up with starvation, warfare, and tyranny. Hunter-gatherers practiced the most successful and longest-lasting life style in human history. In contrast, we're still struggling with the mess which agriculture has tumbled us, and it's unclear whether we can solve it.

Furthermore, civilizations aren't as progressive as they usually appear in the history books. Perhaps 20 agricultural societies have, in the history of this world, progressed to the point of building cities (that's the basic definition of a civilization), the first ones about 5,000 years ago. In all but one, innovation toward widespread technologies was a minor thing, occurring early in the civilization's lifetime (if at all) and then reaching a plateau with little further "progress." Even in the Greco-Roman civilization that lasted from 600 B.C. to A.D. 400, most scientific advances and technological innovations occurred before 250 B.C. In terms of improving people's lives, most agricultural societies were not a clear improvement on the life of the hunter-gatherers. Though, it must be remembered, a half-dozen civilizations did make considerable philosophical-scientific progress, just without translating it into technologies that benefitted people.

In one of the 20 civilizations, during the medieval-to-modern period that followed the Greco-Roman in Europe, technologies became widespread. Even in the "Dark Ages," horse collars and water power became commonplace. And the Renaissance gave birth to a few centuries of intellectual ferment, which led to the

Scientific Revolution and the Industrial Revolution. Their products and some of their ways of thinking spread subsequently to
the older civilizations of Africa, Asia, and the Americas.

Certainly the world since the Renaissance has become a far
better place; I cannot but think of how helpless people have felt
with toothaches, dying children, mental illness, and starvation—
and how much sheer knowledge has improved the situation for
many of us since the "good old days." But the fact that it only
happened to *one* of those 20 civilizations doesn't give us much
reason to assume that the reemergence of a humanity-benefitting
civilization would be inevitable, should we lose our science and
technology in the rampages accompanying a collapse of our civilization. We can't count on a future civilization retrieving what we
lose through poor stewardship.

That men do not learn very much from the lessons of history
is the most important of all the lessons of history.
                                        ALDOUS HUXLEY (1894–1963)

I WAS PUZZLED by some high thin clouds in the sky tonight
above Friday Harbor. They moved around too quickly for a night
with only a light breeze. And one "cloud" developed curtainlike
folds in a matter of seconds, brightened into a whitish-green of
sorts—and then stayed bright for several minutes. Whereupon it
suddenly faded out, disappearing in less than two seconds.

I finally realized what was happening: those weren't clouds
but rather the aurora borealis, the northern lights. I haven't seen
them for three decades, not since my undergraduate years pacing
on the shores of Lake Michigan. There must be a great storm in
progress on the sun, sending even more charged particles stream-
ing out into space. Those that get trapped by the Earth's magnetic field give off light as they slow down, the whitish-green light
coming from excited molecules of oxygen, after a solar particle
has passed by. As much as two-thirds of the sky is sometimes
covered by flickering aurora at one time; you can't miss it.

It is quite a show, those rapid changes in the aurora within
seconds. A friend who grew up in Alaska once told me that they
used to see bands of light darting across the sky, that some people
even claimed to hear it snap and crackle during such whiplash

performances. One wonders what the Paleo-Indians, who hunted and fished their way across the Bering Strait, thought of such displays—whether they attracted them to the northern latitudes or made them hesitant to venture into such a realm. One can imagine the campfire councils of elders in Siberia, debating whether to retreat south or carry on toward those crazy displays in the northeastern skies.

In less than an hour, the aurora has faded out, the performance over. And I am left contemplating the backdrop: the Universe. The waters along the shore are advancing and retreating, like little fast-motion versions of the ice ages. I'm thinking about how any educated person can now know things about where humans come from, about how consciousness might arise, about how the heavens work, about how to prevent deadly diseases such as smallpox. Though imperfect descriptions, many a philosopher of the past would have sold his mother into slavery for a glimpse of them, and kings would have coveted a book describing them.

That our brains are capable of comprehending all this seems a result so out of proportion—at least, compared with the mundane "causes" that are offered as explanations for the evolution of human consciousness. But then emergent properties are usually a surprise, at least until you've seen a few additional examples. Anatomy may seldom take leaps, but physiology more frequently engages in a "conversion of function in anatomical continuity."

OTHERS HAVE CONCLUDED, despairing at what humans are doing to this planet, that the Earth would be better off without us—presumably on the assumption that a wiser creature might evolve from other forms of life if we weren't filling such a big niche.

But, quite aside from my inherent preferences for human companionship and my ingrained suspicion of any counsel of despair, I think that this attitude is a big mistake. It assumes that what we value—intelligence, ethics, creativity, stewardship, alleviation of suffering, whatever—is some universal principle of nature that will inevitably rise to the fore again as the mill of evolution grinds finer.

I also think it dangerous to conclude, as some do, that the "infiltration of mind into the universe will not be permanently

halted by any catastrophe or by any barrier that I can imagine."
It is not merely that one should be skeptical of these on Gould's
Principle ("Always be suspicious of conclusions that reinforce un-
critical hope and follow comforting traditions of Western thought")—
but that such pronouncements soothe us exactly when we should
be alert. There is some evidence for cleverness and reciprocal
altruism as being not-uncommon results of the climate fluctuations
that open up new niches—but no evidence whatsoever that they
regularly lead to intelligence or ethics, much less creativity or
stewardship. Or that if they do, they will be translated into
widely beneficial technologies.

On present evidence (which is approximately sufficient to
suggest that we've still got a lot to learn), I'd have to conclude
that intelligence, ethics, creativity, and stewardship are chance
developments in just one side branch of the great bush of species—
that our ancestors invented them, that they could be easily lost by
happenstance, that the chance of their ever being reinvented
during the lifetime of our sun is nil. We humans invented them
and we can, through poor stewardship, destroy them permanently.

The conservative assumption is that "we are it"—that there
is no backup intelligence who will conserve what we value if we
ourselves let it slip. This is not a counsel of despair—an avowal
that the heavens are lifeless and empty, and humans ephemeral—
but a stratagem of "God looks after those who look after themselves" while we further explore the universe of mind and matter,
acting as responsibly as if we were gods ourselves.

Disturbing thoughts—one hazard of taking a long walk at the
seashore under the starry skies.

*And so as we go whirling and twisting into the future, which
by God we could swear we did not make. . . .*
                                        NORMAN MAILER, 1969

LOOK-AHEAD SCENARIO-SPINNING is one of those uniquely
human characteristics such as music and dance, such as our
versatile language. While chimpanzees may occasionally plan
ahead a few minutes, as in the chimp who deceived his companions
with a false food-cry, we humans are always planning ahead to
tomorrow.

While the ice ages gave us the brains with which to plan ahead, we haven't in fact planned very far ahead in the past, not much further than providing for our children over the next decade. We've recently begun to plan centuries ahead, but only because we know the half-lives of our radioactive waste. Coping with a Dryas-like abrupt climate change, a frigid or arid millennium arriving within a few short years, may be the biggest challenge we have ever faced, and it remains to be seen if we have a brain capable of coping with the situation engendered by our overpollution and overpopulation.

For the last quarter-century or more, we have had the computing power to make working models of the atmosphere, one reason we can now estimate how long it will take for Arrhenius's greenhouse catastrophe to come true if we continue cutting down the forests and burning both them and the fossil fuels. Though a half-life only requires a simple calculation, other predictions are more complicated, as we have to make a working model of the processes involved. This use of simulation is unlike the familiar cockpit simulations for airplanes, which give pilots-in-training the ability to make mistakes harmlessly in real time. Instead we try to speed up time, so as to see what will happen to the system, but in a fraction of the time that the real thing takes to occur. That way we can observe the stabilities and dangerous oscillations after the computer crunches away for hours and days, simulating the complicated mix of processes. In physics, it was once thought that the important processes of the universe could be captured in a series of equations: Maxwell's equations, Einstein's, or those of quantum mechanics. Now we think in terms of simulating the processes, as only simple ones can be captured in equations.

Fast-motion simulation is augmented look-ahead, expanded consciousness. For the greenhouse warming, we've simulated 50 years ahead—and not liked the prognosis. The 12°C (22°F) heating of the high Canadian latitudes suggested by the simulations so far is particularly worrisome, as this seems liable to rearrange the jet stream across the United States, which in turn affects the movement of humid Gulf of Mexico air up into the agricultural Midwest, etc. And to release the tundra's huge quantities of methane (natural gas) upon thawing, thereby augmenting a greenhouse effect even more. From greenhouse to more greenhouse.

Good old positive feedback—or so it would seem. But qualita-tive arguments are always a little iffy, because words can be slippery. They serve to alert you to the need for a quantitative argument, and therefore massive simulations, collapsing decades of real time into months of computer time.

The records of the last 150,000 years . . . scream at us that the earth's climate system is highly sensitive to nudges. . . . By adding infrared-absorbing gases to the atmosphere, we are effectively playing Russian roulette with our climate.
the climatologist WALLACE S. BROECKER, 1989

THE ABRUPT CLIMATE CHANGE in the relatively recent past, merely 11,500 years ago, leads one to ask how often these things normally occur, even without a greenhouse warming. My count of the published records from the Greenland ice cores is roughly 20 cold spikes in the last 120,000 years for the North Atlantic region. And so that is 40 sudden changes, either sudden cooling or sudden warming, every 3,000 years on the average. It seems urgent that we use simulation to help figure out whether we might accelerate mode-switching behavior with our rapid forc-ing of the climate (via greenhouse gases), whether we might (as the first round of such simulations of the North Atlantic Current suggests) trip one of those abrupt climate changes.

I fear that what we're currently doing is the equivalent of one of those Hollywood depictions of a test pilot climbing into the brand-new experimental plane, revving it up, zooming off the runway, doing a few barrel rolls and screaming dives, and then

NORTH ATLANTIC COLD SPIKES
SINCE THE LAST INTERGLACIATION

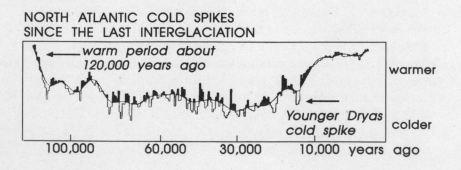

landing to the adulation of television cameras. No test pilot (or employer thereof) would dream of doing such a thing. He would slowly drive down the runway, observing how the plane handled at taxiway speeds. Then a week later he would run the plane up to takeoff speed—but abort the takeoff. After eventually taking off and flying around a little, he'd try slow turns, working up to higher accelerations in slow steps, looking carefully for any signs of instability—and backing off from it. He knows perfectly well, as does anyone experienced with nonlinear systems, that the surest way to discover something that you won't like—say, a tailspin or the airplane shaking itself apart—is to make changes quickly, to do something equivalent to those screaming dives or steep climbs.

Any sensible approach to changing the Earth's climate would emphasize very slow changes, retaining the ability to back off from any sign of an instability. Our present changes are rapid, almost abrupt. *And our ability to back off is limited by the population boom:* Humanity seems to take immediate advantage of any little improvement in living conditions by creating more mouths to feed—and so makes it very hard to back off on our carbon dioxide and methane production.

Various business-as-usual pundits have been heard to say that we should wait before taking action against greenhouse gases, until scientists are "more certain." They fail to recognize that scientists are typically uncertain: like the "But on the other hand" of ordinary discourse, scientific uncertainty is a mental technique that we use to make progress, constantly questioning the adequacy of any explanation that hasn't already survived a few decades; such uncertainty has to be distinguished from the broad scientific consensus that we are seriously polluting the atmosphere and modifying climate. Don't rock the boat of economic boom times, the pundits say, totally missing the point: *continuing the way we are heading is simply reckless*; it means that those leaders are quite willing, in order to maintain present comforts a few more years, to take irresponsible risks with our children's future. It is our *present* course and speed that deserves the pundit's skepticism; with a serious warning of shoals ahead, one slows down the ship rather than waiting for the first sighting. Or impact.

I do not believe in a fate that falls on men however they act;
but I do believe in a fate that falls on men unless they act.
                              G. K. CHESTERTON (1874–1936)

THIS AFTERNOON I heard several commonplace examples of mode-switching behavior as I was reading in the library. First, because the sailboats tend to turn around when they get close to this shore, I heard sails flapping and looked up to see a large sailboat as it was turned into the wind. Anytime a sailor tries to sail too close to the wind's direction, the sails start flapping from one position to another ("luffing"). Sometimes the boom even swings across the centerline when you don't want it to, heading toward a new stable position (and trying to take your head with it).

Then later while I was typing up some notes, I heard an outboard motor being shut down after one of the collecting boats came back to the Labs' dock. I didn't have to look up: I *know* that engine! The motor wouldn't die: it kept restarting itself after coughing to a near-standstill. Auto mechanics call it "run on" and readjust the carburetor so that the engine dies immediately after you turn the key off. Neurophysiologists who study epileptic seizures comment on "motorboating" too: the tonic phase of a seizure runs down the "batteries" of the nerve cells to the marginal point—and so they stop firing, then suddenly resume, then stop again. This is what produces the clonic phase of a tonic-clonic seizure: the patient may first be rigid, and then begins jerking spasmodically. His brain is motorboating (among other things).

Whenever a nonlinear system is changing from one stable state to another, it may go through a transition zone where it chatters back and forth, something like a faulty light switch that cannot decide whether to stay on or off. Chatter can be avoided by good design, as has happened with the most reliable of bistable devices, the flip-flop of digital circuits (which constitutes the basis of modern computer memories). But for most of evolution, including human brains and planetary climate, the good-enough solution hasn't eliminated a chattering zone.

Such may explain the European transition from full glacial times 20,000 years ago to the ice-free conditions of 8,000 years ago: Europe was lagging behind the Southern Hemisphere in warming up during the 15,000- to 13,000- year period. Then, within only a fraction of a century, Europe warmed a few degrees as if catching up: this "warming spike" is what is called the Allerød event at 13,000 years ago. Then, of course, at about 11,500 years, Europe flipped back to cold for 800 years (the Younger Dryas "cold spike"), then suddenly warmed (and continued warming more gradually into the interglacial). So the complete flip up-and-back-and-up-again took 2,300 years.

Most of the cold spikes in the last 120,000 years in the North Atlantic have probably lasted several centuries, rather than the eight centuries of the Younger Dryas. And even more rapid ones could have occurred without our knowing about it yet. Really rapid spikes are something that researchers will be looking for as they analyze cores with newer techniques. Some didn't take Dryas-like flips seriously for decades ("Just noise in those pollen records") because such layers didn't show up in all the various kinds of cores; spurious readings are one of the things that scientists have to guard against. But the seafloor (and likely some lake-bottom) layers had, alas, been smoothed out by the worms; their churning of the ocean floor served to smear

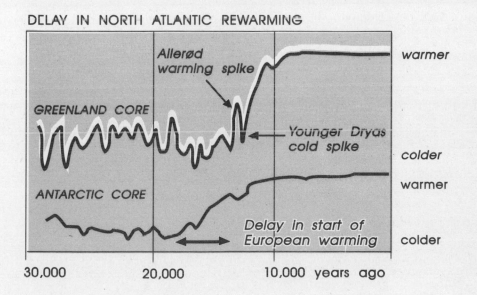

DELAY IN NORTH ATLANTIC REWARMING

The abrupt termination of the Younger Dryas

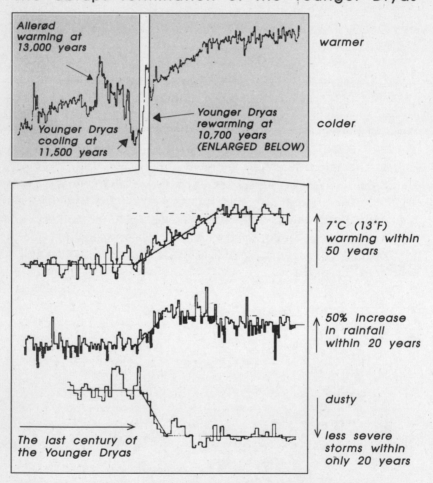

Allerød warming at 13,000 years

Younger Dryas cooling at 11,500 years

Younger Dryas rewarming at 10,700 years (ENLARGED BELOW)

warmer

colder

7°C (13°F) warming within 50 years

50% increase in rainfall within 20 years

dusty

less severe storms within only 20 years

The last century of the Younger Dryas

together the sediments from over 6,000 years, obscuring any rapid fluctuations.

Worms are the original time-averaging machines. While the ice layers and the tree rings haven't been similarly stirred, they too tend to "average" adjacent years, as the layering isn't watertight. And scientists often ignore the rapid change that gets through, if it doesn't fit their notions of slow trends (the most notorious example is when the Nimbus satellite program missed detecting the dramatic "ozone hole" that developed near the South Pole in the early eighties; in analyzing the data radioed down, its scientists programmed their computers to disregard as spurious any departures from the norm of more than a few percent). For many reasons, records of sudden change were likely lost; *we have to assume that abrupt shifts are even more frequent*, that we've seen only the more dramatic ones.

If we gradually change the parameters in the equations, the behaviour of [a typical nonlinear living] system will also change gradually; for example, if the behaviour is to oscillate, then the period and amplitude of the oscillation will change gradually. But ultimately, as we continue to change the parameters, we reach a threshold, or "bifurcation," at which the behaviour changes dramatically: for example, the system may cease to oscillate, and start to grow exponentially [or vice versa]. This, I take it, is a mathematical description of the change from quantity into quality. When one has played with a few systems of this kind, one has a better feel for how things are likely to behave.

the mathematical biologist JOHN MAYNARD SMITH, 1988

FLIPS ARE THE FOREMOST REASON why I worry about the rapid warming of today: we have no information about what modes lie ahead, how our climate might jump. The Earth on its own has never explored the region into which we're heading, at least not in a comparable way, and we have no idea what strange chattering is likely to develop on the way there. Judging from the history of the last Ice Age, Europe is particularly prone to mode-switching—but then the North Atlantic is far better studied via ocean-bottom cores than oceans elsewhere, and it has the wormfree Greenland ice sheets to provide a second glimpse of its history. The Pacific Ocean might well have such mode-switching too, perhaps an exaggerated version of El Niño-to-La Niña cycling.

If climate change happens gradually over a century's time, we can imagine coping—but if it keeps flipping back and forth, we'll be like a country fighting a war on two fronts, frantically shuttling troops back and forth and generally disrupting civilization at the same time. Except we'll be trying to build new dams and pipelines, grow new forests, build new cities—a century's tasks compressed into a decade, all while combatting famines and the political instability that goes with them. And then the climate flips again (probably without warning), and everything has to shift to another front, such mammoth tasks being repeated elsewhere—if we are able to muster the efforts required (a 99 percent decrease in population might be more likely).

About the only way out of the Dryas-style threats to humanity that I can see is if we become considerably more conversant with boom-time reproductive physiology and psychology. And considerably smarter through the use of computers, coming to understand the coupling between the ocean currents and the regional climates well enough to simulate them. Occasionally there is a bonus from predictive simulations: Sometimes you also learn how to give the system a little push in a desired direction. Even in simple systems, such as when pushing a child on a playground swing, there is a right time and place to apply an effective push.

For nonlinear systems such as ocean currents with all their eddies, it is harder to know when and where to push. But modeling may show how to try, suggest the amount of power needed. As chaos studies have illustrated, little changes can sometimes have big effects down the road. Perhaps by heating up an island-sized patch of ocean surface at the critical place and creating some more space-occupying back-eddies, a mode-switch will be prevented by plugging the alternative path. Seeding the clouds, in the manner we try to clear the December fog off airport runways in Seattle, might allow the sunlight to heat up the ocean beneath. Or we might station satellites in space, big mirrors that reflect sunlight down on that patch of ocean. Or we might cool or warm the ocean by managing the plankton's productivity in the surface layers.

If the deep-water production off Iceland became marginal (and some simulations of how greenhouse warming should affect ocean circulation suggest that deep-water production will substantially decrease there in the next few decades) we might encourage the evaporative losses that create the hypersaline sinking (and so attract even more North Atlantic Current up from the tropics) via spreading chemicals on the surface. Augmenting the evaporation rate is what the Israelis do in their southwest corner of the Dead Sea, to speed potash production. If modeling could tell us where and when to spread the surfactants, such a maneuver in the North Atlantic might help stabilize a shaky system, stave off a revisitation of the Younger Dryas.

Via some such maneuver, we could conceivably get ourselves out of this mess, at least for a little while. If we succeed, it will be because we've made a good working model of the system and played around with scenarios for the future, seeing which is best, and figuring out how to implement it. That's the exact same procedure, on a larger scale, as a college student goes through when trying to select a suitable career. It's what family planning attempts to do. It's the business plan that the bank wants to see before lending money.

It is not what the apes do; like people who "live from hand to mouth," apes may plan an hour ahead but seldom organize for tomorrow. These computer models will again extend the time scale of human consciousness: from decades to centuries, perhaps even to millennia. They will get us into the alternative-futures business in a big way. Conceivably this next step in human evolution will also save our civilization.

Abrupt climate change could happen tomorrow, at the rate we're jostling the system via burning fossil fuels, cutting forests, producing methane and refrigerator gases (most of which are secondary consequences of more mouths to feed, not inadvertent technology). So I don't mean to sound optimistic. The state of the modeling art, and the size of computers, is still a generation or more away from this kind of detailed knowledge.

And science itself is far too small an enterprise, given the size of the population and pollution challenges, plus the chattering climatic ones. The allowances that parents give their children for spending on candy and popular music are likely more than governments provide for all of basic science. To combat the problems that overpopulation and overpollution are earning us will probably require a quadrupling of the scientific enterprise, at the least. Plus the kind of public planning that, heretofore, has only occurred in time of war: it's only a little matter of overhauling our entire agricultural-industrial-transportation system, worldwide.

DESPITE OUR PROFESSED CONCERN with the value of human life, we seem to be asking for really serious trouble, of the sort that causes famines and revolutions—and, at the same time, prevents effective technological response by destroying economies and the scientific enterprise. Humanity has greatly overextended itself in the last few decades, largely via population growth and its associated cutting and burning of the forests.

Foresight used to be a frill, a spare-time use of the neural machinery for throwing or language, something our ancestors would occasionally use instead of a traditional, gene-encouraged behavior. Then foresight made possible our plan-ahead consciousness; it greatly expanded our niche and evolved our technological, science-based culture (not to mention greatly expanding worry and suffering). But now an augmented version of foresight has become essential, if we are to extract ourselves from this mess we've made of the Earth and its climate. That we should need major climatic plan-ahead to get ourselves out of the situation created by the minor plan-ahead abilities arising from climate fluctuations—that's the great irony.

The fickle climate giveth, and the fickle climate taketh away. I somehow doubt that we will appreciate the poetic quality of "our just desserts," should we not meet the challenge. The Earth's ocean-atmosphere-biosphere system is reminiscent of an Old Testament God—lots of rules and no mercy.

To go along complacently in the face of greenhouse and population developments recalls *Typhoon*, the Joseph Conrad novel that tells of the imperturbable Captain MacWhirr. He was at sea—and in more ways than one—in the Indian Ocean. This leader of men lacked the wit to imagine the force and ferocity of cyclonic winds. Despite a falling barometer and other ominous portents of a typhoon that would all but sink his ship, MacWhirr kept steady to his course, occasionally murmuring, "There's some dirty weather knocking about."

Here on the level sand
Between the sea and land,
What shall I build or write
Against the fall of night?
Tell me of runes to grave
That hold the bursting wave,
Or bastions to design
For longer date than mine.
          A. E. HOUSMAN (1859–1936)

POSTSCRIPT

I am hardly the first neurobiologist to be attracted by the ice-age puzzles—that was surely Fridtjof Nansen, codiscoverer of the neuron doctrine in 1888, who also made the first crossing of the Greenland ice cap, then led the 1895 Arctic expedition. He readily made the transition to a seemingly distant scientific field because he came from the seafaring culture of Norway, grew up in its ice-scarred landscape. To the extent that this modern neurobiologist has been able to comprehend the scientific fields associated with the ice ages, it is also because of the boost that I have been afforded by my local milieu.

In my case, it is not so much the glacier-carved features of Puget Sound as the unusual Quaternary Research Center at the University of Washington. Its interdisciplinary approach to the problems of the ice ages has made possible my education in areas ranging from geophysics to climatology to paleontology to archaeology. While seemingly far from neurobiology, they are most relevant to understanding the brain modifications that set us apart from the apes. Though I have not been formally affiliated with the center, its faculty have been most helpful; in particular, they have organized an outstanding lecture series each and every year, featuring several dozen visiting speakers. Thanks to them, I have been able to think about some of the ways that brain, behavior, and evolutionary principles interact with climate.

The ideas in this book owe a great deal to my frequent scientific discussions with Katherine Graubard and to my more occasional ones over the years with Douglas Anderson, Myrdene Anderson, Derek Booth, Loring Brace, Stewart Brand, David Brin, Beatrice Bruteau, Iain Davidson, Dan Dennett, John Edwards, Dean Falk, Dan and Esther Gardner, Kathleen Gibson, Susan Goldin-Meadow, Nick Humphrey, Barbara Isaac, the late Glynn Isaac, Harry Jerison, Stan Kater, Kevin Kelly, Marcel Kinsbourne, Karen Landahl, Joan Lockard, John Loeser, Jenny and Ray Lund, Peter MacNeilage, Alex Marshack, William McGrew, George and Linda Ojemann, Astrida Blukis Onat, John Palka, John Pfeiffer, Martin Pickford, Harvey Pough, Howard Rheingold, Vince Sarich, Sue Savage-Rumbaugh, Woody Sullivan, Jill Tarter, Nick Toth, Barbara Wakamoto, Dennis Willows, Jan Wind, J. Z. Young, and Adrienne Zihlman (in case you are wondering, they are not particularly the artificial intelligentsia and the cognitive cognoscenti; they include nine neurobiologists plus five in the neurosurgery-neurology-neuropsychology spectrum, seven archaeologists and six other anthropologists, five primatologists, four scientifically-minded writers, four linguistics types, two philosophers, two astronomers, a novelist, a geologist, a developmental biologist, and an ecologist). Leslie Meredith and Blanche Kazon Graubard have contributed much through their editing of the manuscript and frequent good advice. Kristin Marks Anderson helped out regarding Alaska, Gareth Anderson with the hand axes, and Yuan Wen with some of the illustrations. I thank them all.

I must also express my gratitude to the Rockefeller Foundation for its hospitality in Bellagio, Italy, during our discussions on human consciousness at Villa Serbelloni (located on the cleaver of the ancient glacier that came down Lake Como); the Wenner-Gren Foundation for Anthropological Research for sponsoring the discussions in Portugal on the co-evolution of tools, language, and intelligence; and the International Astronomical Union for a travel grant. Portions of the book were written in the scholarly ambiance afforded by the Marine Biological Laboratory on Cape Cod and the University of Washington's Friday Harbor Laboratories in the San Juan Islands. To the extent that I have achieved some overview of climate and intelligence, it is thanks to the perspective contributed by such friends and places.

W.H.C.

NOTES

1. Following the Gulf Stream to Europe: Tracking Climate Change and Human Evolution

2   ROBERT ARDREY, *The Hunting Hypothesis* (Atheneum, 1976).

4   LIONEL E. JACKSON, JR., and ALEJANDRA DUK-RODKIN, "Geology of the ice-free corridor." University of Washington lecture (19 January 1988). E. JAMES DIXON, "Eastern Beringian paleoindians and the paleoenvironments of the ice-free corridor." University of Washington lecture (1 March 1988). MICHAEL WENDORF, "Diabetes, the ice free corridor, and the paleoindian settlement of North America." *American Journal of Physical Anthropology* 79(4):503–520 (1989). JOSEPH H. GREENBERG, CHRISTY G. TURNER II, and STEPHEN L. ZEGURA, "The settlement of the Americas: A comparison of the linguistic, dental, and genetic evidence." *Current Anthropology* 27(5):477–497 (1986).

5   For the general anthropological background concerning ice-age Europe, see JOHN GOWLETT, *Ascent to Civilization: The Archaeology of Early Man* (Knopf, 1984). For the general background on the ice-age theories, see JOHN IMBRIE and KATHERINE P. IMBRIE, *Ice Ages* (Harvard University Press, 1986); JOHN GRIBBIN and MARY GRIBBIN, *Children of the Ice: Climate and Human Orgins* (Basil Blackwell, 1990); and WALLACE S. BROECKER and GEORGE H. DENTON, "What drives

glacial cycles?" *Scientific American* 262(1):48–56 (January 1990). For the greenhouse, see WARREN M. WASHINGTON, "Where's the heat?" *Natural History* (3):66–72 (1990).

6   Initially, several layers of Dryas pollen showed up in Denmark, but only the more recent of them was seen elsewhere, hence the "Younger Dryas" terminology that is conventional for this period. From a lecture by DOROTHY M. PETEET, "Younger Dryas oscillation: A late-glacial example of abrupt climatic change," University of Washington (28 February 1989).

The basic data on the cold spikes is in: W. DANSGAARD, H. B. CLAUSEN, N. GUNDESTRUP, C. U. HAMMER, S. F. JOHNSEN, P. M. KRISTINSDOTTIR, and N. REEH, "A new Greenland deep ice core." *Science* 218:1273–1277 (1982). For droughts, see F. ALAYNE STREET-PERROTT and R. ROSS PERROTT, "Abrupt climate fluctuations in the tropics: The influence of Atlantic Ocean circulation." *Nature* 343:607–612 (15 February 1990).

COHMAP MEMBERS, "Climatic changes of the last 18,000 years: Observations and model simulations." *Science* 241:1043–1052 (1988).

The timing of the termination of the Dryas at about 10,700 years ago is in W. DANSGAARD, J. W. C. WHITE, and S. J. JOHNSEN, "The abrupt termination of the Younger Dryas climate event." *Nature* 339:532–534 (15 June 1989).

The basics on the carbon budget of the Earth can be found in RICHARD A. HOUGHTON and GEORGE M. WOODWELL, "Global climatic change." *Scientific American* 260(4):36–44 (April 1989).

DAVID A. PEEL, "Ice-age clues for warmer world." *Nature* 339:508–509 (15 June 1989).

WALLACE S. BROECKER, DOROTHY M. PETEET, and DAVID RIND, "Does the ocean-atmosphere system have more than one stable mode of operation." *Nature* 315:21–26 (2 May 1985). WALLACE S. BROECKER, "Unpleasant surprises in the greenhouse?" *Nature* 328:123–126 (9 June 1987). And BROECKER et al, "The chronology of the deglaciation: Implications to the cause of the Younger Dryas cooling." *Paleoceanography* 3:1–19 (1988). RICHARD G. FAIRBANKS, "A 17,000-year glacio-eustatic sea level record: Influence of glacial melting rates on the Younger Dryas event and deep-ocean circulation." *Nature* 342:637–642 (7 December 1989). E. JANSEN and T. VEUM, "Evidence for two-step deglaciation and its impact on North Atlantic deep-water circulation." *Nature* 343:612–616 (15 February 1990). HANS OESCHGER and C. C. LANGWAY, editors, "The Environmental Record in Glaciers and Ice Sheets." *Dahlem Workshop* 8 (Wiley, 1989). HANS OESCHGER and H.

U. Dütsch, "Ozone and the Greenhouse Effect." *Nature* 339:19 (4 May 1989). Robert J. Charlson, James E. Lovelock, Meinrat O. Andreae, and Stephen G. Warren, "Oceanic phytoplankton, atmospheric sulphur, cloud albedo, and climate." *Nature* 326:655–661 (1987). And the news stories regarding cloud cover and albedo, "Pinning down clouds" in *Scientific American* 260(5):22–24 (May 1989) and "Cloudy concerns" in *Science News* 136:106–110 (12 August 1989).

8   Irish elk, from Anthony D. Barnosky, "Paleoecology and extinction of Irish elk (*Megaloceros giganteus*)," lecture at the University of Washington (13 February 1990); see also his " 'Big game' extinction caused by climatic change: Irish elk (*Megaloceros giganteus*) in Ireland," *Quaternary Research* 25:128–135 (1986).

9   Quotation from Edwin Dobb, "The big picture." *The Sciences* 29(2):44–50 (1989).

9   Volcano ash potentially rewarming Earth by changing albedo: it all depends on how thick it is, whether it warms or insulates. The dark medial stripes of many glaciers, from where lateral debris has collected as two smaller glaciers merge, often causes the underlying ice to melt *slower* than the surroundings. Glacial "tables" provide another example: If a rock on the glacial surface cannot warm up enough during the day to transmit heat to the underlying ice, then the surrounding ice will melt faster, leaving the rock atop a pedestal. I thank the geologist Neil Fahy for pointing this out to me in the Gulf of Alaska.

9   Stephen E. Zebiak, "Ill Winds: How events in the tropics throw the world's weather out of whack." *The Sciences* 29(2):26–31 (1989). And for historical data, the news article "La Niña's big chill replaces El Niño," *Science* 241:1037–1038 (26 August 1988).

14   W. S. Broecker, letter in *Science* 245:451 (4 August 1989).

2. Incrementing Intelligence: A Principle of Nature?

16   Francis Bacon, *The Advancement of Learning* (1640).

17   Brain/body ratios, see Harry Jerison, *Evolution of the Brain and Intelligence* (Academic Press, 1973), for hominid brain/body estimates, see Robert Foley and Robin Dunbar,

"Beyond the bones of contention," *New Scientist* 1686:37–41 (14 October 1989), especially the boxed data from HENRY MCHENRY and LESLIE AIELLO.

20   Ants are a particularly good example of how "intelligent" behavior seems to be the collective property of a minimum number of contributors. See THOMAS D. SEELEY and ROYCE A. LEVIEN, "A colony of mind: The beehive as thinking machine." *The Sciences* 27(4):38–43 (1987). NIGEL R. FRANKS, "Army ants: A collective intelligence." *American Scientist* 77:139–145 (March-April, 1989).

Dictionary definitions of intelligence, cleverness, etc., are of little help. Some of the more thoughtful distinctions regarding intelligence are to be found in HORACE B. BARLOW's "Intelligence, guesswork, language," *Nature* 304:207–209 (1983), and his entry "Intelligence: The Art of Good Guesswork" in *The Oxford Companion to the Mind*, edited by RICHARD L. GREGORY, pp. 381–383 (Oxford, 1987). But pigeons are pretty good at guessing new perceptual categories, one of the reasons why I emphasize inventing and judging "novel courses of action" as a basic aspect of human intelligent behavior.

22   W. H. CALVIN, *The Cerebral Symphony: Seashore Reflections on the Structure of Consciousness* (Bantam, 1989), chapter 1. In that book and the present one, I have started the evolution story with the animals of the last 100 million years; for a more complete time scale of evolutionary processes, see my third book, *The River That Flows Uphill: A Journey from the Big Bang to the Big Brain* (Macmillan, 1986; Sierra Club Books softcover edition, 1987).

24   For a view that says language is the big step to becoming intelligent, see E. MACPHAIL, "Vertebrate intelligence: The null hypothesis." *Philosophical Transactions of the Royal Society of London* B308:37–51 (1985). Tool use isn't necessarily "intelligent": BENJAMIN B. BECK, "Tools and intelligence." In: *Animal Intelligence*, edited by R. J. HOAGE and LARRY GOLDMAN, (Washington, D.C., Smithsonian Institution Press, 1986) pp. 135–147.

24   OLIVER SACKS, *Seeing Voices: A Journey Into the World of the Deaf* (University of California Press, 1989), p. 40. Many prelingually-deaf children raised without Sign will, however, develop their own "home sign" system of much greater sophistication than that of their caregivers: see SUSAN GOLDIN-

MEADOW and H. FELDMAN, "The development of language-like communication without a language model." *Science* 197:401–403 (1977). While this indicates that the developing brain can "invent" language without hearing speech, the prospects of such children are still bleak.

27   W. H. CALVIN, "The brain as a Darwin Machine." *Nature* 330:33–34 (5 November 1987). An interesting predecessor from the computer science community to the Darwin Machine concept can be seen in JOHN H. HOLLAND, K. J. HOLYOAK, R. E. NISBETT, and P. R. THAGARD, *Induction: Processes of Inference, Learning, and Discovery* (MIT Press, 1986). Though neither draws explicitly on the serial-ordered aspect of DNA bases and of antibody amino acids that characterize darwinism in our best-understood systems, Holland's genetic algorithms is the closer analogy to Darwin Machines creating strings of movement commands than is the "neural darwinism" seen in GERALD M. EDELMAN, *The Remembered Present: A Biological Theory of Consciousness* (Basic Books, 1989). My review of Edelman's earlier book draws some distinctions: W. H. CALVIN, "A global brain theory," *Science* 240:1802–1803 (24 June 1988).

29   NICHOLAS KEYNES HUMPHREY's book *The Inner Eye* (Faber and Faber, 1986) is a good exposition on the role of social life in shaping up intelligence, and FRANS DE WAAL's *Peacemaking Among Primates* (Harvard University Press, 1989) has many examples of "look-ahead" in a social setting. If you want more, there is *Machiavellian Intelligence*, edited by RICHARD BYRNE and ANDREW WHITEN (Oxford University Press, 1988). More conventional analyses of animal mentality can be found in HOAGE and GOLDMAN (1986); and DONALD R. GRIFFIN, *Animal Thinking* (Harvard University Press, 1984).

33   CHARLES DARWIN, *On the Origin of Species* (John Murray, 1859), p. 194.

34   HERBERT A. SIMON, *Models of Thought* (Yale University Press, 1979; first appeared in a 1956 paper), p. 20. Closely related to satisficing is *good-enough engineering*, whose physiological implications are discussed by LLOYD D. PARTRIDGE, "The good enough calculi of evolving control systems: Evolution is not engineering," *American Journal of Physiology* 242:R173–R177 (1982).

34   Copernicus's sun-centered model actually wasn't simpler than Ptolemy's Earth-centered one, because Copernicus used circu-

lar orbits. It wasn't until Kepler used ellipses that things simplified. See JAMES TREFIL, *Reading the Mind of God* (Scribner's, 1989).

36   Increasing body size is another drive toward behavioral complexity, in the analysis of JAMES TYLER BONNER, *The Evolution of Complexity* (Princeton University Press, 1988). But body size is surprisingly labile: A. M. LISTER, "Rapid dwarfing of red deer on Jersey in the last interglacial," *Nature* 342:539–542 (30 November 1989). And, for an excellent example of how predation changes the rates of somatic growth and reproductive maturity (and makes bodies much larger and longer-lasting), see TODD A. CROWL and ALAN P. COVICH, "Predator-induced life-history shifts in a freshwater snail," *Science* 247:949–951 (23 February 1990). For a survey of dwarf species on the Mediterranean islands, see PAUL SONDAAR, "The island sweepstakes," *Natural History* 95(9):50–57 (September 1986).

Some of the Hungary-specific material in this chapter first appeared in somewhat different form in my article, "Fast tracks to intelligence (considerations from neurobiology and evolutionary biology)," in *Bioastronomy—The Next Steps*, edited by G. MARX (Kluwer, 1988), pp. 237–245.

37   DARWIN (1859), p. 191.

40   Flickers, cited in DAVID P. BARASH, *The Hare and the Tortoise* (Viking, 1986), p. 84.

41   Chewing ends of sticks: Y. SUGIYAMA et al., "Ant-catching wands of wild chimpanzees at Bossou, Guinea." *Folia Primatologica* 51(1):56–60 (1988).

42   Much has been made of the tendency for behavior to lead the way in evolution ("Free will can guide the evolutionary process" and other such upbeat pronouncements). It was first formulated (in somewhat more obscure terms) in 1896 when three different scientists discovered it: James Mark Baldwin, Henry F. Osborn, and Lloyd Morgan. Today it tends to go under the name "the Baldwin Effect" or the motto "form follows function." It marks the last big discovery of the nineteenth-century followers of Charles Darwin, who clearly laid the foundation for how we now think about thought processes (I describe animal decision-making and human Darwin Machines more fully in *The Cerebral Symphony*). But

their work was largely forgotten when the early mutations-are-everything geneticists turned their backs on Darwin and the psychologists became so enamored of the behaviorist and Freudian extremes that they could tolerate no other way of looking at things. Population thinking, that concern with the changing statistical profile of whole groups which is the key feature of Darwinism, does not come naturally to most humans, who more readily identify with an "essence," that "typical type." For the Baldwin Effect, see ROBERT J. RICHARDS, *Darwin and the Emergence of Evolutionary Theories of Mind and Behavior* (University of Chicago Press, 1987), p. 452.

44   DARWIN (1859), p. 182. LOREN EISELEY, *The Man Who Saw Through Time*, (Scribner's, 1973), p. 95.

3. Finding a Fast Track to the Big Brain: How Climate Pumps Up Complexity

46   PAUL GAUGUIN, as quoted by HUMPHREY (1986), pp. 172–173.

47   Reconstructing hominid evolution using cues from the great apes: see the various contributions in *The Evolution of Human Behavior: Primate Models*, edited by WARREN G. KINZEY (State University of New York Press, 1987).

48   KENNETH BOULDING, quoted in *The Environmental Crisis*, edited by HAROLD W. HELFRICH (Yale University Press, 1970), p. 160.

49   RUSSELL H. TUTTLE, "The pitted pattern of Laetoli feet." *Natural History* (3):60–65 (1990). R. H. TUTTLE, D. M. WEBB, and M. BAKSH, "The pattern of little feet." *American Journal of Physical Anthropology* 78(2):316 (1989). "The Laetoli G prints are indistinguishable from those of habitually barefoot *Homo sapiens*."

51   SUE TAYLOR PARKER and KATHLEEN RITA GIBSON, "A developmental model for the evolution of language and intelligence in early hominids," in *Behavioral and Brain Sciences* 2:367–408 (1979), identify "extractive foraging of embedded foods" as creating selection for tool use, and so on to intelligence.

51   Chimpanzee sign language references, see *Teaching Sign Language to Chimpanzees*, edited by R. ALLEN GARDNER, BEATRIX

T. GARDNER, and THOMAS E. VANCANTFORT (State University of New York Press, 1989).

51   Hay plays an interesting role midway in civilization, as FREEMAN DYSON notes in *Infinite in All Directions* (Harper and Row, 1988). The Roman Empire didn't need to cut grass in the autumn and store it for winter "grazing" because in the Mediterranean basin grass grows well enough in winter for animals to graze; the idea of hay was unknown to the Roman Empire but was known to every village of medieval Europe. Keeping large numbers of horses and cows alive through the winter aided in the development of the northern population centers such as Paris and Berlin, whose economies came to dominate the Mediterranean ones.

53   RONALD M. NOWAK and JOHN L. PARADISO, *Walker's Mammals of the World*, 4th edition (Johns Hopkins University Press, 1983). Black bears have litters of one to four, usually two or three.

57   Mutation rate, see J. S. JONES, "A tale of three cities." *Nature* 339:176–177 (18 May 1989).

59   LOREN EISELEY, *The Immense Journey* (Doubleday, 1957), p. 51 and p. 54.

60   The illustration of the last five major ice ages has been adapted from figures 40 and 48 in IMBRIE and IMBRIE (1986); based on cores from the floor of the Indian Ocean, these records have less regional bias than the Greenland ice cores (which tend to reflect the surface temperature of the North Atlantic Ocean) used for similar illustrations in chapters five and ten.

61   HERBERT A. SIMON, *Reason in Human Affairs* (Stanford University Press, 1983), p. 44.

61   Woodpeckers' empty niche, see ERNST MAYR, *Animal Species and Evolution* (Harvard University Press, 1963), p. 87.

62   *Epidemic* originally meant to spread beyond the local deme; *endemic* means only within a local population, as in "this deme is the only one that exists anywhere," a species unique to the locality.

65   MATT CARTMILL, "Misdeeds in anthropology: A review of *Bones,
            Bodies, Behavior,* edited by GEORGE W. STOCKING, JR." *Science*
            244:858–9 (1989).

66   ERIK ERIKSON, *Identity: Youth and Crisis* (Norton, 1968).

68   MAYR (1963), p. 371.

68   Most such refuges have been logged off, their ecosystems
            greatly disrupted, but a few remain. A conflict between dif-
            ferent branches of science occurred in the late 1980s, when
            astronomers wanted to build yet another telescope atop the
            mountains of southern Arizona in the midst of one of the last
            Pleistocene refugia, misrepresenting the biologists' ancient
            ecosystem concerns as a fight over "just one more kind of
            squirrel." The U.S. Congress, familiar with squirrels but not
            with ecosystems, overrode the environmental protection laws
            in 1988 at the request of Arizona politicians concerned that
            the construction and operations money might go to some
            other deserving state without a Pleistocene refuge to destroy.
            A partial account can be found in *The Scientist* (22 January
            1990), pp. 4–5.

71   LEWIS THOMAS, *Late Night Thoughts on Listening to Mahler's
            Ninth Symphony* (Viking, 1983), p. 15.

4. Neandertal Country:
Some Consequences of a Fickle Climate

72   HEINZ PAGELS, *The Dreams of Reason* (Simon and Schuster,
            1988), p. 161.

75   JOHN IMBRIE and KATHERINE P. IMBRIE, *Ice Ages* (Harvard Uni-
            versity Press, 1986); the Milankovitch quote is from pp. 102–103.

76   R. E. EDWARDS, J. H. CHEN, T.-L. KU, and G. J. WASSERBURG,
            "Precise timing of the last interglacial period from mass spec-
            troscopic determination of Thorium-230 in corals." *Science*
            236:1547–1553 (19 June 1987).

77   The illustration of encephalization quotient is taken from the
            work of HENRY MCHENRY and of LESLIE AIELLO featured in
            the *New Scientist* of 14 October 1989, p. 39.

77   ERIK TRINKAUS, "The fate of the Neandertals." Lecture at
        University of Washington (6 February 1990); see his "The
        Neandertals and modern human origins," *Annual Review of
        Anthropology* 15:193–218 (1986).

77   Stature in aboriginal groups, see K. L. BEALS, C. L. SMITH,
        and S. M. DODD, "Brain size, cranial morphology, climate,
        and time machines." *Current Anthropology* 25:301–330 (1984).

80   Gracile chimpanzees, see ADRIENNE L. ZIHLMAN, JOHN E.
        CRONIN, D. L. CRAMER, VINCENT M. SARICH, "Pygmy chim-
        panzee as a possible prototype for common ancestor of hu-
        mans, chimpanzees and gorillas." *Nature* 275(5682):744–746
        (1978). RANDALL L. SUSMAN, "Pygmy chimpanzees and com-
        mon chimpanzees: Models for the behavioral ecology of the
        earliest hominids," in *The Evolution of Human Behavior:
        Primate Models*, edited by WARREN G. KINZEY (State Uni-
        versity of New York Press, 1987), pp. 72–86.

82   CHARLES DARWIN, as quoted by ERNST MAYR in *Scientific
        American* (March 1990), p. 37.

82   "Juvenile playing-around tendencies" may be useful for dis-
        covering a new niche, but aren't as likely to be important for
        the maintenance of it, if culturally enlightened robusts can
        equally well exploit it. My guess is that shortened generation
        time was typically the major factor, with some other aspect of
        juvenilized brains maintaining the gracile form in the face of
        harder times.

83   The quote is from STEPHEN JAY GOULD's column in *Natural
        History* (November 1986), p. 28. The basic reference on brain/
        body ratio is JERISON (1973).

84   "Features by which humans differ from apes. . . ." For start-
        ers, see the list in RICHARD D. ALEXANDER's *Darwinism and
        Human Affairs* (University of Washington Press, 1979), pp.
        209 ff.

84   ALISTER HARDY's hypothesis can be best read in ELAINE
        MORGAN's *The Aquatic Ape* (Stein and Day, 1982); see her
        regular updates in *New Scientist*. For some aspects of aquatic
        ape proposals and their chronology, see Mile 136–137 of my
        1986 book, *The River that Flows Uphill*. For bonobos (the
        gracile chimpanzees) as evidencing some aquatic adaptations,

see FRANS DE WAAL's *Peacemaking Among Primates* (Harvard University Press, 1989), pp. 183–186.

84   Savannah theory restatement: C. OWEN LOVEJOY, "The origin of man." *Science* 211:341–350 (23 January 1981).

86   "20 percent of land covered . . ." About 10 million square miles of land are covered at the peak of an ice age (see IMBRIE and IMBRIE, 1986). My calculation goes as follows: Subtracting 5 million for uninhabited Greenland, Canada, and the northern U.S. leaves 5 million for covering northern Europe and Asia. Europe-Asia-Africa total 32 million square miles, though perhaps a third of Africa and of Central Asia is only marginally habitable. Thus 5 million reduces the inhabitable 25 million by 20 percent; a meltback would expand the remaining core by 25 percent.

86   Latitude effect on stature summarized by BEALS et al. (1984).

87   Calories from gathering vs. hunting, see RICHARD B. LEE, in *Man the Hunter*, edited by R. B. LEE and I. DeVORE (Aldine, 1968), pp. 30–48.

87   No, I'm not slighting the southern mid-latitudes in temperate zone roles: neither New Zealand nor Chile-Argentina had hominids until 1,200 and 31,000 years ago, respectively, after modern *Homo sapiens* arrived.

88   "This pump is even simpler than Darwin's": Note, however, that this expand-the-periphery-but-compress-the-center principle won't work in every case of population fluctuation. The dramatic frontier-type advantage is dependent on the relative rates of frontier movement (the no-land-rush qualification); it may not apply to the end of a drought where the remaining population can quickly space itself out to occupy the newly productive land. And it depends on shaping up a somewhat different frontier genome by special selection pressures (the annual round of selection associated with winter); the margins of a drought-devastated region are unlikely to present opportunities comparable to the herds of megafauna attracted by the good grazing on the glacial margins.

Still, though dramatic accelerations of gradual evolution depend on such qualifications about the rates at which frontiers move and specialize, pumping the periphery of the habitat may be a more general principle relevant to the slower evolution of many species: selection pressures are always the most severe where the species is precariously adapted to its niche, such as at the margins of a habitat. Because climates are always fluctuating to cause substantial alterations in the habitat size and thus population levels (e.g., El Niño causes population crashes among Pacific birds and fish), the frontier-type representation in the total genome may be pumped up repeatedly even in the general case.

This is a simple model, assuming a doughnutlike arrangement: a ring around the outside of the main population with 15 percent of the total area. In real life, it was surely more complicated, if only from the geography having inhabitable areas. As the crows of Europe demonstrate, temperate zone species may be pushed south into refugia that are isolated from one another (eastern and western Mediterranean peninsulas), rather than continuously spread around a single ring. While there is some tendency for temperate zone and central populations to constantly mix, this stirring of the gene pool will be minimized during the expansion phase, the crucial period for this analysis. The invention of boats during the most recent glaciation may have promoted greater mixing of peripheral and central populations.

Fragmentation of the frontier has two consequences, both of which speed up evolution even more. Speciation becomes more likely, as in the crows. And secondly, the contracted population has more of its population living on a margin of the habitat than they would joined into one continuous ring—and if one lives on the margins of the range, living conditions are marginal. The perimeter-to-population ratio (just a special case of surface-to-volume ratio reasoning) would be even higher, with a higher percentage of the population living in marginal circumstances that speed up natural selection's modifications to the population.

FRANCIS BACON and CHARLES DARWIN speculated on reasons for the frequent dominance of northern faunas over southern: see LOREN EISELEY, *Darwin's Century* (Doubleday, 1958), pp. 10–11. For flora, however, Europe is something of a special case, with many fewer species of plants than North America or east Asia. As the British botanist CHARLES TURNER explained ("Plant extinctions of the European Quaternary," lecture at University of Washington, 9 January 1990), this is probably because the Mediterranean limits the southern retreat of species during an ice advance, so that species go extinct more readily there rather than surviving in refugia. For a review of how gene flow and regional specialization interact, see N. H. BARTON and G. M. HEWITT, "Adaptation, speciation, and hybrid zones," *Nature* 341:497–503 (12 October 1989).

88   Speciation is, in a sense, more common in the relatively static tropics—the way that every valley in Hawaii seems to have its own endemic species of fruit fly. But my argument on reproductive quasi-isolation in islandlike refugia seems particularly appropriate to temperate-zone hominid evolution, given that the various isolated groups are always coming back to potentially intermix with each other at each major meltback: whatever reproductive isolation is achieved during geographic isolation will serve to limit backsliding during boom times.

90   Because there is no land for interglacial expansion in Africa, southern Africa might house the most conservative type in spite of its borderline-temperate climate; because of the bottleneck at Suez, Africa might also be invaded more slowly from Eurasia than in a simple model. Southern Africa does have one of the oldest types of mtDNA: REBECCA L. CANN, MARK STONEKING, and ALLAN C. WILSON, "Mitochondrial DNA and human evolution," *Nature* 325:31–36 (1 January 1987). "All these mtDNAs stem from one woman who is postulated to have lived about 150,000 years ago, probably in Africa." But just as an English surname may disappear from the church records following generations of all female offspring, so a woman with a rare mtDNA allele may fail to pass it on if only her sons grow up to reproduce. Such loss of alleles in clonal lineages reduces variability; one would expect such loss to be exaggerated in small temperate-zone populations, compared to the tropical demes. Such effects could give rise to a substantially different interpretation of where ancestors lived.

The "Eve" interpretation of the mtDNA analyses is quite misleading; to say that all modern peoples have one common ancestor that lived about 150,000 years ago is only to restate the initial *assumption* of genetic drift. There were many women then living, and their *nuclear* DNA is to be found in all of us. It's just that the mtDNA inheritance is odd in two ways: the genes aren't regularly shuffled, and they are inherited only from one's mother. Because of this, some variants die out. In a population of n mothers, each of whom produces on average one daughter, it will take about $2n$ generations for the mtDNA from n-1 of the orginal mothers to die out via having only sons at some generation along the way. Though the tree-making model itself is most helpful in suggesting when migrations might have occurred, focussing on its singular root is nonsensical; all it tells you is that the genetic drift method is useless for dates older than 150,000 years (just as the carbon-14 dating methods are no good for dates older than about 70,000 years).

91   Punctuated equilibrium: STEPHEN JAY GOULD, in *Perspectives on Evolution*, edited by R. MILKMAN (Sinauer, 1982), pp. 83–104.

91   Note that the selection pressures seasonally present at the margins of the habitat could be far more influential than the everyday selection pressures of the average habitat, e.g., infrequently used hunting skills might evolve more rapidly than frequently needed gathering skills in the total population, simply because of ice-age cycling. For hominid evolution, this disassociation promises to create severe difficulties for interpreting fossils: the living conditions when bones were deposited in the African savannah might be unrepresentative of those at the distant margins of the habitat where features were most effectively shaped. Similarly, where less-modified genes can still be found need not mean that this locale was where the ancient genome was shaped up, or where speciation occurred.

92   Dating of the earliest spread of hominids out of Africa is reviewed by RICHARD G. KLEIN in his text *The Human Career* (University of Chicago Press, 1989).

94   LOREN EISELEY, *The Immense Journey* (Doubleday, 1957), p. 55.

5. Over the Pole: Surveying the Ice Ages from a Seat in Heaven

96   ROBERT ARDREY, introduction to EUGÈNE N. MARAIS, *The Soul of the Ape* (1969), p. 21 of the 1973 Penguin edition.

97   PETER WADHAMS, "Evidence for Thinning of the Arctic Ice Cover North of Greenland," *Nature* 345:795–797 (28 June 1990).

97   A brief introduction to the glaciations is JOHN GRIBBIN, "The end of the ice ages?" *New Scientist* 1669:48–52 (17 June 1989). The extensive popular treatment is JOHN IMBRIE and KATHERINE

P. IMBRIE, *Ice Ages* (Harvard University Press, 1986), pp. 102–103. D. R. LINDSTROM and D. R. MACAYEAL, "Scandinavian, Siberian, and Arctic Ocean glaciation: Effect of Holocene atmospheric CO_2 variations." *Science* 245:628–631 (1989). The beginning of the ice age at 2.5 million years is dated by N. J. SHACKLETON, J. BACKMAN, H. ZIMMERMAN, D.V. KENT, M. A. HALL, D. G. ROBERTS, D. SCHNITKER, J. G. BALDAUF, A. DESPRAIRIES, R. HOMRIGHAUSEN, P. HUDDLESTUN, J. B. KEENE, A. J. KALTENBACK, K. A. KRUMSIEK, A. C. MORTON, J. W. MURRAY, and J. WESTBERG-SMITH, "Oxygen isotope calibration of the onset of ice-rafting and history of glaciation in the North Atlantic region." *Nature* 307:620–623 (1984). But, as would be expected from their origins in the Earth's orbital cycles, the Milankovitch rhythms were present long before that, and can be seen as cycles of deep-sea anoxia: T. D. HERBERT and A. G. FISCHER, "Milankovitch climatic origin of mid-Cretaceous black shale rhythms in central Italy." *Nature* 321:739–743 (1986). The precession and tilt (though not eccentricity) rhythms were faster, back when the moon's orbit was closer to Earth: ANDRE BERGER, M. F. LOUTRE, and V. DEHANT, "Pre-Quaternary Milankovitch frequencies." *Nature* 342:133 (1989).

99   FRIDTJOF NANSEN: See my notes in *The Cerebral Symphony*, pp. 352–353.

100   M. MILANKOVITCH, *Canon of Insolation and the Ice Age Problem* (Königlich Serbische Akademie, 1941; English translation by the Israel Program for Scientific Translations, 1969). JOSEPH ADHÉMAR history from WALLACE S. BROECKER and GEORGE H. DENTON, "What drives glacial cycles?" *Scientific American* 262(1):48–56 (January 1990), p. 49.

100   Iceland's volcanos, see JOHN MCPHEE's *The Control of Nature* (Farrar, Straus & Giroux, 1989).

104   For the fourfold rate differences, see JOHN IMBRIE and JOHN Z. IMBRIE, "Modeling the climatic response to orbital variations," *Science* 207:943–953 (1980). There are, however, some significant nonlinearities associated with melting. The coastal glaciers provide an important example of modes of operation. Even when rainfall and temperature are shared by neighboring glacial systems, as at Glacier Bay National Park near Juneau, Alaska, some will be in "retreat mode" and others in "advance mode." If a glacier has retreated far enough back up

its valley, the next advance will plow a terminal moraine—that serves as a coffer dam when reaching the sea, allowing the glacial snout to push far offshore. This makes it difficult for seawater to erode beneath the glacier. When water finally comes in over the top of the coffer dam, one gets a "tidewater glacier." They are an anomaly, cliffs ten stories high above the waterline dropping blocks of ice into the sea. They may have twice as many stories below sea level, with the submerged snout extending far out from the "shoreline." Once sea-water does penetrate beneath the submerged section of glacier (and great icebergs begin popping to the surface!), the glacier will rapidly retreat until only a tip is touching the shoreline—and be unable to advance again to form an ice cliff, at least until retreating far enough to build up another terminal moraine. There may be similar state-dependent situations in the ocean-ice-atmosphere system more generally.

104   Intermediate meltoffs best correlated with June–July perihelion: from a lecture by the French glacial expert, ROBERT J. DELMAS, "Climatic and environmental information from ice cores." Lecture at University of Washington (14 February 1989).

105   Greenhouse warming and the chance of triggering another Dryaslike shutdown of the North Atlantic Current: UWE MIKOLAJEWICZ, BENJAMIN D. SANTER, and ERNST MAIER-REIMER, "Ocean response to greenhouse warming," *Nature* 345:589–593 (14 June 1990), do not discuss the Dryaslike episodes, but their simulations of ocean currents do show the decreased North Atlantic deep water production and decreased salinity of surface waters there that BROECKER et al. (1985) identify as precursors of a shutdown.

105   PAUL HOFFMAN's piecing-together of the mosaic geology of Archean North America, Greenland, and Scandinavia is covered in a news story in *Discover* (February 1990), pp. 26–27.

105   W. R. PELTIER, "Slow changes in the earth's shape and gravitational field: constraints on the glaciation history and internal viscoelastic stratification." *Space Geodesy and Geodynamics* (Academic Press, London, 1986), pp. 75–109.

106   JOHN GRIBBIN and MARY GRIBBIN, "Climate and history: the Westviking's saga." *New Scientist* 1700:52–55 (20 January 1990). Settlement of Greenland and windows of opportunity from climate change in the North Atlantic.

107   When northern glaciers melt back in response to changes in summer sunshine, so do the southern hemisphere glaciers of South America and New Zealand, as STEPHEN PORTER points out. That suggests that the northern meltoff is affecting global climate in a big way, overriding the effects of the minimal summer sunshine of the Southern Hemisphere.

108   Aurora, see SYUN-ICHI AKASOFU, "The dynamic aurora." *Scientific American* 260(5):90–97 (May 1989). Solar output also varies, with implications for climate: RICHARD R. RADICK, G. W. LOCKWOOD, and SALLIE L. BALIUNAS, "Stellar activity and brightness variations: A glimpse at the sun's history." *Science* 247:39–44 (5 January 1990)

111   Ice-free corridor opening dates: LIONEL E. JACKSON, JR., and ALEJANDRA DUK-RODKIN, "Geology of the ice-free corridor," talk at University of Washington (19 January 1988), and JOHN IVES, ALWYNNE B. BEAUDOIN, and MARTIN P. R. MAGNE, "Evaluating the role of a western corridor in the peopling of the Americas," *Circum-Pacific Prehistory Conference* (Lecture in Seattle, 3 August 1989; to be published by Washington State University Press). The illustration of the ice-free corridor and Clovis-Folsom sites was adapted from the more detailed figure of WENDORF (1989).

113   Earliest human habitation dates in the Americas: ROGER LEWIN's news article "Skepticism fades over pre-Clovis man." *Science* 244:1140 (9 June 1989). And ELIOT MARSHALL's news article, "Clovis counterrevolution," *Science* 249:738–741 (17 August 1990).

114   RICHARD E. LEAKEY on widespread disappearance of predecessor hominid populations: lecture in Seattle, Washington (25 February 1989).

116   BENJAMIN THOMPSON (Count Rumford), quoted by WARREN M. WASHINGTON in *Natural History* (March 1990), p. 68.

116   The illustration of winter ice extent was adapted from Fig. 6 in the review of BROECKER et al. (1985).

117   WALLACE S. BROECKER and GEORGE H. DENTON, "What drives glacial cycles?" *Scientific American* 262(1):48–56 (January 1990), pp. 55–56. For a paleosalinity story, see DAVID A. ANATI, "Red Sea salinity." *Nature* 339:20–21 (4 May 1989).

121   Rebounding bluffs, from a lecture by STEPHEN C. PORTER, director of the Quaternary Research Center, University of Washington (May 1989).

122   Seattle tombstone-*cum*-park-bench: ROBERT FULGHUM, in *It Was On Fire When I Lay Down On It* (Villard, 1989), pp. 209–210, may have remembered the quotation incorrectly—but not the sentiments! The tombstone is not entirely anonymous: the surname WHITEBROOK can be inferred from the family plot.

122   Puget lobe of Cordilleran glacier, see ROBERT BURNS, *The Shape and Form of Puget Sound* (University of Washington Press, 1985); THOMAS A. TERICH, *Living with the Shore of Puget Sound and the Georgia Strait* (Duke University Press, 1987). Ocean circulation theory, see BROECKER and DENTON; their figure on p. 52 shows the advance and retreat of Washington State glaciers.

6. Mount Rainier:
Growing Up in a Boom Time

126   CHARLES DARWIN, *On the Origin of Species* (John Murray, 1859), pp. 481–482.

131   JAMES HANKEN, "Development of evolution in amphibians." *American Scientist* 77:336–343 (July 1989). R. D. SEMLITSCH and H. M. WILBUR, "Artificial selection for paedomorphosis in the salamander *Ambystoma talpoideum*." *Evolution* 43(1):105–112 (1989).

131   STEPHEN JAY GOULD, *Ontogeny and Phylogeny* (Harvard University Press, 1977), pp. 177 ff.

132   WALTER GARSTANG, *Larval Forms With Other Zoological Verses* (Basil Blackwell, 1951), p. 62.

133   Adult development finally implementing typically truncated features, see ALDOUS HUXLEY's cautionary novel *After Many a Summer Dies the Swan* (Harper, 1939).

133   Juvenile advantages in adulthood: I discuss this in *The Throwing Madonna: Essays on the Brain* (Bantam, 1991), chapter 3.

133   The first species to fill a "new niche" may, of course, not be
        able to hold it, e.g., the grasslands-to-forest succession.

135   CLIFFORD J. JOLLY and JANE E. PHILLIPS-CONROY, "Bulls,
        bears and baboons: The evolutionary significance of develop-
        mental plasticity." *American Journal of Physical Anthropology*
        75(2):227 (1988). ROBERT M. SAPOLSKY, "Lessons of the
        Serengeti." *The Sciences* (May/June 1988). See also his "Junk-
        food monkeys," *Discover* 10(9):48–51 (September 1989). JEANNE
        ALTMANN has shown that garbage-fed baboons mature faster
        and have more babies, and SAPOLSKY has found that they
        have cholesterol levels one-third higher than savannah baboons
        (see *Natural History*, May 1990, p. 107 for a picture).

136   Animals that adjust their reproductive policy, see PAUL
        COLINVAUX, *Why Big Fierce Animals Are Rare* (Princeton
        University Press, 1978), p. 16.

139   Supernormal releasers and attractors, see DAVID P. BARASH,
        The Hare and the Tortoise (Viking, 1986), pp. 84–86, and
        ANNIE DILLARD, *The Writing Life* (Harper and Row, 1989), p.
        18. These behavioral attractors are quite different from the
        "strange attractors" of chaotic systems, more like the attrac-
        tions of quicksand than the "gravitational centers" of chaos.

141   Adolescent growth spurt, see J. M. TANNER, *Foetus into
        Man: Physical Growth from Conception to Maturity* (Har-
        vard University Press, 1978), p. 14. Growth in general (and
        models for the adolescent growth spurt associated with sexual
        maturity, in particular): BARRY BOGIN, *Patterns of Human
        Growth* (Cambridge University Press, 1988). For juvenile pe-
        riods of various species, see P. H. HARVEY and T. H. CLUTTON-
        BROCK, "Life history variation in primates." *Evolution*
        39:559–581 (1985).
            Juvenilization, neoteny, and paedomorphism are not re-
        ally synonymous. See BOGIN (1988, p. 71), GOULD (1977, p.
        179), ASHLEY MONTAGU, *Growing Young* (McGraw-Hill, 1981),
        and F. HARVEY POUGH, JOHN B. HEISER, and WILLIAM N.
        McFARLAND, *Vertebrate Life*, 3rd edition (Macmillan, 1989, p.
        68).
            My own summary of the confusing terminology: what is
        here called *paedomorphosis* ("child-shaped") or *juvenilization*
        is simply descriptive of the appearance of the end-product,
        without implication of mechanism. Lately *neoteny* has been
        used by some, but not all, authors to refer to the slowing

("retardation") of somatic development. *Progenesis*, on the other hand, refers to paedomorphosis associated with accelerated somatic development plus the truncation of ontogeny. Thus, compared to the apes, we are both neotenized (somatic development retarded to half the pongid rate) and paedomorphic. But compared to modern-type *Homo sapiens* earlier in the last ice age, we exhibit progenesis in the same sense as, compared to wild-types, the domestic animals exhibit progenesis.

142   DAVID BRIN, "Neoteny and two-way human sexual selection" (unpublished manuscript, 1990). Brin's suggestion that juvenilized appearance in females might preferentially attract nurturing males has several interesting consequences, as he points out: it helps to explain the unusual (compared to the mammals) amount of attention-attracting female adornment (which currently supports an enormous cosmetics and fashion industry), and it helps to explain pedophilia. If male preference for juvenile appearing females coevolved with paedomorphosis, then one might expect more than the usual (for other primates) amount of misplaced sexual attraction toward juveniles. Brin suggests that the unusual-for-mammals breasts of the human female (which are 85 percent fat pad) might serve as a sexual releaser, helping the sexually-interested male to distinguish between appropriate and inappropriate juvenile appearing females.

142   For the invertebrate-to-chordate transition, see Q. BONE, *The Origin of Chordates* (Oxford University Press; Carolina Biology Readers #18, 1979), or p. 70 of POUGH (1989).

144   C. LORING BRACE, KAREN R. ROSENBERG, and KEVIN D. HUNT, "Gradual change in human tooth size in the late Pleistocene and post Pleistocene." *Evolution* 41:705–720 (1987). And C. LORING BRACE, *The Stages of Human Evolution*, 3d edition (Prentice-Hall, 1988)—though, as KATHLEEN GIBSON notes (personal communication, Cascais, Portugal, 22 March 1990), simple truncation of tooth growth by precocious puberty will not explain tooth size reduction, as tooth size is seemingly determined much earlier in childhood. JAMES M. CALCAGNO, *Mechanisms of Human Dental Reduction* (University of Kansas Publications in Anthropology No. 18, 1989). One of the hazards of the simplified treatment of early puberty which I and others utilize is that it leads us to think of early puberty occurring as if the living conditions suddenly improved at the time of truncation—when, of course, they

are usually spread out over the previous decade and influence somatic growth as well as menarche.

146   ROSE E. FRISCH, "Fatness and fertility." *Scientific American* 258(3):88–95 (March 1988). See also *Science* 185:949–951 (13 September 1974), and 199:22–30 (6 January 1978).

146   Deer on the Kaibab Plateau of Arizona, see JOHN P. RUSSO, "The Kaibab North Deer Herd," a 1964 publication of the Arizona Department of Fish and Game.

147   Humans perhaps too *K*-selected, see LOVEJOY (1981).

149   JEROME KAGAN, J. STEVEN REZNICK, and NANCY SNIDMAN, "Biological Bases of Childhood Shyness." *Science* 240:167–171 (8 April 1988).

149   VICTOR H. DENNENBERG, "Hemispheric laterality in animals and the effects of early experience." *Behavioral and Brain Sciences* 4(1):1–50 (March 1981).

150   RICHARD D. ALEXANDER, *The Biology of Moral Systems* (Aldine de Gruyter, 1987), p. 23.

151   The "28-year-old grandparent" phenomenon has been commented upon by people who work in hospital maternity wards, e.g., MELVIN KONNER, *Becoming a Doctor: A Journey of Initiation in Medical School* (Viking, 1987).

152   SUSAN OYAMA, *The Ontogeny of Information: Developmental Systems and Evolution* (Cambridge University Press, 1985), p. 188.

7. Whidbey Island:
Ratcheting Up Brain Size

154   LEONARD A. SAGAN, "Family ties." *The Sciences* 28(2):20–29 (March 1988).

157   RUTH KIRK with RICHARD DAUGHERTY, *Exploring Washington Archaeology* (University of Washington Press, 1978). Note that ice-age fishing villages would have been covered up by rising sea level, unless the land uplifted at a faster pace.

There are some sites along the Alaskan panhandle coastline where uplift could have preserved an early Holocene fishing village: BRUCE F. MOLNIA, "Glacial history of the northeastern Gulf of Alaska: A synthesis." In *Glaciation in Alaska: The Geologic Record*, edited by T. D. HAMILTON, K. M. REED, and R. M. THORSON (Alaska Geological Society, 1986), pp. 219–236.

160   Death in childbirth, see SUE ARMSTRONG, "Labour of death," *New Scientist* 1710:50–55 (31 March 1990). "All but 1 percent of these maternal deaths take place in the Third World, where the average lifetime risk of dying as a result of pregnancy is between one in 25 and one in 50; this compares to a lifetime risk of between one in 4000 and one in 10,000 for a woman in the developed world."

160   Hat size and IQ, see STEPHEN JAY GOULD, *The Mismeasure of Man* (Norton, 1981).

160   Kin selection by big heads, see W. H. CALVIN, "The great encephalization: Throwing, juvenilization, developmental slowing, and maternal mortality roles in prehuman brain enlargement." *Human Ethology Newsletter* 5(3):4–6 (September 1987). And also W. H. CALVIN, "Of fast teeth and big heads." *Nature* 328:481 (6 August 1987).

162   Despite our perceptual abilities to guess a racial designation from a collection of traits such as skin color, hair color and stiffness, eye color, and facial shape, the serious study of the subject suggests that we are simply inventing pigeonholes ("categorical perception") along a continuous distribution of traits. There is, however, a tendency called assortitive mating where people tend to pick mates for themselves or their children on the basis of physical similarity; this tends to *maintain* distinctive groupings of physical traits that might arise by chance. Such considerations of "beauty" may be simple sexual selection with no rhyme or reason—but sexual selection often has some natural selection rationale, however exaggerated and inappropriate the extremes to which it is taken (those long or iridescent bird tails probably started out as simple female preference for mates healthy enough to grow new feathers; women in many parts of the world prefer tall men as mates, stature being an indirect indicator of successful childhood development).

And the birth canal bottleneck could be the rationale for

some such human mate selection, given how obstetricians worry about difficult deliveries when the wife is petite and the husband isn't. Any random (but heritable) tendency to select a body type similar to one's parents or siblings would be reinforced by improved survival of offspring and mothers. And so the birth canal bottleneck might have helped maintain local standards of "beauty" (and, alas, reinforced racism).

163   Heritability of early menarche: TANNER (1978), p. 126.

163   HERBERT A. SIMON, *Reason in Human Affairs* (Stanford University Press, 1983), p. 50.

163   F. BROWN, J. HARRIS, R. LEAKEY, and A. WALKER, "Early *Homo erectus* skeleton from west Lake Turkana, Kenya." *Nature* 316:788–792 (1985).

163   Secular trend in height, see TANNER (1978), p. 150.

165   PETER K. STEVENS, *Patterns in Nature* (Little, Brown, 1974), p. 25.

167   THEODOSIUS DOBZHANSKY, "Discussion." In *Insect Polymorphism*, edited by J. S. KENNEDY (Symposia of the Royal Entomological Society, 1961), p. 49.

168   JAMES LOVELOCK in *The Ages of Gaia* (Norton, 1989) gives a nice treatment of those population boom-and-bust equations for general readers.

168   Oscillations in population size, see PAUL COLINVAUX, *Introduction to Ecology* (Wiley, 1973), pp. 483–485.

169   The enormous plasticity of adult body size can be seen in the poorly understood reduction in body size of mammals in isolated demes; pygmy races of elephants and rhinoceros have been found on islands. But it wasn't until someone studied fossils of the European red deer on Jersey that we realized how fast body size could change, absent artificial breeding: During the last interglacial about 128,000 years ago, a range of hills in western Normandy was isolated by rising sea level, becoming the island of Jersey. And within a time span of only 6,000 years (during which mainland deer didn't change, and hadn't for the previous 400,000 years, either), the body size of

the deer inhabiting the island dropped to about one-sixth of their original size. A. M. LISTER, "Rapid dwarfing of red deer on Jersey in the last interglacial," *Nature* 342:539–542 (30 November 1989). Was this due to resource limitations? Lack of predators? No one is sure; were there a boom-time due to omission of predators or pathogens from the new island, juvenilized variants that reach reproductive age sooner might come to eventually dominate the gene pool (because they have more offspring per century than those with standard menarche). Note that lack of certain pathogens (one of the virtues of isolation) might allow small adults to more successfully raise offspring; lack of predators per se is not required. After the glaciers again lowered sea level to reconnect Jersey to the mainland, the dwarf deer disappear from the fossil record.

169   How might domestication thoroughly embed a juvenilized form of the species if natural selection operated upon the *r*-shift itself? This is somewhat like asking why those invariably aquatic axolotls might have evolved from those conditionally aquatic *Ambystoma*—again it is a question of how the conditional feature might have been lost without natural selection for losing it.

It's potentially like that recessive gene which, when two are present, causes sickle-cell anemia—but when only heterozygous, protects against malaria (and so is selected for, in low-lying tropical areas with the mosquitos that spread malaria). Only in my theory, the homozygous condition causes sure-fire acceleration rather than the conditional-on-climate acceleration of the heterozygous case.

Ordinarily you'd think that the natural selection would operate on the flexibility, so that the body features would spring back to the old average once the climate stabilized at a new mean. But there are some ways in which accelerated maturity might become unconditionally established despite an origin in a series of conditional *r*-shift events. Suppose we have one version (allele) of a developmental rate gene that, when homozygous (the individual has two copies and so no other choices), leads to accelerated maturity. When neither allele at this position in the chromosome is the special allele, one gets average developmental rates. But if one version is present, and the other is the standard allele, one gets a precarious balance between acceleration and standard. And so the special accelerated version is conditionally used: the occasions being when the environment improves (the better nutrition, increased daylight, higher population density, or whatever). Since the phenotypes will be more successful under such conditions, the allele will become more and more common in the general population. Some individuals will become homozygous for it, and thus always accelerated in maturity, unconditionally juvenile in adult appearance.

171   EISELEY (1957), p. 125, pp. 129–131.

8. Hand-ax Heaven:
The Ambitious Ape's Guide to a Bigger Brain

174   ERNST MAYR, *Toward a New Philosophy of Biology* (Harvard University Press, 1988), p. 95.

175   Mastodon: KIRK and DAUGHERTY (1978), p. 28.

176   ERNST MAYR, "Descent of man and sexual selection." In *L'Origine dell' Uomo* (Academia Nazionale dei Lincei, 1973), pp. 33–61.

177   Tool-use by animals, see pp. 575–578 of *The Oxford Companion to Animal Behaviour*, edited by DAVID MCFARLAND (Oxford University Press, 1987).

177   CHRISTOPHE BOESCH and HEDWIGE BOESCH, "Sex differences in the use of natural hammers by wild chimpanzees: A preliminary report." *Journal of Human Evolution* 10:585–593 (1981), and film shown at *Tools, Language, and Intelligence: Evolutionary Perspectives* workshop in Cascais, Portugal (19 March 1990).

178   Cooperative hunting: SHIRLEY C. STRUM, "Baboon cues for eating meat." *Journal of Human Evolution* 12:327–336 (1983). GEZA TELEKI, "The omnivorous chimp." *Scientific American* 228(1):32–42 (1973). FRANS X. PLOOIJ, "Tool-use during chimpanzee's bushpig hunt." *Carnivore* 1:103–106 (1978). C. BOESCH and H. BOESCH, "Hunting behavior of wild chimpanzees in the Taï National Park." *American Journal of Physical Anthropology* 78:547–573 (1989).

178   Throwing by chimpanzees, see PLOOIJ (1978); JANE GOODALL, *In the Shadow of Man* (Houghton Mifflin, 1971) and *The Chimpanzees of Gombe* (Harvard University Press, 1986), p. 550; and FRANS DE WAAL, *Chimpanzee Politics: Power and Sex Among Apes* (Harper & Row, 1982).

178   Chimpanzees throw in a variety of humanlike styles, see JANE GOODALL, "The behaviour of free-living chimpanzees in the Gombe Stream Preserve." *Animal Behaviour Monographs* 1(3):161–311 (1968), at p. 203. But, as SUE SAVAGE-RUMBAUGH pointed out to me, many of those postures are associated with male threat displays and are unlikely to be associated with "get set" styles that might lead to precision throwing.

179   The illustration of Acheulian "hand axes" is adapted from drawings by C. O. WATERHOUSE at the British Museum (Natural History). The smaller one is a "twisted ovate" from St. Acheul, France. The larger is the one associated with the Swanscombe skull in England. While the Acheulian tool kit went out with *Homo erectus*, bifaces shaped like Acheulian hand axes are also seen in *Homo sapiens* tool kits, e.g., the one from Le Moustier at Musée de l'Homme in Paris).

180   H. G. WELLS, *Tales of Space and Time* (Doubleday and McClure, 1899); for a general introduction to hand axes and the associated toolmaking styles, see JOHN GOWLETT, *Ascent to Civilization* (Knopf, 1984), pp. 60 ff.; EILEEN M. O'BRIEN, "The projectile capabilities of an Acheulian handaxe from Olorgesailie." *Current Anthropology* 22:76–79 (1981); and "What was the Acheulean hand ax?" *Natural History* 93:20–23 (1984). Spin for throwing into flocks of birds: M. D. W. JEFFREYS, "The hand bolt." *Man* 65:154 (1965).

181   Hand axes in dried-up ponds, etc.: GLYNN LL. ISAAC, *Olorgesailie* (University of Chicago Press, 1977). F. CLARK HOWELL, "Isimila: A Paleolithic site in Africa." *Scientific American* 205:118–129 (1961). M. R. KLEINDIENST and C. M. KELLER, "Towards a functional analysis of handaxes and cleavers: The evidence from East Africa." *Man* 11:176–187 (1976).

181   WILLIAM D. HAMILTON III, "Geometry for the selfish herd." *Journal of Theoretical Biology* 31:295–311 (1971).

182   WILLIAM H. CALVIN, "A stone's throw and its launch window: timing precision and its implications for language and hominid brains." *Journal of Theoretical Biology* 104:121–135 (1983). And my subsequent book *The River That Flows Uphill: A Journey from the Big Bang to the Big Brain* (1986).

185   The big cats sometimes leap onto the back of a much larger herd animal and bring it down; the cat's claws might activate the same withdrawal reflex that lowers the hindquarters.

185   PATRICK D. WALL, "On the relation of injury to pain." *Pain* 6:253–264 (1979).

186   "Killer Frisbee": ALBERT LEO of Pomona College suggested this name (June, 1988), which is sure to be disavowed by anthropologists.

187   "Manuports," see MARY D. LEAKEY, *Olduvai Gorge*. Vol. 3 (Cambridge University Press, 1971).

187   BARBARA ISAAC, "Stone throwing and human evolution." Unpublished MS; see news article in *Discover* 7(6):6–7 (June 1986).

190   Pruning of connections in cerebral cortex is reviewed in *The Cerebral Symphony*, pp. 165, 362. The loss of neurons is from J. B. LOHR and D. V. JESTE, "Studies of neuron loss with age in three different brain regions in humans," *Society for Neuroscience Abstracts* 15:22 (1989). For monkey motor cortex, see J. TIGGES, J. HERNDON, and ALAN PETERS, "Neuronal changes in Area 4 during the life span of the rhesus monkey," *Society for Neuroscience Abstracts* 15:259 (1989); they report that this movement control area of the leg loses nearly a third of its neurons between infancy and early adulthood [my wife suggests that the monkeys must have killed off their clumsy neurons!].

190   PAUL CHENEY and EBERHARD E. FETZ, "Comparable patterns of muscle facilitation evoked by individual corticomotoneuronal (CM) cells and by single intracortical microstimuli in primates: evidence for functional groups of CM cells." *Journal of Neurophysiology* 53:786–804.

190   The illustration of synaptic density in visual cortex uses the human data of P. R. HUTTENLOCHER, "Synapse elimination and plasticity in developing human cerebral cortex." *American Journal of Mental Deficiency* 88:488–496 (1984). The monkey data is from P. RAKIC, J.-P. BOURGEOUS, M. F. ECKENHOFF, N. ZECEVIC, AND P. GOLDMAN-RAKIC, "Concurrent overproduction of synapses in diverse regions of the primate cerebral cortex," *Science* 232:232–234 (1986). I have replotted the data to normalize peaks and used a logarithmic time scale starting at about 120 days after conception and ending about ten years after birth. In addition to breaking synapses and withdrawing axon collaterals, there is also some cell death in cerebral

cortex during the same period. The lateral shift in the human curve relative to the monkey curve would be consistent with a two- to three-fold slowing of human somatic development.

192   Not all hunters are male: see A. ESTIOKO-GRIFFIN, "Daughters of the forest." *Natural History* 95(5):36–43 (1986).

195   EISELEY (1957), p. 140

9. San Juan Ferry:
Does Consciousness Emerge from Cortical Consensus?

203   DEAN FALK, "Brain evolution in *Homo*: The 'radiator' theory." *Behavioral and Brain Sciences* (in press, 1990).

205   JEFFREY T. LAITMAN, "The anatomy of human speech." *Natural History* 93(8):20–27, 1984. And PHILLIP LIEBERMAN, *The Biology and Evolution of Language* (Harvard University Press, 1984)

211   From an entirely different perspective, involving cortical injuries and developmental abnormalities, the neuropsychologist MARCEL KINSBOURNE also arrives at the suggestion that conscious attention corresponds to the widespread activation of many regions of cerebral cortex (the quote is from "Integrated field theory of consciousness," in *Consciousness in Contemporary Science*, edited by A. J. MARCEL and E. BISIACH (Clarendon Press, Oxford, 1988), pp. 239–256. The philosopher DANIEL C. DENNETT emphasizes that consciousness perception takes time, much more than any of the component processes; again, this can be predicted from Darwin Machine reasoning applied to both sensory and movement schema sequences, as it takes many Darwin Machine generations to achieve a widespread consensus (Bellagio workshop on consciousness, 26–31 March 1990). Hierarchies, such as the acoustics-phonemes-syntax-semantics levels of analysis which seem to help us understand sentences, may be helped by Darwin Machine architectures that can be parasitized for language uses and staged appropriately.

     The bar-code analogy also helps one understand why various attempts to measure this consensus might succeed or fail. Were the representation a string in time (as when the optical wand is swiped across the bars), and the strings in various areas synchronized in time, we might see the EEG from various regions move up and down in synchrony (the EEG *coherence* is a measure of this). But if the strings were out of phase with one another (if I were designing such a system, I'd do that to prevent out-of-control oscillations such as seizures), it might be much harder to detect string consensus in various regions. And if the representation were instead spatial (like the bar code on the package), merely repeating in the manner of wallpaper designs, we might require a very sensitive imaging method to detect the consensus.

215   OSWALD SPENGLER, *The Decline of the West* (Knopf, 1926), vol. 1, p. 166 of the abridged edition.

10. Friday Harbor:
Has Intelligent Life Evolved Yet?

218   ALISON JOLLY, "The evolution of purpose." In *Machiavellian Intelligence*, edited by RICHARD W. BYRNE and ANDREW WHITEN (Clarendon Press, 1988), pp. 363–378, p. 378.

219   CHIEF SEATTLE, 1854, quoted from a U.S. National Park Service exhibit in Seward, Alaska.

220   ALFRED W. CROSBY, *Ecological Imperialism: The Biological Expansion of Europe, 900–1900* (Cambridge University Press, 1986). Role of disease, firearms in conquering virgin continents.

227   EDWIN DOBB, "The big picture." *The Sciences* 29(2):44–50 (1989), at p. 49.

227   Gaia, alas, is only capable (at most) of keeping things suitable for plants and simple animal life—not intelligent life. See JAMES LOVELOCK, *The Ages of Gaia* (Norton, 1988).

228   PAUL R. EHRLICH and ANNE H. EHRLICH, *The Population Explosion* (Simon and Schuster, 1990). "The critical prerequisites to reduced fertility are five: adequate nutrition, proper sanitation, basic health care, education of women, and equal rights for women. The first four factors reduce infant mortality, allowing a reasonable expectation that a given child will survive to adulthood. Female education is an especially interesting and in some ways the most unexpected finding. Women will apply even a few years of schooling to improving life for

their families by providing more nutritious, balanced meals
and better home health care and sanitation . . . Improving the
home situation reduces infant and child mortality, making
men and women more receptive to the idea of smaller families. And the women's education makes them more open to
contraception and better able to employ it properly. Finally,
when women have sources of status other than children, family size often decreases."

229   Alas, those breakwaters exist no more, thanks to an ill-
conceived plan to double the width of the Northwestern University campus by filling in the lake. Inelegant riprap, a
jumble of broken concrete slabs representing the throw-away
building era, has replaced the sand beaches. Northwestern
has created a lagoon in the midst of its landfill, though with
the unmistakably uniform contours created only by bulldoz-
ers. But the outer strip of walkway between lagoon and lake
has some of the sense of the old breakwaters.

231   JARED DIAMOND, "The worst mistake in the history of the
human race," in *Discover* (May 1987), pp. 64 ff. See also MARK
N. COHEN and GEORGE J. ARMALAGOS, editors, *Paleopathology
at the Origins of Agriculture* (Academic Press, 1984).

231   History of technological civilizations from a lecture by Professor JON BRIDGMAN, University of Washington (25 May 1989).

233   Paleo-Indians as searching for the source of the aurora: This
variant on "looking for the pot of gold at the end of the
rainbow" occurred to me when I noticed that the magnetic
pole was east and north of the Mackenzie River delta, east of
those North Slope oil fields and wildlife refuges. Indians in
Siberia following the aurora would have been led to the Bering Strait; once within Alaska, they would have been led up
north around the mountains that, during the ice age, blocked
other routes east and south. And so they could have discovered the ice-free corridor to Montana, just by initially trying
to find the most intense "root" of the northern lights.

233   "Infiltration of mind into the universe. . . ." FREEMAN DYSON,
Infinite in All Directions (Harper & Row, 1988), p. 118.

234   "Gould's Principle. . . ," see STEPHEN JAY GOULD, *The Fla-
mingo's Smile* (Norton, 1985), p. 401.

234   NORMAN MAILER, in accepting the 1969 National Book Award for *The Armies of the Night*.

235   STEPHEN H. SCHNEIDER, "The greenhouse effect: Science and policy." *Science* 243:771–781 (10 February 1989). And his book *Global Warming: Are We Entering the Greenhouse Century?* (Sierra Club Books, 1989). See the "Managing Planet Earth" issue of *Scientific American* (September 1989).

236   W. S. BROECKER, letter in *Science* 245:451 (4 August 1989).

236   The illustration of the cold spikes in the North Atlantic Ocean since the last interglaciation is adapted from the Camp Century core (east of Thule, Northern Greenland) shown in Figure 4 of DANSGAARD et al. (1982). It is based on the oxygen isotope ratio; seen in ocean floors, the slow trends in this ratio tend to reflect ice volume (filtered by mixing times) but the rapid changes from ice cores may be due to the surface temperature of the North Atlantic Ocean at the time of evaporation in the mid-latitudes (higher temperatures aid in the "launch" of the heavier water molecules containing the oxygen-18 isotope); this water subsequently fell on northern Greenland as snow and was compacted into ice layers. Rapid fluctuations may also be influenced (e.g., FAIRBANKS 1989) by surges of fresh water into the Atlantic from ice dams breaking and draining huge lakes of meltwater via the St. Lawrence River.

239   The illustration showing the end of the last glaciation, as seen from northern Greenland (Camp Century) and from Antarctica (Byrd Station) ice cores. Adapted from Fig. 2 of the BROECKER et al. (1985) review; data from S. JOHNSEN, W. DANSGAARD, H. CLAUSEN, and C. LANGWAY, *Nature* 235:429–434 (1972).

240   The illustration of the Allerød-Dryas chattering, and the speed of the end of the Younger Dryas, was adapted from Fig. 1 of DANSGAARD et al. (1989) and utilizes the ice core at "Dye 3" in southern Greenland.

241   JOHN MAYNARD SMITH, *Did Darwin Get It Right? Essays on Games, Sex, and Evolution* (Chapman and Hall, 1988), p. 37.

242   Simulations of North Atlantic Current's deep water production: UWE MIKOLAJEWICZ, BENJAMIN D. SANTER, and ERNST

MAIER-REIMER, "Ocean response to greenhouse warming."
Nature 345:589–593 (14 June 1990). This is only the first
round of such simulations of ocean-atomspheric linkage; successor models will hopefully simulate the Current in more
detail and analyze its stability.

244   Most governments are still treating scientific research in the
ocean-atmosphere systems as if it were just another aspect of
routine agricultural research. Or of improving weather forecasting. Hardly as serious a matter as, say, the perceived
need for yet another new "defense" system, or bailing out the
Chrysler Corporation, or rescuing the savings-and-loan-
association gamblers. Those examples from recent U.S. history involve industries that, unlike science, contribute mightily
to politicians' campaign funds as a way of gaining a hearing
for their industry's problems. They may not be able to buy
solutions, but they can keep their problems from getting
placed on a back burner via contributions and high-priced
lobbyists. And their problems are, relatively speaking, easily
comprehended. Getting the politicians' attention is sometimes
hard for scientific-based agendas, given that the politicians
are mostly lawyers who avoided science courses in college,
who think mostly in terms of creating prohibitions rather than
plans, using penalties rather than preparedness.

244   "Like an Old Testament god with lots of rules and no mercy"
is, I confess, what JOSEPH CAMPBELL said in his interview
with Bill Moyers on Nova (1988)—but about personal computers, not climate!

244   Another redirected characterization: I have adapted the Conrad bad-weather-ahead tale from that (this time regarding
nuclear terrorism) by LUTHER J. CARTER, *Nuclear Imperatives and the Public Trust*, excerpted in *Issues in Science and
Technology* (Winter 1987), p. 60.

246   A. E. HOUSMAN, lines 9–16 of "Smooth between sea and
land." In *More Poems* (Knopf, 1936), p. 64.

INDEX

ABOUT THE AUTHOR

WILLIAM HOWARD CALVIN was born in 1939. He studied physics at Northwestern University, doing an undergraduate thesis on a neural-network model of the retina, graduating with honors in 1961. He spent a year at the Massachusetts Institute of Technology and Harvard Medical School making the transition from physics to biophysics, then moved to Seattle, where he studied the primate visual system and cellular neurophysiology, receiving a Ph.D. in physiology and biophysics in 1966 from the University of Washington. Following his doctorate, he remained at the University of Washington School of Medicine, joined the faculty of Neurological Surgery, and also taught in Physiology and Biophysics; in the 1980's, he moved to the Biology Program, also teaching in the Department of Zoology and the Honors Program of the College of Arts and Sciences.

In the 1960s, he was elected a member of the American Physiological Society, the Biophysical Society, and Sigma Xi. In the 1970s, he was a founding member of both the International Association for the Study of Pain and the Society for Neuroscience; he was elected to the International Brain Research Organization and was selected as a Fogarty International Fellow of the National Institutes of Health (and was visiting professor of neurobiology at the Hebrew University of Jerusalem). In the 1980s, he was elected to the New York Academy of Sciences, the International Society for Human Ethology, the American Anthropological Association, and the Language Origins Society. In the 1990s, he was elected to membership in the American Association of Physical Anthropologists and Commission 51 of the International Astronomical Union.